AF560685

Contents

Introduction

An earlier book I had edited in 2004 was called *Will Secular India Survive?* The general elections of 2004 did emphatically underline the secular aspirations of the people. Neerja Gopal Jayal in her paper in this book underlines the many ways in which this was a unique election. With the UPA-led coalition coming into power, the face of the Indian state at least, was once again, a secular one. Despite the BJP's electoral defeat, Hindutva as a specific construction of majoritarian communalism represented by political outfits such as the BJP and Shiv Sena, and organizations like the RSS and VHP, survives. The spate of Hindu-Muslim riots in some parts of Uttar Pradesh, notably in Aligarh, is a telling reminder of the tatters in which the secular fabric of the country now lies. The question that we must now ask is: 'How will secularism survive?' What are the covert and overt ways in which the monster of communalism continues to affect our lives and threaten the plural, syncretic culture of our country?

The papers in this book examine the many community and communal formations and configurations of Hindus and Muslims in India and their contribution to notions of citizenship. They introspect on the changing nature of communities in their encounter with colonialism, postcolonialism, globalization and modernity. They reflect on the shrinking of shared spaces between communities that nurture the pluralist traditions of India.

The Nehruvian consensus around which India as a modern state was sought to be created even after the trauma of Partition addressed the question of a secular state in a country which is deeply religious. The essays in this volume raise many questions about this consensus. Was it Nehru's soft secularism that led to the ever-increasing flabbiness of the Congress party's commitment to the secular agenda? Is it worthwhile to continue with the framework of nationalism at all, or is there a need to move into a postnationalist framework? There were many nationalisms in the national movement but what was common to all of them was a concern with the 'most numerous and the most poor'. In the post-1980s era of strident Hindu nationalism, according to Amir Ali, rather than revive one or the other nationalism – Nehruvian, Gandhian, Marxist or Ambedkarian, it may be better to posit a 'constitutional patriotism'. All nationalisms are structurally weighted against a minority. While nationalism is effective in the anti-colonial, anti-imperialist phase, it may have outlived its uses. There is also the belief that the secular project's inclusivism actually implies the dissolution of the 'other', leaving no space for a genuine pluralism constituted by distinct identities and entities. If the 2002 Gujarat pogroms put under erasure the belief in the Indian state as a secular one, it was constitutional bodies like the Election Commission that brought forth a faith, literally, in 'constitutional patriotism'.

Several papers in the volume discuss the rise and spread of Hindutva and its implications for minorities in India. They outline three phases of Hindutva in its post-1980s *avatar*: The first phase (1986-92) coincides with the Congress government's decision to open the gates of Babri Masjid and ends with its demolition. The second phase (1993-8) witnesses the showcasing of Atal Behari Vajpayee as the BJP's liberal face. BJP then comes to power and forms the government as the main partner in a coalition. The third phase (1998-2002) sees 'ethnic cleansing' in Gujarat, in which an estimated 2,000-5,000 Muslims were killed, women violated sexually on a scale not witnessed before, and state power used openly to contribute to the riots. According to Anwar Alam, Hindutva is more dangerous than Nazism because it has a huge network of educational and cultural organizations and does not always rely on state power for propagation. It successfully covers its fascist nature and exhibits flexibility in its strategies.

Two papers focus specifically on the Bajrang Dal and the RSS. The jointly authored paper by Smita Gupta and Christophe Jaffrelot traces the Bajrang Dal's rise to becoming the militant arm of Hindutva in the 1990s. It had been founded in 1964, was an offshoot of the VHP, its youth wing, and differed from the RSS in its use of systematic violence that could also target Hindus. The members of the Bajrang Dal, who numbered 1.25 million in 2001, learn judo, karate, climb ropes, go through circles of fires. They are adept in the use of rifles, pistols and trishuls. Over the years, the Bajrang Dal has shifted focus from mobilizing support for the Ram Temple to 'problem solving'. The problems have been identified as terrorism in Jammu & Kashmir, the influx of refugees from Bangladesh referred to as 'infiltration', and conversions to Christianity. Their main target has been the Muslim community. The Dal has hunted Muslim and Hindu artists for practicing what it perceived as anti-Hindu art and acts as an unofficial censor organ, particularly in matters of history-writing.

Vasundhara Srinate examines the demonization of the Muslim community by the RSS and the conceptualization of citizenship that it proposes. Citizenship is viewed in liberal thought as the individual's membership of the nation state. According to Srinate '. . . othering/ demonisation/ essentialisation is understood as a political act that aims specifically at the social and political exclusion of Muslims from mainstream politics and national life'. Their notion of citizenship drew on Orientalist discourse; they were also able to adapt Nazi theories of racial superiority to the Hindu caste system. M.S. Golwalkar's *We, Our Nation Defined* (1939) praises the Germans for 'othering' Jews and persecuting them. The first mark of Hindu identity for Savarkar is by paternal descent within the geographical space called India. The second criterion of citizenship was the 'bond of common blood', by being born to Hindu parents. Muslims for him were actually Hindus who had to be brought back into the fold from their conversion.

Many of the papers written for this volume introspect on the changing nature and role of the 'Muslim community'. Although diverse as a community with regard to region, beliefs and practices, they are constructed as a monolithic collective in the Hindutva imaginary. There is also a reciprocal 'othering' of Hindus, which has led to stricter orthodoxy. Yogendra Sikand's paper examines the new *shariah*-centred Sufism that the Tablighi Jamaat has introduced in Mewat, where it had a significant sphere of influence among the Meos by the end of the 1940s. The Tablighi Jamaat advocates conformism and a resistance to reform: 'Rather than seeking to critically engage with the multifarious challenges that modernity poses the thrust of the Tablighi Jamaat is to encapsulate Muslims in their own cultural world, insulating them from the rapidly changing developments in the world around them by stressing the need to conform as closely as possible to the model of the Prophet and his Companions'.

Arshad Alam's paper on the directions Indian Islam is taking describes the local, micro-processes of change in response to changing socio-economic conditions through the workings of two different denominational *madrasas*, the Deobandi and Barelwi. These denominations created a public of their own to propagate their own versions of Islam. The Barelwi has catered to rural Muslims and Deoband to the semi urban petty bourgeoisie. The seminaries were established not only to challenge the onslaught of British systems of education, but also to negotiate new power structures. *Madrasas* of both denominations practice not just pedagogy, but exercise different forms of control. The Dar ul-Ulum Madrasa at Deoband established in 1866 became the most popular *madrasa* in South Asia. Barelwi Islam, in contrast to the Deobandi school, consists of a large repertoire of practices around shrines and other customs. Alam argues that we are witnessing the Deobandization of Islam; 'Migration to urban areas is a common phenomenon in India . . . in the urban areas they come in contact with the Deobandi Islam. They see for themselves that richer and better educated Muslims follow this variety of Islam and they start questioning their own understanding of religion. . . . The urban lifestyle demands a less ritualistic routine that Deoband offers them.' The increased allegiance to Deoband also means that in inter-communitarian terms, the lines between Hindus and Muslims are more sharply drawn. Barelwi Islam prospers when identities between communities are not sharply drawn.

The resignation of Muslims to the overpowering presence of Hindutva has also resulted in a resistance to reform because of the perceived threat to identity as well as the desire of those in privileged positions to protect their positions. Rather than participate in broader democratic struggles, the Muslim leadership has played the politics of identity. There is also the fear of upper class Muslims that participation in such struggles will be counterproductive to their own hegemony in their community.

Many of the writers point out that Indian Muslims are ill-equipped to actively support secularism. Since the 1980s there has also been a tendency among secular Muslims to exhibit their religious identity. There is also a growing belief that they should withdraw from the national political process and concentrate like the Jews on the betterment of their own community.

Muslims are the largest religious minority group in India and the second largest Muslim population in the world. The issues of education, employment, gender relations and intercommunity relations are the grids on which the functioning of democracy is tested.

In their paper 'Investing in the Future', the Jefferies point out that the situation with regard to education has worsened in the 1990s. Their paper studies the political economy of schooling in Uttar Pradesh, the impact of the saffronization of education, the problem of the education of Muslim girls. The state has failed to provide affordable and comprehensive education with adequate buildings and teaching material to the rural poor and these problems are even more acute in Muslim and SC dominated areas.

> Although the direct threat to minority schooling has retreated, now that the BJP has lost power both at the UP and national levels, the state is unlikely to act to remedy this situation. Because of the fiscal crisis in UP, the state education system is collapsing. Alongside the liberalization of the economy, the inequalities of the market are untrammeled and on the rise. The general privatization of social provisions leads to elitism, diversification, and the fragmentation of schooling with further emphasis on social distinction. Increasingly, government schooling is serving only those groups who cannot get access to better, more expensive, non-state alternatives. Because the new non-state institutions are beyond the means of most north-Indian Muslim parents, their children seem likely to be left behind in the race to be part of new India.

Sylvia Vatuk's paper discusses the debates on dowry in south Indian newspapers in the 1990s. In the last three decades there has been a change in marriage transactions among Muslims. The traditional trousseau given to the bride by her parents is now supplemented with material gifts to the groom and in-laws. Traditionally among Muslims, the asymmetry in the exchange of gifts between bride-givers and bride-takers was not as pronounced as it was among Hindus. Now, however, it is on the increase. The debate in the newspapers, rather than condemn dowry outright, tends to veer around how this Hindu custom is inimical to an Islamic identity.

While many of the contributions to in this volume refer to the increasingly rigid boundaries being drawn within and between communities, S.M.A.K. Fakhri's paper charts out the relationship between Tamil Muslims and the Self-Respect movement between 1925 and 1947. The shared space between Tamil Muslims and Dalits in a single movement challenged Brahmin dominance and the caste-system. As Tamil speakers and non-Brahmins, Muslims in the region were, by implication, Dravidian. Dalits converted to Islam because of untouchability. This did not stop them from being part of their own specific milieu. A Tamil-Muslim matrix was thus produced. The Muslims responded to this inclusion by upholding Tamil as their liturgical language and participating in anti-Hindi agitations in 1937-8. The nationalist movement was led by upper castes and all power accruing to them had to be opposed. Ramasamy's leadership, therefore, forged a unity not on religious community lines but on a Dravidian and lower caste platform. Ramasamy's political strategy was to blur distinctions between oppressed groups.

Ramasamy however, believed that gender problems and the status of women transcended all religious boundaries and the *mullas* often performed the same conservative role that the Brahmin priesthood performed in Hinduism.

The Congress adopted the policy of introducing Hindi as the national language from 1918 onwards, when the Dakshin Bharat Hindi Prachar Sabha was founded in Madras to spread knowledge of Hindi in south India. Ramasamy opposed Hindi as the Sanskritic imposition of Brahmins. Tamil Muslims, therefore rejected the proposition that adoption of Hindi would promote Hindu-Muslim unity. This was in contrast to the Dakkhani Muslims, who accepted this proposition more easily because their mother-tongue was Urdu.

This paper illustrates the many ways in which Indian Muslims in India are diverse as a community and the ways in which alliances with progressive intent cutting across religious boundaries can be forged. There has been a political assertion of Dalits and Muslim OBCs in the last decade as a consequence of the loss of faith of Muslim masses in the traditional leadership after the demolition of Babri Masjid. There is once again a possibility of their coming together in a national secular consensus in the wake of the perception that militant Hindutva is the handiwork of upper caste Hindus.

Zoya Hasan traces the complex history of reservations in India. There was a national consensus in the 1950s in favour of reservations for scheduled castes and tribes in the sphere of education and employment. According to Zoya Hasan, over the past 50 years, the world's largest democracy has developed an affirmative action programme which is unprecedented in both its scope and intent. Despite this, she points out that social inequality has functioned on four axes: caste, tribal status, religion and gender. While the reservation quotas on the caste axis continue to expand, religious minorities and women remain outside the ambit of reservation. There is also vexed issue of whether caste applies to Muslims at all, since caste is against the tenets of Islam. It might be better for the government to include sections of the Muslim community in the backward class category or else evolve affirmative action policies that target the socio-economically deprived sections of the community. She argues that in the absence of a provision for an economic criterion for affirmative action, Muslims need to be included in the OBC list.

This volume should be read as a sequel to my previously edited book *Will Secular India Survive?* (2004) The common theme that runs through them is the future of secularism and the place of religious minorities, mainly Muslims, in the secular and democratic arrangements. This book should command scholarly interest for two additional reasons. First of all, its arguments and interpretations reflect maturity, understanding, and sensitivity to the dangers to the secular consensus. Second, many of our contributors are being drawn into the debates on secularism and communalism for the first time. They have not been heard before, and yet they speak with authority and conviction. I hope their voices will be heard loud and clear so that we can explore new ways of engaging with an old theme—the future of pluralism and composite living.

MUSHIRUL HASAN

1

Competing Interests, Social Conflict and Muslim Reservations

ZOYA HASAN

Over the past fifty years, the world's largest democracy, has developed an affirmative action programme, which by any standards is unprecedented in both its scope and extent. In India social inequality revolves around three main axes: caste/tribal status, religion, and gender; but caste far and away remains the crux of the government's elaborate scheme of reservations for the disadvantaged. Even as caste quotas are expanding continuously, women and minorities fall outside the purview of the state's framework and policies for the alleviation of disadvantage. Neither group is adequately represented in influential decision-making bodies, legislatures, political parties, media, and so on. Religious minorities have been frequently discriminated against but this is less well recognized and hence not part of the public debate on social inequalities. Today, some of these inequalities are a matter of great concern for reasons of both distributive justice and because ethnic inequalities may lead to social conflict and violence.

The Andhra Pradesh Government Order of 5 July 2005 reserving 5 per cent seats in educational institutions and government jobs for Muslims has raised a controversy.[1] Issued by the Backward Classes Welfare Department, it created a new category, E, among the Backward Classes and gave 5 per cent reservation to Muslims. This is in addition to the existing reservations for backward classes. The recommendation was based on a study of the living conditions, occupational profile, income and literacy levels. The participation in social activities of

Muslims shows the prevalence of high levels of illiteracy and poverty and this justified the reservation.[2] A High Court stay on this move seems to have set off a national debate on the pros and cons of community quotas despite the Sangh Parivar's strident opposition to reservations for Muslims as 'divisive and communal'.

The furore over the Andhra Pradesh Government decision to reserve 5 per cent seats in educational institutions and government jobs for Muslims harks back to the unresolved tensions in the government policy of reservations for various categories/groups. These tensions relate in large part to the contradictory notions of equality that the Indian state has adopted in promoting social justice in a highly stratified and unequal society. For its part state policy has been attempting to strike a balance between its commitment to an overarching notion of equality and justice for all, and the imperatives of the established framework of reservations in favour of historically depressed and socially backward sections of society (scheduled castes and tribes and backward classes defined in largely in caste terms). In effect, the post-independence state promoted a two-pronged strategy to advance equality: social equality for the low castes through non-discrimination and reservations in education and jobs, and cultural rights for the minorities through the protection of religious personal laws. Recently electoral considerations have led political parties, particularly the Congress, to woo Muslims with promises of reservations, but this has exacerbated social conflict among potential beneficiaries and those who perceive themselves to be losers in this process. This is because any extension of reservations cuts into their quotas or else because some are not going to get reservations anyway.

Like affirmative action policies in other countries, preferential policies in India are a system of quotas designed to increase opportunities in employment, education, and legislatures for disadvantaged groups. These policies are targeted at specific groups identified by the government as disadvantaged, essentially on the basis of caste. The public controversy over these policies centers on both equity and identity issues—redistributive effects as well as the difficulty of defining the relevant groups on the basis of caste, which bars other groups.[3] However, the official identification of people is extremely important as it has an impact on access to opportunities. Official identification has created new arenas of conflict over definitions and the criteria used to identify beneficiaries. The disagreements speak to the relationship of caste and community, on the one hand, and community and class, on the other, and the ways in which state and group conceptions of backwardness tend to evade or circumvent the complex relationship between these categories. Caste, class, and religious identities are varied and multifaceted and official policies frequently fail to capture this complexity.

This paper approaches the question of reservations for Muslims from the standpoint of state policy towards religious minorities in the public sphere. It will examine this issue through an analysis of the claims and counter claims for reservations for Muslims and the response of the government to these contending claims and its implications for the political discourse on backwardness. The aim of this paper is four-fold. First, it reflects on the conceptual framework of backwardness and its application to non-caste groups; second, it examines the conflicting Muslim response to these changes; third, it discusses the shifts in the conception of backwardness resulting in the inclusion of Muslims in the OBC list; and fourth, it makes a plea for broad-based policies of affirmative action for Muslims on the ground of inter-group disparity and under-representation in public services. I argue that religious quotas are dangerous and we must steer clear of them. It might be better for the government to include sections of the Muslim community in the backward class category or else evolve affirmative action policies that target the socio-economically deprived sections of the community. Since there is no provision for an economic criterion for affirmative action, the inclusion of Muslims in the OBC list is the most viable option. This inclusion, which began with Mandal Commission including Muslims in the OBC list, has been an important step with the potential of contributing a rethinking about disadvantage and backwardness. In other words, by adopting established categories of classification used by the government, Muslim groups are challenging the official boundaries of the scheduled castes, scheduled tribes and OBCs, and also the identity driven description and designation of the Muslim community in the political discourse.[4]

THE DYNAMICS OF RESERVATION POLICIES

Affirmative actions refer to at least three kinds of measures available to help the socially disadvantaged: affirmative action, positive discrimination, and strict quotas in school/college admissions and jobs. Affirmative action can take many forms: setting up special schools or vocational guidance facilities, and even declaring that the government will encourage specific groups to apply for jobs, etc. In Part XVI (Special Provisions Relating to Certain Classes), the Constitution has provided for the reservation of seats in the legislatures as also in public employment and educational institutions funded by the state; and for the creation of a body to monitor all these safeguards. These policies reserve government jobs, college and university admissions and scheduled tribes. In addition, we need to make a distinction between federal (central) and state policies on reservations. Several state governments, especially in south India, have gone beyond the 50 per cent limit for reserved jobs fixed by the 1994 Supreme Court verdict (Indira Sawhney case) by invoking exceptional circumstances. Tamil Nadu, Karnataka and Kerala have had reservations for backward classes that at times exceed 70 per cent.

The issue of reservation in the sense of preferential treatment has obviously been a controversial one over the past few decades. In the 1950s there was a clear national consensus in favour of reservation for the scheduled castes and tribes in the sphere of education and employment. Though the government's position was that only these two groups are entitled, reservations have been extended to the OBCs in education and public employment since 1994. The rationale of the Mandal Commission (1990) was to break the upper caste monopoly on government jobs and the professions, unchanged by two centuries of modern education and nearly half a century of democracy. This policy has proved to be controversial and has given rise to resentment that reservation benefits were not going to the really backward.[5] Since then middle class support has diminished, though it is still widespread among those directly affected. Most disadvantaged groups including religious minorities, who have not benefited significantly despite now being classified as backward, continue to actively support this policy. Much of the debate both in scholarly writing and various public forums are animated by political stands on the primacy of social justice and questions of individual *versus* group rights, and the potential conflict between merit or efficiency and social justice. But these issues do not figure in the public debate over reservations for minorities, rather the strong opposition to separate electorates tends to overshadow the debate and the focus is on the potential for communal conflict and social division.

Though the constitutionality of the use of religion as a criterion for selecting backward classes has not been explicitly under challenge, the government and courts have rejected its application in practice. Hence, minority groups were not identified as backward for the purpose of special safeguards for the disadvantaged.[6] There are two main reasons for this: In the absence of a caste system among Muslims there was no overt social discrimination suffered by them to justify special measures. This argument derived from the perception that minority religions are different in the specific sense that they do not accept the caste system and reservations were principally a matter of social justice or reparation for those who were the victims of oppression and discrimination arising out of the Hindu caste system.[7] Since Muslims do not recognize caste there was no ground for discrimination against them. The second argument is that reservations like separate electorates before Independence can be socially and politically divisive and could undermine national unity. This argument had precedents in the nationalist positions articulated in the Constituent Assembly debates. The general apprehension articulated then, and the sense of unease that continues to reflect in government policy, led to a concern that since any form of special representation or reservation for minorities might be divisive and had in fact led to Partition, any policy proposals aimed at increasing minority representation in government and so on might once again give an impetus to political division and separation. This was because of the apprehension that issues of representation raise the bogey of separatism and partition, and special rights would weaken efforts to promote national unity and cohesion. Before Independence, the British had inducted communities into the political process by granting separate representation to the Muslim community in various legislative bodies.

The decisive shift occurred during the Constituent Assembly debates. Labouring under the shadow of Partition, the Assembly swiftly jettisoned any talk of special representation for Muslims. To begin with, minorities were an inclusive category encompassing religious minorities, as well as the scheduled castes and scheduled tribes. It was only later in the process of the drafting the Constitution that the term itself came to be renegotiated and redefined. It was widely agreed that the only these two groups deserved to be the beneficiaries of a system of affirmative action so as to bring them to the same level as the rest of the country. Their backwardness was on account of their being segregated and excluded from social and political life. Their protection was in no small measure due to the earlier Assembly resolution that had implicitly declared them Hindus. Religious minorities and lower castes were distinguished, and the latter were seen as part of the Hindu community and therefore different from the religious minorities. The concept of minority was dropped altogether as inappropriate for purposes of affirmative action policies. Social discrimination of a group in the Hindu caste system was the only legitimate ground for group-preference provisions. However, in 1956 Sikhs fought for their rights and they were included with Hindus in reservations for scheduled castes. Again in 1990 Buddhists were accommodated with Hindus and Sikhs in this category. Only Muslims and Christians were left outside the reservation umbrella. Conversion to Christianity or Islam legally disqualified Dalits from the benefits of reservation given to scheduled castes.

The elimination of reservations on the basis of religion did signal the resolve to get rid of colonial categories like 'Muslim' in favour of the liberal vision of free individuals acting together with the state. Yet, group categories of different kinds, especially the category 'minority' staged a comeback in the context of secularism, contradicting the liberal goals. Even as Partition applied complete closure on job or educational reservations for Muslims on the basis of religion, it renewed the commitment to the construction of a secular state to accommodate the religious rights of millions of Muslims who had opted to stay in India. This secular vision was incompatible with reservations on the basis of religion. At the level of institutional structures, the Constitution goes on to acknowledge the presence of several diverse communities and minorities. Thus, separate personal laws were retained for different communities and rights were provided to minority communities to protect their linguistic and cultural identity. This distinctive arrangement resulted in a reification of certain kinds of group identities and a discourse where citizenship rights are linked to group identities rather than being dissociated from it. This arrangement had the imprimatur of approval of the Muslim religio-political elite, a kind of quid pro quo between them and the state. The national political leadership may well have believed that since it was giving equality in one sphere through protection of personal laws, it was somehow absolved of the obligation to provide equality in the public domain, which is the domain of economic opportunities and employment.

This framework can be traced to the pre-Independence period, when the Muslim religious elite such as the Deobandi *ulema* bargained with the colonial state and subsequently with the Congress, which they had supported in the freedom struggle. The religious elite was mainly interested in the private domain, the protection of personal laws. Congress was more than willing to accommodate this particular interest. This was part of the reason why it was unwilling to consider equality in the public domain. Moreover, issues pertaining to equality in the public domain had already been raised by the Muslim League and therefore could be conveniently dismissed as having the potential to divide in the country. In the process, the majority-minority syndrome overtook the idea of social equality of citizens qua citizens in actual politics and practice. Indian politics acknowledged and accepted Muslims only as a supplicant minority, not as full citizens. In most cases the state gives selective benefits to integrate a disadvantaged group into a wider process and co-opt it; but 'in the case of Muslims, the resources of the state were meant to reinforce their status as minority, not to integrate them fully into the political process'. Consequently, Muslims were effectively alienated from the political process itself. This alienation from public life has created a vicious cycle resulting in the denial of equality in one sphere and affirmation in the other. Refusal to countenance any suggestion of affirmative action is rooted in this idea of differentiated spheres of equality, which is being extended in one even as it is denied in the other. The benefits that are likely to accrue from the protection and promotion of cultural diversity are often considered adequate compensation for the disregard of other rights, notably equal opportunity. The distinctive feature of this approach is that while there is a great deal of emphasis on diversity and plurality, it does not seek to ensure that the polity adequately reflects the ethnic and social diversity found in society.

India has more Muslims than any other nation except Indonesia. Muslims are the single largest minority and in 2001 they comprised 13.4 per cent of the population. Indian Muslims form the largest group of Muslims in any country where they are not a majority. They are widely dispersed and unevenly spread throughout India. Sixty per cent of India's Muslims are concentrated in the Uttar Pradesh, Bihar, and West Bengal. They are a majority in the state of Jammu & Kashmir; five states have a population higher than the national average: Assam (28.43 per cent), Kerala (23 per cent), and West Bengal (23.16 per cent), Uttar Pradesh (17.3 per cent) and Bihar (16 per cent). Another state with a sizeable Muslim population is Karnataka (11.6 per cent).

Despite the success of some individuals and the high visibility of celebrities in cinema, sports, and music, Muslims on the whole have not done well since Independence in areas such as education, government service, and formal sector jobs. There are a number of educational and employment benefits for religious minorities that are implemented through special agencies, but there is no assessment of the role of social inequality in job opportunities, much less the role of religion in access to jobs. The disadvantage in various development indicators and access to services such as health and education is now well recognized. Available information points to the exceptionally low participation of Muslims in education and public employment. Indeed, the defining characteristic of the Muslims is their dismal educational and socio-economic status and their minuscule presence in public employment. Muslims have been traditionally concentrated in certain occupations and self-employment.[8] Their socio-economic status can be gleaned from a cursory analysis of the 50th and 55th rounds of the National Sample Survey Organization (NSSO) in 1993 and 1999-2000. The data show that on all major socio-economic indicators, Muslims are worse off than their counterparts in the majority community. Widespread illiteracy, low income, irregular employment, and a low asset base are common features.[9] In urban areas Muslims are at a distinct disadvantage in formal jobs.[10] If a salaried job in urban India makes it more likely that a household will have steady income and will enjoy a better economic position then again Muslims are clearly at a disadvantage. Only 27 per cent of Muslim households in urban areas had a working member with a salaried job (43 per cent in Hindu homes), whereas 52 per cent were self-employed. With low levels of education and no reservations in government jobs, Muslims have a marginal presence in the organized sector—which includes both public and private sector employment.[11] Their representation in all spheres of public life: parliament, police, civil service remains far below what their numbers would warrant. Muslims are under-represented in the Indian Administrative Services (2.8 per cent), the police (2.8 per cent), the railways (2.6 per cent) and the nationalized banks (2 per cent).[12]

BACKWARDNESS POLICY AND INCLUSION OF MUSLIMS IN THE OBC LIST

India has become much more representational in its approach than it was under Nehru or Indira Gandhi, but Muslims have not benefited from this. The major exception to this pattern of exclusion was the Mandal Commission, which had declared over 80 Muslim groups to be backward. The principles implicitly put down by the Mandal Commission were: (1) caste membership rather than individual class should determine beneficiaries; (2) low social ranking in the caste hierarchy of Hindu society rather than individual per capita income or other economic criteria should be the principal consideration for inclusion in the OBC list; (3) inadequate representation in government services and in the fields of trade, commerce and industry; (4) religious and linguistic identity no matter what the economic condition should not qualify for inclusion in the backward class category. The Commission drew up a list of 400 castes, and classified them as backward; most of them belonged to the Shudra varna. The Commission declared over 80 Muslims groups backward and categorized half of the Muslim population as backward.[13] According to the data used, Muslims constituted a little over 8 per cent of the 27 per cent OBC population; backward caste Muslims were over half of the total Muslim population of 11.2 per cent; and those specified as backward included groups such as weavers, oil crushers, carpenters, and dhobis (washermen).[14] In a major policy shift the Mandal Commission made provisions for reservations for these groups. Various states have been directed to implement these provisions; the proportion of reserved positions that would go to them has been left to state governments to decide.

The Mandal Commission objected to declaring Muslims as a whole a backward community, enjoying the same status as scheduled castes or tribes.[15] The official policy is premised on the principle of social and educational backwardness of any class, and such backwardness must be established by certain defined criteria. It recognizes specific communities cutting across religion as backward on the basis of the time-tested criterion of backwardness evolved by different states. According to this understanding, any religious community comprises a backward and a non-backward section. As in the case of Hindus, there are caste-like formations among Muslims, which the Commission recognized as the Muslim counterpart of a backward class. However, it is unclear whether the Muslim OBC category refers to the backward-forward division or was it meant to include all occupational groups and all converts of lower ranks known as *ajlaf* (low-born) and simply excluding some advantaged groups at the top. This is important, because in the case of minorities the issue is not just intra-group inequality but also inter-group inequality.

As things stand, the Muslim OBCs have been included in backward lists at the central and state levels. But they are not getting the full benefits of this provision. This should be obvious from the continued under-representation of Muslims in the central services. In 1981, they were 2.98 per cent among a total of 3,883 IAS officers, while in 2000 they were marginally less at 2.83 per cent.[16] A guaranteed minimum within the 27 per cent OBC quota would increase the likelihood of Muslims getting reserved jobs. As of now, the most prosperous among the backward castes have been able to secure a disproportionate share of benefits, and those at the bottom, including the majority of Muslims, have got very little.[17] 'This is a natural consequence of bundling unequals together. Various OBCs are in different stages of educational development. So if they compete against each other, obviously the "forwards" among them will take the cake. . . . This is why Muslim OBCs can never receive their due as part of a conglomerate because they suffer under double jeopardy – backwardness and communal prejudice', argues Syed Shahabuddin.[18]

Thanks to the policy of a few state governments to include Muslims in the category of backward castes/classes, some Muslim groups enjoy reservations in Kerala, Tamil Nadu, and Karnataka, and now in Andhra Pradesh. In Kerala 12 per cent of government jobs are currently reserved for Muslims, who account for 22 per cent of the state's population. But this benefit is available to those who come from families earning less than Rs. 2.50 lakhs annually. In Tamil Nadu, Muslims are entitled to reservation under the 30 per cent category earmarked for OBCs. Karnataka brought in 4 per cent reservation for Muslims in 1994; again the benefit is given to applicants who come from families that have an annual income below Rs. 2 lakhs or hold land below a certain ceiling or do not have a gazetted officer as parent.

By contrast, states with high demographic concentration of Muslims have been tardy in giving them reservations, which means that Muslims do not have the benefit of reservations where they most need it because 60 per cent of India's Muslims live in Uttar Pradesh, Bihar, West Bengal, and Assam. They are socially and educationally backward compared to their counterparts in the southern states but these states have been halfhearted in implementing reservations to Muslims. Applying the 50 per cent formula envisaged by the Mandal Commission, Muslim OBCs who are roughly 12 per cent of Uttar Pradesh's OBC population should be getting 6 per cent of all appointments in the public services. But they do no get even half of this because in the absence of a fixed quota, the more affluent OBC corner jobs disproportionately in comparison to the more backward.[19] Given that Muslims have been included in the backward class category the key issue is whether actual benefits have accrued to them from inclusion in the OBC list.

ARE MUSLIMS A CASTE OR A COMMUNITY?

It is necessary at this juncture to advert briefly to the controversy between caste and community that is frequently alluded to in the debate on reservations for Muslims. Assuming that Muslims are entitled to reservations because they are socially and economically backward, would it be proper to define all of them as backward for this purpose? The key issue is whether religion together with backwardness is as constitutional a basis for reservation as is caste coupled with backwardness. This would depend on the understanding of whether caste divisions or community homogeneity is more pervasive. If caste divisions are a feature of the Muslims community then religion qua community quota becomes impossible, while if the backwardness of the community is emphasized, caste-based reservations become indefensible.

Two levels of equality are at stake: intra-group and inter-group. Some Muslims are more interested in inter-group equality and hence press to be classified along religious community lines, while the vast majority are demanding that caste stratification be used for the classification of Muslims for the purpose of reservations.

While the caste system is conventionally associated with Hinduism, all religions in India, including Christianity and Islam, display inter-group disparity akin to the caste system. The basic issue is whether caste applies to Muslims. 'Caste is against Islam but still a factor in Muslim society' stated a Muslim MP. Such a contradiction surprises many since caste has become so strongly associated with Hindu society. Caste, class and religious identities are so contingent and complex that the official group based policies are constantly thrown into question. Caste-like differences exist among Muslims and marriages take place strictly within specific castes. 'When there is so much division on caste lines, how could they be bracketed as just Muslims when it comes to giving reservations' asked many Muslims at a national consultation on Muslim backwardness in New Delhi in 2002.

Taking the view that all Muslims are backward, an influential section of the Muslim leadership argues for reservations for the community on this basis. Led by Syed Shahabuddin, founder of the Association for Promoting Education and Employment of Muslims, Muslim leaders have sought to promote reservations for Muslims qua community in the civil service and education (but not legislatures), rather than backward caste or Dalit Muslims. With the tacit support of the Congress, this demand was stated at a Convention on Reservation in New Delhi in 1994 where this section of Muslims asked (1) for the whole community to be declared a backward class countrywide;

(2) the benefits of reservations should accrue first by priority to Muslims notified as OBCs and that candidates belonging to other Muslim groups (for example, *ashraf*) be admitted to those benefits only if the Muslim quotas remain unfilled.[20] Supporting a separate quota for Muslims, they emphasize the necessity of 'cutting the cake' not just horizontally by class and caste, but also vertically by religion, to evenly distribute opportunities. This is because in their view the 'entire Muslim community in the country forms a backward class'. Others among this section of the leadership believe the philosophy and structure of caste, as a superstructure of social discrimination, is wholly contradictory to the basic beliefs of Islam, which implicitly emphasize equality and universal brotherhood.[21] In other words, there are no vertical social faultlines within the community but they are as a community backward in comparison with others. The elite are therefore not in favour of inclusion of Muslims in the OBC lists, which would exclude them and they would stand to lose unless the entire community is declared backward.

This proposal has been strongly opposed by the backward castes among Muslims, who claim that Muslim elites have monopolized the benefits of even token representation in government jobs. The 2001 publication of a book, *Masawat ki Jang* (Battle for Equality)[22] sparked an intense debate with regard to the status of internal discrimination against backward castes among the Muslims. The book makes a strong case for constitutional recognition of reservations for backward class Muslims by countering two popular arguments. First, it contends that caste among Muslims has been a pervasive reality for centuries and is not the result of colonial government policies, which have favoured the so-called upper caste Muslims. Second, Congress promoted elite Muslims at the expense of backward caste Muslims even though they form 80 per cent of the Muslim population. In short, marginalization of the backward Muslim castes is of the same order as the marginalization of a Muslims as a whole vis-à-vis the Hindus. As a result, backward Muslims find themselves out of legislative assemblies and government employment. They are totally opposed to the classification of the whole community as backward, and call for reservations in employment and education mainly for the backward among them.[23] The backward classes already included in the lists of

OBCs fear that affluent and educated sections will usurp reservation benefits under a Muslim quota and their opportunities for upward social mobility would be severely curtailed. Additionally, lower caste or Dalit Muslims are demanding recognition as scheduled castes on a par with the lower castes in Hindu society.[24] (At present the Muslim equivalent of the scheduled castes are in the OBC list.) The leaders of this movement have demanded reservations for Dalit Muslims based on the concept of positive discrimination enshrined in Article 341 of the Constitution, which authorizes the President to declare certain castes as castes for special benefits. All these groups are opposed to the demand for religious quotas, and prefer to press for a caste quota for OBC and Dalit Muslims. Shabir Ansari, President of the All India Muslim OBC Organization, rejects the idea of community reservations and argues for caste-based reservations. Ejaz Ali also opposed the demand for a religious quota. Their demand for a Muslim OBC quota has brought them into direct confrontation with the traditional Muslim leaders, no matter what party they belong to, and also with the BJP, which resists the demand for reservations for Muslims, just as it opposes job quotas for Dalit Christians.

These groups argue that the caste-less Muslim is a complete myth.[25] But the Congress party has gone out of its way to promote 'upper caste' Muslims at the expense of backward caste Muslims even though the latter form 80 per cent of the Muslim population. Leaders of Muslim OBC reservations draw attention to the fact that Muslims are not a homogeneous group and are divided by caste and status distinctions. Indeed, the latest Census has shown that the low caste Muslims are worse off in terms of education and social conditions than their counterparts among Hindus.[26] But clearly the whole community is not educationally and socially backward, hence, the demand for a community quota is not consistent with the established policy of OBC reservation. But it has raised issues with regard to the rationale of OBC reservation.[27] The official policy is premised on the principle of social and educational backwardness of any class. To satisfy Article 15 (4), the class must be both socially and educationally backward, and such backwardness must be established by certain defined criteria. As there are castes among Hindus there are caste like formations among

Muslims and Christians, which have a low social status within the community.[28]

RECENT CONTROVERSIES

Recently, the Andhra Pradesh Government to implement 5 per cent reservation for Muslims in education and government employment has predictably raised a storm of protests, from the BJP and its allies. The Andhra High Court quashed the government order on the ground that the identification of Muslims as a separate reservation category has not been done on the recommendation of the State Commission for Backward Classes.[29] Second, the government order did not make a distinction between the relatively well off and the deprived Muslims thus not heeding the rule about excluding the better off among them. As the term of the Backward Classes Commission expired in September 2002, the government reconstituted it and referred the reservation issue to it. The Commission made three major recommendations in its report submitted on 14 June 2005: Muslims as a class are educationally and socially backward and may be given 5 per cent reservation creating a separate 'E' category; the well-off should be excluded from reservations; and Muslim sects such as the Dudekula, Laddaf, Pinjari/ Noorbash and Mehtar categories respectively, should be included instead in the proposed 'E' group to make it homogeneous.[30] The government accepted the first two recommendations and felt there was no need to disturb the existing arrangement by acting on the third. Reservation in the state adds up to 46 per cent, and the 5 per cent quota for Muslims will take it beyond the judicially imposed 50 per cent ceiling. However, the state government plans to fight any legal challenge to the extension beyond the stipulated 50 per cent on the grounds of extraordinary compulsions arising out of the backwardness of a very large segment of Muslims.[31]

The key point is not the opposition to job reservations for minorities, but the lack of thinking about constitutional remedies or policy initiatives to redress disadvantage in the public sphere. In the absence of any meaningful policy intervention on behalf of minorities, the hostility to reservations for Muslims appears to be unfair, given the willingness of most governments to broaden the categories of people eligible for preferential treatment and going beyond the accepted notions of social-structural disadvantage. Major arguments against reservations for Muslims on the other hand continued to involve concerns about disadvantaged groups, namely lower classes and castes. One argument was that inequalities faced by Hindu lower castes outweighed those facing the Muslims. The BJP leader, Madan Lal Khurana, suggested that reservations for Muslims would occur only at the cost of Scheduled Castes and Scheduled Tribes.[32] A second and more powerful argument had precedents in the nationalist positions articulated in the Constituent Assembly debates. The general apprehension articulated at that time and the sense of uneasiness which continues to reflect in government policy led to a concern that since any form of special representation or reservation for minorities might be divisive. The subject of affirmative action for minorities invariably raised the spectre of national disintegration in the wake of the fact that official distinctions were made between groups that are religion-based and other social groups. L.K. Advani, Deputy Prime Minister (2002-4) and President of the BJP (1996), has repeatedly criticized reservations for Muslims on the ground that it was divisive issue and might re-create Partition-like conditions.[33] In all, the divisiveness associated with colonial categories persists in contemporary India.

In the particular case of Andhra there are signs of a Muslim-backward class divide, which the BJP has been trying to take advantage of to challenge the very idea of extending benefits of reservations to Muslims. The national leadership of the BJP called the move a conspiracy to divide society. Once again, Advani said that the move would not only be 'harmful to the country, but to the Muslim community as such. It will have a catastrophic cascading effect.'[34] Rajasekhara Reddy, however, countered by arguing that:

> Keeping Muslims or for that matter any community, backward will have a catastrophic effect and not the move to uplift them. . . . Are they forgetting that development will not be possible if a large chunk of the population remains backward? Muslims constitute 9.2 per cent of the State's population. Nearly 80 per cent of them live in abject poverty. Let us give them a chance to come up in life. Reservation in education and employment is the least we can do. We promised to work for the poor and the downtrodden in our manifesto. To think that Muslims have no nationalistic fervour is criminal. And there is no greater farce than calling reservation based on backwardness a religious reservation.[35]

WHAT CAN BE DONE

A key test of democracy is the treatment of minorities. The economic, educational, social and political status of minorities is the standard for judgment. Many multi-ethnic societies exhibit a tendency for ethnic inequality. Notwithstanding the existence of a slew of policies to deal with issues of inequalities, India is not an exception with regard to this tendency. The key issue is not whether Muslims should have reservations or not, but rather that the widespread practice of reservations for others disadvantages them further since reservations leave fewer places for which they can compete. As Martha Nussbaum argues: 'Affirmative action always makes things somewhat more difficult for people who are not its beneficiaries. It is one thing to limit opportunities for an amorphous number of economically underprivileged upper castes in order to redress an urgent social problem of discrimination. But it is quite another to be selective in the way one singles out the social problems of disadvantage, leaving out one or two groups, chronic victims of discrimination, on the outside of all the elaborate machinery of state protection.'[36]

We can argue that making governing elites more plural or power sharing in governance and administration is an important objective that is well worth pursuing, even if it does not result in increasing the weight attached to the concerns of the disadvantaged or does not radically alter outcomes for the disadvantaged, it still has an independent symbolic weight in a polity with a diverse citizenry. However, the most effective solution to this call to pluralize public institutions are policies of preference in selection to desired positions, that is, affirmative action policies of which quotas are only one part. Even those concerned about the alienation of Muslims from India's public institutions and the discrimination against them in public institutions have rightly cautioned against religious quotas, which would be counter-productive. Enacting religion-based reservation has the potential to fracture the national fabric; it will unleash a politics of communal competition and is likely to provoke a reaction that can spark off new tensions that might weaken democracy. Above all, it will serve to further division and provoke a strong response from the Hindu right, which opposes the very idea of any special treatment of minorities and remains completely opposed to reservations for Muslims.

In view of this there are two strategies available. The first is to acknowledge caste stratification among Muslims and identify the least advantaged on this basis as has been done by the Mandal Commission and several state governments. This approach is practical and has less potential to alienate other groups. Most of all, it has found favour with state governments that have shown willingness to extend reservations to Muslims on the basis of caste, but not on the basis of religion. Bihar and Uttar Pradesh governments have preferred to follow this approach. The second approach is to identify disadvantaged groups on the basis of a mix of economic and social criteria. The governments of Kerala, Karnataka, and Tamil Nadu have adopted this approach to give reservations to Muslims on this basis. It is noteworthy that these states are not giving reservations to all Muslims, which means they have kept away from religious quotas. In addition, they have been more successful in implementing the principle of proportionality by giving public employment and government jobs to Muslims. They have got around the tricky issue of caste stratification and at the same time reached out directly to the disadvantaged by circumventing the Muslim elite through a policy of affirmative action rather than reservations. The distinctive element of the approach is the emphasis on an economic criterion and a provision for a guaranteed minimum for Muslims fixed by the state governments.

Affirmative action is a way of ensuring access for Muslims to education and employment opportunities. This is grounded in the understanding that affirmative action policies have contributed, both directly and indirectly, to increasing the participation and access of the scheduled castes, scheduled tribes, and backward classes, to resources and benefits. Such an approach strengthens equal citizenship and the democratic process. This can be justified on two grounds. One, there is a sense of 'otherness' to Muslims that secular India has not been able to reconcile. For example, for most inhabitants in Uttar Pradesh, as one recent study has shown, Muslims are an imagined other, essentialized as 'child breeders, dirty, violent, fundamentalist, sinister looking, poor, illiterate and so on'.[37] These prejudices, imbibed from the public sphere and the media, were elevated to be transcendent truths. The preoccupation with the Muslim 'other' is partly responsible for the strong opposition to affirmative action for Muslims, which is seen as special treatment of Muslims, notwithstanding the fact that caste, class and religious boundaries intersect and sustain one another to create a vicious circle of poverty and deprivation for Muslims just as they do for the scheduled castes and tribes.

Second, their historical status as the 'other' adversely impacts on their prospects of getting public employment. Lack of education and discrimination on account of their status as the largest religious minority and their status as the 'other' are major factors in their exclusion from the government sector. The prejudices mentioned above influence the production of national level ideologies and policies. One effect of this essentialization is discrimination, as state agencies imagine Muslims in the same stereotypical ways as the rest of the public, rather than as part of the dispossessed and disadvantaged population. As a result, the public space for educated and professionally trained Muslims shrinks. Yet, the exclusion of Muslims from public employment has not received the attention it deserves, except from intellectuals in the community who for a long time have been lamenting the poor representation of Muslims in civil service and politics.

One last point. Affirmative action policies will be effective only when supplemented by policies that encourage and support educational progress and occupational mobility. Thus, priority must be given to the inclusion of minorities in all schemes that are aimed at expanding opportunities for citizens: education, employment, and so forth. On this front the Indian state needs to give a credible commitment, which it has not done adequately. Government policy must address the issue of inclusion of minorities more forcefully, or else the effects can be disastrous.

NOTES

1. No. 33 (G.O. 33) of 12 July 2005.
2. The National Sample Survey 55th Round Report on *Employment and Unemployment Situation among Religious Groups in India 1999-2000* indicates that among those with a monthly per capita expenditure below Rs. 300 in the rural areas, about 21 per cent are Muslims. In the urban areas, more than 39 per cent of those with monthly per capita expenditure below Rs. 425 are Muslims. In a state where only 8.5 per cent of the population is Muslim, this clearly shows that levels of poverty are high.

3. Laura Dudley Jenkins, *Identity and Identification in India: Defining the Disadvantaged*, London: Routledge Curzon, 2003.
4. Ibid.
5. K.C. Suri, 'Competing Interests, Social Conflict and the Politics of Caste Reservations in India', *Nationalism and Ethnic Politics*, vol. 1, no. 2, 1995.
6. Marc Galanter, *Competing Equalities: Law and the Backward Classes in India*, Delhi: Oxford University Press, 1984.
7. Jenkins, *Identity and Identification in India*, op. cit., 2003.
8. Khandker, John Harris, Shariff, Mushirul Hasan.
9. This section on disparities draws upon the analysis of the NSSO data on inter-group disparity by Rammanohar Reddy, 'Deprivation affects Muslims more', *Hindu*, 12 and 13 September 2002. Also see Abusaleh Shariff, 'Socio-economic and Demographic Differentials between Hindus and Muslims in India', *Economic and Political Weekly*, 18 November 1995.
10. Maitreyi Bordia Das, 'Muslim Women's Low Labour Force Participation in India: Some Structural Explanations', in Zoya Hasan and Ritu Menon (eds.), *In a Minority: Essays on Muslim Women in India*, Delhi: Oxford University Press, 2005.
11. A.R. Momin, *The Empowerment of Muslims in India: Perspective, Context and Prerequisites*, Delhi: Institute of Objective Studies, 2004.
12. Ibid.
13. Marc Galanter, 'Group Membership and Group Preferences in India', in his *Law and Society in Modern India*, Delhi: Oxford University Press, 1994.
14. *Report of the Backward Classes Commission*, 1980 known as the Mandal Commission, pp. 60-1.
15. D.L. Sheth, 'Reservations: No Provision for Communal Quotas', *Alpjan Quarterly: A Chronicle of Minorities*, vol. IV, no. 3, 2004.
16. A.R. Momin, *The Empowerment of Muslims in India*, p. 63.
17. Syed Shahabuddin, 'Reservation of Muslims: Constitutional and Socially Necessary', *Alpjan Quarterly: A Chronicle of Minorities*, vol. IV, no. 4, 2004, p. 8.
18. Ibid., p. 8.
19. Ibid.
20. Theodore Wright Jr., 'A New Demand for Muslim Reservations in India', *Asian Survey*, September 1997, vol. 37, no. 9.
21. Shabbir Ansari cited in Jenkins, p. 116.
22. Ali Anwar, *Masawat ki Jang* (Battle for Equality), Delhi: Vani Prakashan, 2001.
23. See the series of articles in the *Economic and Political Weekly*, 15 November 2003, especially, Anwar Alam, 'Democratization of Indian Muslims: Some Reflections'; Irfan Ahmad, 'A Different Jihad: Dalit Muslims' Challenge to Ashraf Hegemony'.
24. Yoginder Sikand, 2003.
25. Imtiaz Ahmad (ed.), *Caste and Stratification among Muslims in India*, Delhi:

Manohar, 1976. Also see *Family, Kinship and Marriage among Muslims in India; Ritual and Religion Among Muslims in India*, Delhi: Manohar, 1980 and 1981.

26. For an analysis of the Census data see Abusaleh Shariff, 'On the Margins: Muslims in a State of Socio-economic Decline', *The Times of India*, 22 October 2004.
27. D.L. Sheth, 'Reservations: No Provision for Communal Quotas', *Alpjan Quarterly: A Chronicle of Minorities*, vol. IV, no. 3, April-June 2004.
28. The rediff.com reported incidents of backward or lower caste Muslims being denied entry for burial in graveyards by the upper caste Muslims, forcing the lower caste Muslims to bury their dead outside the graveyard.
29. *The Hindu*, 2 August 2004.
30. W. Chandrakanth, 'A Reservation Row', *Frontline*, 15 July 2005.
31. Ibid.
32. Cited in Jenkins, op. cit., p. 135.
33. Ibid., p. 135.
34. Quoted in *Frontline*, 15 July 2005.
35. Ibid.
36. Nussbaum, op. cit., p. 36.
37. Kathinka Froystad, *Blended Boundaries: Caste, Class and Shifting Faces of Hinduness in a North Indian City*, Delhi: Oxford University Press, 2004, p. 212.

2

The Reformist Sufism of the Tablighi Jamaat: The Case of the Meos of Mewat

YOGINDER SIKAND

The twentieth century witnessed the emergence of a number of movements for religious revival and reform among Muslims all over the world. One of these, probably the largest Islamic movement in the world today, is the Tablighi Jamaat (TJ), which has a major presence in India.[1] Although it has its roots in the South Asian Muslim environment, with which it is still closely identified, the TJ is now said to be active almost in every country with a significant Sunni Muslim presence.[2] Its founder, the charismatic *alim*, Maulana Muhammad Ilyas (1885-1944), believed that Muslims had strayed far from the teachings of Islam.[3] Hence he felt the urgent need for Muslims to go back to the basic principles of their faith, and to strictly observe the commandments of Islam in their own personal lives and in their dealings with others. This alone, he believed, would win them the pleasure of God, who would then be moved to grant them 'success' (*falah*) in this world and in the life after death.

Although not identified as a specifically Sufi movement as such, the TJ emerged from out of the reformist Sufi project represented by the renowned Dar ul-Ulum Madrasa located at the town of Deoband, not far from Delhi. It first took root in the area of Mewat, south of Delhi, in the mid-1920s, among a community of Muslim peasants known as the Meos. The Meos continue to be closely involved in the work of the TJ, although this has somewhat declined in recent years as the movement has assumed global proportions. Yet, as TJ ideologues and activists see it, Mewat is said to be the most successful experimental ground of the movement.

This paper examines the reformist Sufi project of the TJ as it has come to express itself among the Meos of Mewat, using this as a case study to illustrate the working of the TJ among Muslim communities elsewhere in India. It begins with a brief description of the Meos and the early twentieth century Meo popular religion. It then discusses the intervention of the TJ in Mewat, looking at what this has meant for popular Sufism in the region. It goes on to examine the new form of Islam—reformist, *shariah*-centred Sufism—that the TJ has sought to introduce in the region, examining the ways in which the Meos have sought to incorporate the TJ's project in their daily lives. I also consider the implications of this new conceptualization of Islam, particularly what it has meant for how religious authority is imagined, understood, and articulated. Finally, it examines how, in the face of growing urbanization, education, and the intervention of the modern state, in short the challenge of modernity, Meo attitudes towards the TJ are undergoing a steady transformation. Although not identical, similar processes are at work among other Muslim communities in India where the TJ is active.

THE TJ AND THE REFORMIST SUFI TRADITION

The TJ had its origins in the reformist Sufi project represented by the Dar ul-Ulum Madrasa at Deoband. Established in 1867, the Deoband *madrasa*, as Metcalf discusses in her excellent study, set in motion a powerful movement of reform of popular tradition, exhorting Muslims to closely follow the Prophetic model and to abandon what it condemned as 'un-Islamic' customs.[4] This entailed a fierce attack on those beliefs, customs and practices seen as having no sanction in the *shariah* and the practice of the Prophet, and which were consequently declared *bidaat* or wrongful 'innovations'. At the same time, it also entailed the definition of what constituted 'orthodox' Islam. As the Deobandis saw it, 'true' Islam lay simply and entirely in the classical scripture comprising the Koran and the canonical collections of Hadith or Prophetic traditions, and also the writings of the Hanafi *ulama*. As strict *muqallids*, they insisted on rigid *taqlid* of the *ijma* of the Hanafi *ulama*, and even went to the extent of condemning inter-*mazhab* eclecticism. They were fiercely opposed to Western culture, represented by the British colonial regime, which they saw as threatening the integrity of Islam. They roundly condemned Muslim modernists who advocated reforms in the historical *shariah* in the name of *ijtihad*. In other words, they saw modernity as seducing Muslims away from faithful adherence from their religion. Yet, they did not oppose modern technology or modern forms of organization as such, and in fact willingly embraced modern methods of communication, such as the printing press, in order to spread their doctrines to a wider audience.

At the same time as they insisted on the need for Muslims to closely abide by the *shariah* and internalize its norms, the *ulama* of Deoband also sought to cultivate a rich inner life. Leading Deobandi *ulama* also acted as Sufi *shaikhs*, the spiritual preceptors of many of their students, and initiating them into various Sufi orders. Metcalf's book deals extensively with the reformed Sufism of the Deobandis, and so this does not need to be repeated here. To summarize, the Deobandis were particularly concerned to reconcile the *tariqat* with *shariah*, the inner mystical journey with the externalist path of the law. This entailed new definitions of what constituted 'orthodox', and hence acceptable, Sufism in the Indian context.

The founder of the TJ, Maulana Ilyas, was himself a student of several of the leading *ulama* of Deoband, including a number of its founding fathers. He was born in the town of Kandhla, district Muzaffarnagar, in the erstwhile United Provinces, not far from Delhi, in 1885. His family claimed Arab origins, and was known for having produced numerous leading Islamic scholars. In 1897, at the age of 12, Ilyas traveled to the town of Gangoh, not far from Kandhla, then a major centre for reformist Islamic learning. After staying nine years there in the service of the renowned Deobandi *alim*, Maulana Rashid Ahmad Gangohi (1829-1905), he went on to Deoband. There he studied Hadith with Maulana Mahmud ul-Hasan (known to his followers as Shaikh ul-Hind or 'The Teacher of India'), to whom it is claimed that he gave an oath (*baiat*) of *jihad* against the British. While at Deoband he also came into contact with other leading Deobandi *ulama*, including Maulana Ashraf Ali Thanwi, arguably the greatest reformist Sufi of his times, and Maulana Shah Abdur Rahim Raipuri. Later, Ilyas would refer to them as his 'very body and soul'.[5] Ilyas' years at Gangoh and then Deoband instilled in him a deep reverence for the Deobandi *ulama* and their mission, inspiring him to later launch his own powerful movement of Islamic scripturalist reform in the early 1920s. Ilyas would later insist that the TJ aimed to spread the reformist doctrines of the Deobandis, albeit using different means of popular preaching.

ILYAS' REFORMIST SUFI PROGRAMME

The Tablighi Message

Ilyas himself wrote almost nothing about his own project of reformed, *shariah*-centred Sufism, stressing that 'practical work' (*amali kam*) for the sake of Islam was more important that merely writing about it. In this, of course, he carried on in the path of the early Sufi masters, who insisted that Sufism was, above all, a practical rather than intellectual discipline. Yet, some of Ilyas' disciples collected his letters (*maktubat*) and utterances (*malfuzat*), which they later published after his death.[6] These form important traditional genres of Sufi writing, and provide us with valuable insights into Ilyas' own understanding of the work which he was engaged in.

Ilyas' *malfuzat* and *maktubat* reveal a man passionately concerned with the fate of the Muslim community, both its worldly conditions as well as what he saw as its digression from the Prophetic model. The community's fortunes, Ilyas was convinced, critically depended on strict observance of the *shariah*. As he saw it, the Muslims' plight owed simply to their having strayed from the path of God's law and having adopted the ways of the 'disbelievers'.[7] The eagerness that he saw many Muslims display in seeking to emulate the British greatly distressed him. Modernity, as it came to be embodied in the colonial project, appeared to Ilyas a threat to the integrity of Islam. Muslims, he warned, must cease to imitate their 'enemies', for their only way to salvation was to strictly follow in the path of the Prophet. Equally distressing to Ilyas was the widespread practice among many Muslims of what he saw as 'Hinduistic', and, therefore, 'polytheistic' customs, and he regarded the need for the reform of popular tradition as particularly urgent. In this, of course, he was not alone. Early twentieth century Indian Muslim reformists of all hues, including the Deobandis as well as Islamists and Muslim modernists, railed against popular customary practices, exhorting Muslims to 'return' to the path of the 'authentic' Islamic tradition. Although the ways in which they envisaged Islamic 'orthodoxy' and 'authenticity' varied considerably, and were often mutually opposed to each other, the reformists were united in their opposition to rituals, which they roundly castigated as 'un-Islamic'. Yet, whatever their concern for 'orthodoxy', the entire effort seems to have been also deeply influenced by an overriding concern on the part of Muslim reformers to draw rigid boundaries between Muslims and others (mainly 'Hindus') as part of a wider project of constructing an 'imagined community' of Muslims. This must be seen in the context of Muslim marginalization following the collapse of Mughal political authority, and the growing challenge of Hindu 'nationalism' that threatened to absorb the Indian Muslims into the Hindu fold. In Ilyas' particular case, it appears that the growing success of the Arya Samaj in bringing into the Hindu fold large numbers of those seen as 'nominal' Muslims (generally referred to as *nau musalman* or 'new Muslims') goaded him on to realize the importance of inculcating an adequate sense of unity among Muslims of all classes based on a common commitment to the *shariah*. Only in this way, he believed, as we shall later discuss, could Muslims stave off the Arya challenge and preserve their faith and identity intact.

In other words, the growing stress that late nineteenth- and early twentieth-century Indian Muslim reformists placed on *shariah*-centred Islam and their attacks on popular custom must be seen as intimately related to the particular political context of colonial north India, one characterized by growing and increasingly fierce rivalry between Hindu and Muslim elites. It is important to note in this regard that the concern of Muslim elites with the *shariah* as a symbol of identity that united Muslims while at the same time distinguished them clearly from Hindus, had much to do with the fact, which the reformists lamented, that the Muslims of India (like the Hindus) did not actually constitute a single community. Sharp divisions of language, locality, ethnicity, sectarian affiliation, and even caste divided the Muslims of the country, and in no sense of the term could they be considered a homogeneous group. The attack on local customary practices, and their replacement by commitment to the universal, normative standard of *shariah*-centred scripturalist Islam thus served as a powerful resource in the process of constructing a pan-Indian Muslim community transcending internal divisions. At the same time, by attacking customary practices that were condemned as borrowings from 'infidel' Hindus, the reformers helped undermine traditions of popular religiosity and religious culture that brought Hindus and Muslims together in a shared cultural universe. Stressing the distinctions between Muslims and their Hindu neighbours, reformists exhorted Muslims to remain deeply conscious of their separate communal identity, for only then could they effectively meet the perceived threat of being absorbed into the Hindu fold by organized Hindu revivalist groups. This had its counterpart on the Hindu side as well, as Hindu reformers strongly condemned the visiting of Sufi shrines by Hindus and the widespread observance of what were seen as 'Muslim' practices. In turn, these attacks on popular religious traditions bolstered the process of constructing sharply defined boundaries between Muslims and Hindus.

Ilyas' own reformist Sufi project grew out of these powerful concerns for identity and normative Islam of the Muslim reformers of his time. As he saw it, the decline of Muslim political authority in India, and what he referred to as Muslim 'degeneracy',[8] owed entirely to Muslims having strayed from the path of strict observance of scripturalist Islam. By having abandoned that path, and having 'adopted' what he saw as un-Islamic customs, which he traced to their Shia and Hindu neighbours, they had courted God's wrath. Also branded as 'un-Islamic', and occupying a central place in customary tradition, was the domain of popular Sufism. This included practices related to worship at the shrines of saints, such as prostration before their graves, musical sessions, and the unrestricted mixing of men and women. Equally condemnable were a range of beliefs and associated practices relating to the authority of the Sufis, whether living or dead. The notion that a buried Sufi was still alive and could intercede with God to grant one's requests was fiercely condemned as 'un-Islamic' and akin to *shirk*, the sin of associating partners with the one God. It was also said to be a reprehensible innovation that had no legitimacy in Islam. Likewise, the notion that one could attain unity with God, which the *wujudi* Sufis stressed, was branded as heresy. As Ilyas saw it, the *shariah* must set the parameters of normative Islam. Practices associated with popular Sufism that were regarded as exceeding those boundaries were 'un-Islamic' and hence to be abandoned.

In other words, Ilyas did not condemn Sufism outright, as did, for instance, the followers of the Ahl-i Hadith, a group of reformists who emerged in the late nineteenth century, who identified themselves with the Wahhabis of Arabia. Ilyas' *shariah*-centred Sufism insisted on the unity of the *shariah* and the *tariqat*. Ilyas, like many of his Deobandi masters, functioned as both an *alim* as well as a Sufi, and in the latter capacity as a guide to his followers on the spiritual path. His *maktubat* and *malfuzat* are replete with Sufistic terms, such as *lutf* (joy), *sukun-i qalb* (peace of heart), *nur-i basirat* (the light of insight), *marifat* (gnosis) and so on,[9] but these are to be understood as states experienced in the course of missionary work, abiding faithfully by the *shariah* and exhorting others to do the same, not in mystical flights of fancy and self-absorption. Several of the practices that Ilyas enjoined upon his followers are clearly associated with Sufism. The 'six points' (*chhe batein*) that he laid down for his followers, which now serve to encapsulate the Tablighi programme, have remarkably Sufi associations. The first of these was the *kalima shahada*, the Islamic creed of confession of the faith (*la ilaha il allah muhammadur rasul allah*). Muslims were first to memorize the *kalima shahada* and learn to pronounce it properly. Then, they were to internalize it, seeking to realize its essence—that God alone is the Master of all, which means that His will alone, as expressed through His Prophet, should be obeyed. The second point was *namaz* (Arabic: *salah*), or ritual worship. Muslims were to learn the rules of *namaz* and regularly perform it. This was to go along with the cultivation of the appropriate inner attitude, for it was not enough simply to go through the worship as a mere physical exercise. The third point was *ilm-o zikr* (knowledge and remembrance). Muslims were to seek to acquire knowledge of the faith, particularly of the *shariah*, and also to engage in various *zikr* practices, many of these being clearly Sufi in substance and form. Fourth was *ikram-i muslim*, or 'respect for [all] Muslims'. The ideal Muslim was one who loved and respected all fellow believers, overlooked their follies and ignored their bad qualities, focusing, instead on the good that they might possess. Fifth, *tashih-i niyyat* meant 'purification of intention'. All actions, whether worldly or religious, were to be motivated by pure intention, that is by the desire to win God's favour, to do His will and to earn merit (*sawab*) in the hereafter. This meant that one's actions were to be untainted by worldly motives. Last came the *tafrigh-i waqt* (spending time). A true Muslim was one who actively worked for the cause of the faith, taking time off from his worldly responsibilities to travel to engage in *tabligh* or missionary work, both in search of religious knowledge as well as to impart that knowledge to others. Ideally, a Muslim was to spend three *chillahs*[10] a year doing *tabligh* work. Overall, the *chhe batein* reflect an activist, *shariah*-centric Sufism that, borrowing heavily from the Sufi heritage, seeks to root itself within the boundaries of normative or scripturalist Islam.[11]

POPULAR *VS. SHARIAH*-CENTRED SUFISM

Ilyas' reformed Sufism, as expressed in the form of the TJ, had crucial implications for the constitution of religious authority. By attacking popular custom, the TJ directly challenged the authority of the custodians of the Sufi shrines (*sajjada nashin*), who were seen as having a vested interest in preserving popular custom, for their own claims to authority rested on these. Since a true Muslim was sought to be defined as one who carefully followed the *shariah* in his own life, the claims of the *sajjada nashin* to authority on the basis of their special links with the buried saints (generally as relatives or descendants) were effectively challenged. As Kelly Pemberton perceptibly notes, by making access to fundamental texts and the teachings of scripturalist Islam available to all Muslims, the TJ, like the Deobandis, 'sought to undercut the intercessionary role of the Sufi *shaikh*'.[12] This did not, however, mean doing away with the position of the *shaikh* altogether, but, rather, recasting his role from that of an intermediary between God and man to that of a teacher of the *shariah*. In other words, the TJ put forward a new basis of religious authority. Authority to speak for and to represent Islam was, Ilyas suggested, to be sought to be earned through personal effort, by strict compliance with the *shariah*, rather than simply gained through inheritance from one's ancestors. Every Muslim, Ilyas insisted, no matter what his status in life, could be considered a true *wali* or friend of God, provided he followed the *shariah* faithfully. One did not require the 'right' family connections for that, contrary to what many *sajjada nashin* claimed. As Ilyas saw it, since it was one's faithful observance of the *shariah* alone that qualified one to be considered a *wali*, the claims of the *sajjada nashin* to authority, based on the reports of the miracles (*karamat*) performed by the saints whose shrines they tended, were effectively dismissed as ultimately of little worth. Punctilious observance of the *shariah*, and not *karamat*, was, Ilyas stressed, the only way to rise in God's eyes. Even 'despicable' non-Muslims were said to be capable of performing miracles, and so that could not constitute a basis for authority. One's claims to religious authority, Ilyas suggested, also had nothing to do with mediating between God and man, as in the case of popular Sufi cults, for this was 'un-Islamic'. Rather, Ilyas seems to have believed, one earned religious authority by strictly following the *shariah* and dedicating one's whole life to the propagation of Islam. In other words, the role of the Sufi *shaikh* was now no longer that of an intermediary, but that of a guide. Alongside this, the ways in which the Sufi path was understood also underwent a crucial transformation. The *shariah*, rooted in this-worldly practices, took over from the mystical quest of abandoning the world or absorbing oneself in God. There could thus be no contradiction between the *shariah* and the *tariqat*.

In other words, in the TJ the locus of authority was sought to be transferred from the deceased Sufi or the *sajjada nashin* to the charismatic community, the roving *jamaat*, or preaching party of Tablighi missionaries. It was within the *jamaat*, rather than in a Sufi hospice (*khanqah*) associated with a particular order (*silsilah*) that the Sufi discipline was to be cultivated, and it was in the course of one's work in the *jamaat* that God was believed to grant His blessings and even sometimes arrange for suitable *karamat* to happen. In a sense, then, the TJ represented a significant democratization of religious authority, at least in comparison to the closely controlled and steeply hierarchical cults of the Sufis centred on the shrines. All Muslims were exhorted to gain knowledge of Islam, and access to the resources of scripturalist Islam was no longer to be regarded as a closely guarded monopoly of the *ulama* or high-ranking Sufis. All Muslims could, indeed should, be actively involved in the 'work' for the faith. *Tabligh* was no longer to be regarded as the duty of the *ulama* and Sufis alone. From being earlier considered as a *farz-i kifaya*, a duty considered fulfilled if even a section of the community, *tabligh* was now to be considered as *farz-i ayn*, a responsibility binding on every member of the community, no matter how humble his or her origins. One's stature in God's eyes was said to be dependent not on family origins, wealth, or power, and not even on Islamic knowledge, but simply on one's dedication to Islam and to the work of *tabligh*, expressed in the form of faithfully following the dictates of the *shariah* in one's own life. Naturally, such a stance worked to undermine the influence of the *sajjada nashin* and even of many *ulama*, even as it sought to impose the vision of one section of the *ulama*—those associated with the TJ—as hegemonic.

THE MEO POPULAR TRADITION: FROM *BIDAAT* TO *SHARIAH*

Ilyas' reformist project was first launched in a culturally distinct region south of Delhi called Mewat, comprising large parts of the Alwar and Bharatpur districts of Rajasthan and the Gurgaon and Faridabad districts of Haryana. Mewat is the land of the Meos, a Muslim community for the most part peasants, who today number about a million. The Meos were regarded, and still, in some sense continue to be seen, as *nau*-Muslims or neo-Muslims, although their first contact with Islam goes back several centuries. The Meos claim to be of 'high' caste Hindu Rajput origin, but although it may well be that some of them are indeed of Rajput stock, it appears that the vast majority are descendants of 'low' caste and tribal converts, who now claim a different origin.

Mewat's first encounters with Islam dates to the twelfth century, when, living in the vicinity of the imperial capital of the Sultanate of Delhi, they often came into conflict with the Turkish Sultans. Sometimes, drought and famine would force hordes of Meos to attack and loot Delhi, which then brought on them violent reprisals. On several occasions, forcible conversion to Islam was sought to be imposed on them as a punishment and as a means to combat Meo lawlessness. Yet, if the Sultans seem to have been rather ineffective in bringing about the conversion of the Meos, numerous Sufis who entered the region and settled there seem to have been more successful. Today scores of Sufi shrines dot the Mewati countryside, testifying to the many centuries of Sufi presence in the area. It was under the influence of these Sufis that the vast majority of the inhabitants of Mewat came to identify, at least nominally, with Islam. Yet, Meo forms of Islam continued to be deeply rooted in popular traditions, leading observers to comment that the Meos were Muslim only in name. Writing in the last quarter of the nineteenth century, Major Powlett, the British settlement officer of the Alwar state, was provoked to remark:

> The Meos are now all Musalmans in name, but their village deities are the same as those of the Hindus, and they keep several Hindu fasts. . . . Meos, in their customs, are half Hindu. The Meo places of worship are similar to those of their Hindu neighbours. . . . As regards their own religion [Islam] the Meos are very ignorant. Few know the *kalima*, and fewer still the regular prayers, the seasons of which they entirely neglect.[13]

According to another source, in Mewat:

> Reading of the Qur'an was less popular than reading the Hindu epics Ramayana and Mahabharata. Hindu shrines far outnumbered mosques in Mewat. Few Meos prayed in the Muslim manner, but most of them performed the *puja*—worship at the shrines of the Hindu gods and goddesses.[14]

As an almost entirely peasant community, the Meos had few religious specialists of their own. Instead, they sought the help of Hindu *pandits* as well as Muslim *faqirs*, custodians of the Sufi shrines, for various ritual purposes. Meo religion was, above all, practical, rooted in specific life cycle events, as well as geared to the propitiation of deities, including (but not exclusively) Allah, and a host of spirits and hidden saints for favours or to ward off misfortune. As for the way the Meos identified themselves, the notion of 'Muslim' as clearly district from 'Hindu' was quite unknown.

From the late nineteenth century onwards, and gaining particular momentum from the 1920s, a complex set of developments set in motion a process of radical redefinition of Meo self-perceptions, including religious identity. I have dealt with this process in detail elsewhere, and this need not detain us here.[15] Suffice it to say that these included the introduction and spread of reified notions of religion and community identity popularized by colonial administrators, particularly census officers, as well as Muslim and Hindu elites; growing competition between Hindu and Muslim elites, leading to Hindu-Muslim conflict in large parts of northern India; a series of Meo peasant revolts during the Great Depression of the 1930s that the Hindu rulers of the Bharatpur and Alwar states saw as 'Islamic' movements and accordingly sought to brutally crush; the role of external Muslim organizations and leaders in assisting the Meos in their revolt and articulating their grievances to a wider audience; and, finally, the role of Ilyas and his movement in the area from the mid-1920s, in order to save the Meos from the threat of being absorbed into the Hindu fold at the hands of the Hindu revivalist Arya Samaj. All these seem to have made for an increasing stress on the Islamic aspect of Meo identity. The TJ had a crucial role to play in this process, with its call for the Meos to identify with and observe the rules of the *shariah* striking a receptive chord among many who now sought to clearly distinguish themselves from their Hindu neighbours. Yet, it was only in the aftermath of Partition in 1947, and the resultant bloody rioting in which tens of thousands of Meos were killed, that the TJ really took off in a major way among the Meos. Faced with the fierce hostility of their Hindu neighbours, most Meos found in the TJ a source of strength, and its call to eschew 'Hindu' customs and beliefs was now certainly more acceptable than before.[16]

In order to understand the success of the TJ in Mewat, it is pertinent here to examine how the TJ sought to root itself among the Meos, and, in particular, how it related itself to the Meo popular religious tradition, one that, as we have seen, had for centuries resisted the pressure to conform to normative understandings of Islam. Ilyas insisted on a gradual process of Islamization, and in this he was only following in the footsteps of his Sufi forebears. The Meos were not to be forced to accept and follow the entire edifice of the *shariah* all at once. Rather, Ilyas stressed, they must be first encouraged to follow the *chhe batein*, this being based on a firm cultivation of their faith (*iman*) in Islam. Once their faith had been sufficiently fortified, he argued, they would themselves work for the creation of a 'truly' Islamic society, replacing their 'un-Islamic' practices and institutions with those that were in line with the *shariah*. TJ missionaries were asked simply to focus their preaching on the great divine rewards (*fazail*) that the Meos would receive if they followed the *shariah*, with promises of immense blessings (*sawab*) being assured for 'reviving' even the most minor *sunnat* or practice of the Prophet. The missionaries were to clearly avoid, in matters other than ritual worship, the *masail* or detailed aspects of Islamic jurisprudence and law, which in many respects conflicted with Meo customary practice. This was particularly important, given the deep-rootedness of the Meo tradition, and reflected Ilyas' astute awareness that to combat that tradition directly, even if it constituted a flagrant violation of the *shariah* in many crucial respects, would inevitably result in stern Meo opposition to his movement. Put differently, Ilyas insisted that in their missionary work TJ activists must avoid all reference to what he called *ikhtilafi* issues, or matters which might promote dissent and conflict. Instead, they must focus only on *ittifaqi* issues, matters such as the need for piety and prayer, on which there could be no dispute or opposition.[17]

Given Ilyas' pragmatic missionary strategy, the TJ was able to establish a firm foothold in Mewat by the end of the 1940s, responding to the growing quest on the part of the Meos for a more unambiguously 'Muslim' identity built in opposition to what had now come to be seen as the menacing Hindu 'other'. This process was given a further boost in the aftermath of the bloody events of 1947, when several thousand Meos were slaughtered by Hindu mobs. Today, with the growing spread of Hindu militancy in large parts of India including Mewat, association with the TJ and its programme of *shariah*-centred Islamic reformism has much to do with Muslim insecurities and fear that their lives, faith, and identity are under grave threat. Formal affiliation or identification with the TJ has now become, in a sense, an integral part of Meo identity. This does not mean, however, that the TJ has been able to make much headway in bringing the Meos to lead their personal and collective lives in accordance with the *shariah*. Several pre-Islamic customs and institutions of the Meos still remain deeply rooted, and in the case of many Meos their commitment to TJ-style reformism is nominal. It appears that this has much to do with the TJ's own style of missionary activism, leading to an only very partial acceptance, in actual fact, of its total message on the part of most Meos. As we have seen, TJ workers are strictly forbidden from raising 'controversial' (*ikhtilafi*) matters, restricting themselves instead *to ittifaqi masail* or matters on which all are agreed. In the Meo case, the stress on the *fazail* and the *ittifaqi*, as opposed to the *masail* and the *ikhtilafi*, has meant that the TJ has been able to accommodate itself in Mewati society without major controversy, but also that many practices that are seen as un-Islamic by TJ activists are not directly challenged or opposed. By ignoring the *ikhtilafi masail*, it spares deep-rooted 'un-Islamic' traditions and institutions of the Meos from direct attack, and lets them, in effect, continue unopposed. These include the traditional Meo prohibition of cross-cousin marriage (the preferred form of marriage for many other Muslim groups in South Asia), the custom of dowry paid to the groom by the bride's family, the working of women in the fields in the presence of 'strange' men, and the almost universal denial of inheritance rights to women, all of which have no sanction in the *shariah*.

THE TJ AND MODERNITY

The TJ's response to the manifold challenges that modernity poses is a complex one, fraught with tensions and ambiguities. On the one hand, in line with the general Deobandi position on the matter, the TJ enjoins strict *taqlid* or following precedent in matters of *fiqh* or Islamic jurisprudence. *Ijtihad*, or creative reasoning and development of *fiqh* in accordance with changing conditions, is explicitly condemned as threatening to dilute Muslims' faith and destroy the *shariah*, which is believed to have been revealed by God, while claiming to reform it. Such changes are regarded as dangerous *bidaat* or 'innovations' that are to be fiercely condemned, for every such 'innovation' is said to lead to hell-fire. In other words, in several crucial respects the TJ appears vehemently hostile to the changes that modernity brings in its wake, including changing value systems and laws. Modernity, for many Tablighi activists, is seen as inculcating religious indifference or laxity as well as crass materialism and sexual licentiousness. It threatens to seduce Muslims from faithful adherence to Islam. Rather than seeking to critically engage with the multifarious challenges that modernity poses, the thrust of the TJ is to encapsulate Muslims in their own cultural world, insulating them from the rapidly changing developments in the world around them by stressing the need to conform as closely as possible to the model of the Prophet and his Companions down to the smallest detail of dress and personal etiquette.

This said, it is also the case that Meo identification with the TJ today also has much to do with distinctly modern concerns, and in this sense the TJ might actually be promoting an incipient, yet inadvertent modernity. Thus, the TJ's opposition to the cults centred on the Sufi shrines ties in with contemporary Meo aspirations for equality and self-respect. As a Meo respondent, an active TJ worker, puts it:

In the past, we served the *faqirs* of the shrines, for they insisted that they were of pure Muslim descent and that we were Hindu converts. They claimed that they had special access to the Sufis whose shrines they looked after, and through those saints to God. We would serve them to pass on our requests to God through the saints. In return we had to pay them regular sums of money and a share in our harvest. Despite that, they treated us as lowborn, almost like their own servants, and looked upon us as uncivilized and uncouth.

In contrast, the TJ is seen as considerably more democratic, challenging the notion of the privileged access of the Sufis and the *faqirs* to religious knowledge and authority. As the Meo respondent quoted above adds:

In the work of the *jama'ats* there is no high and low. All of us are equal, being fellow Muslims. It does not matter in Allah's eyes how much money you have, how much land you own, how many degrees you have earned or even how many books you have read on Islam. Without faith and willingness to work for the sake of Islam, all such things are useless. Here, in our movement, even the poorest Muslim feels he is the equal of a rich landlord and can exercise the right to gently admonish him when he does something wrong.

The *shariah*-centred form of Islam that the TJ represents is also seen as relieving the Meos of a heavy economic burden, which has come to be associated with popular Sufism. The TJ makes no financial demands on its followers, other than exhorting them to spend on going out themselves on *tabligh* work. Generally, this is not a very expensive affair, as activists sleep in mosques and cook their own food or are entertained by local Muslims. This is often presented as in sharp contrast to pre-Tablighi Meo popular religion centred on the Sufi shrines. Thus, a Meo respondent explains:

In the past, each time we went to a shrine, which was very often because we always wanted something from the saints who are buried there, we were expected to pay something to the *faqirs* and the other *sajjada nashins*. Sometimes we would give them wheat or vegetables or maybe a chicken, and at other times cash. If you didn't pay you were often made to feel that you were not welcome. Some *faqirs* would even quarrel with us, demanding to be paid more. And then, we had an extra burden of expenses each time we organized a festival, and there were so many, as we celebrated both Hindu and Muslim festivals. There are so many *dargahs* [Sufi shrines] in Mewat, and each shrine has its own large annual festival. So, sometimes poor Meo families landed deep in debt to meet the expenses involved in these festivals and the payments to the shrine custodians. But there's nothing of this sort at all in the Tablighi Jama'at. In fact, it seems that Allah has sent the *jama'at* to rescue us from our economic plight.

Association with the TJ today also represents new and distinctly modern ways of imagining Muslim communal identity. In the years after Partition, Mewat gradually opened up to the wider world and the developments taking place in it. This led to an increasing crisis of an identity tied to local cults of saints and folk heroes and godlings, and a consequent further shift to a 'world religion' as represented by the *shariah*-centred Islam of the TJ. The Meo popular tradition was clearly inadequate to confront the new challenges that modernity posed and the tools provided by the reified Islam of the TJ seemed far more effective and useful. The state established a number of schools in the region, which led to the gradual emergence of a class of literate Meos, literacy having been almost non-existent among the community earlier. This, and the improved means of communication with the outside world meant that Meos could now seek to establish closer links with the wider Indian Muslim community. These links were often facilitated through the Tablighi network, for gradually, by this time, the TJ had expanded from its confines in Mewat to become an India-wide movement, and with a significant presence in several other countries as well. Influenced by the TJ, growing numbers of Meo students took admission in *madrasas* or Islamic schools in other parts of India, thus facilitating a crucial process of geographic as well as upward social mobility for many Meos. Going on missionary tours to other parts of India and, increasingly, abroad as well, has led not simply to new understandings of Muslim identity, and a growing commitment to global Muslim unity and Islam, but also to distinct worldly benefits for several Meos. As one Meo respondent says:

In theory Tablighi activists are meant to travel simply to increase their knowledge of Islam and to impart that knowledge to others. Indeed, that is what many of them actually do. However, travelling to other places on *tabligh* work naturally opens up the minds of many of the activists. They see new places, new things, meet new sorts of people and come to know how other people live. They come to know of the whole world outside Mewat, about new developments in the rest of the world, which can really open their minds. Some of them might even strike business deals with people they might meet on their journeys or establish business contacts or get new business ideas, although the Tablighi elders actually strictly forbid this.

In matters of education, gender relations, and inter-community relations, three areas of particular concern to Muslims living as a minority in India today, the TJ advocates what might seem a rigid conformism and a stern refusal to recognize the need for change or reform. Thus, for instance, Ilyas is himself said to have condemned the first modern school in Mewat, set up in 1923 at the town of Nuh, as a 'Satanic institution',[18] warning the Meos to stay away and to send their children to Islamic *maktabs* instead. Even today, many TJ leaders insist, to quote a Meo *alim*, the 'only form of education that is valuable in God's eyes is knowledge of the *shariah*, which alone can win success for Muslims in this world and in the hereafter'. In Mewat's leading *madrasa*, the Madrasa Moin ul-Islam at Nuh, founded in the early 1940s by Maulana Ilyas himself, no 'worldly' subjects are taught, and students are even forbidden to read newspapers, for fear that they might be attracted by the snares of the world.[19] Some Meo *maulvis* associated with the TJ are even said to go so far as to declare that learning English and Hindi are *haram*, strictly forbidden in Islam.[20] In matters of gender relations, too, the TJ betrays a distinctly anti-modernist impulse. It represents an extremely patriarchal understanding of Islam, one in which women are subordinate to men.[21] Many Meo TJ leaders and activists continue to condemn modern education for girls, seeing it as threatening to tempt them away from commitment to Islam and opening the doors for all manner of *fitna*, worldly temptation, strife, and insubordination. Female Meo literacy rates remain among the lowest in India, estimated at no more than 5 per cent, and this owes much to the distinct lack of enthusiasm on the part of TJ activists in Mewat for girls' education. Likewise, in matters of inter-community relations, the TJ's position might seem to militate against modern sensibilities. It refuses to recognize the truth claims of other faiths, insisting that Islam, as it understands it, is the only way to win God's favour and enter paradise. All other religions are regarded as either man-made or else are said to represent distorted versions of divine religions that have become corrupted over time. Other religions are, therefore, false and their followers doomed to hell. TJ activists are constantly reminded that non-Muslims, no matter how pious and noble they might be, are all veritable 'enemies of God'. However, despite this, TJ activists are expected to behave with courtesy and kindness with non-Muslims, although strictly within the limits set by the *shariah*. It is hoped that thereby non-Muslims might be suitably impressed by Islam and might then even consider accepting it.

A common refrain heard in TJ circles is that the movement is concerned 'only about the heavens and the grave below, and never about the world in-between'. This is often employed as an argument to convince others that the TJ has no political or worldly motives. Yet, it is precisely because of what is seen as a distinct lack of concern for the worldly affairs of Muslims that today a small, yet growing number of Meo youth are today increasingly voicing their protest against its rigid understanding of Islam, which they regard as contributing to the further marginalization and impoverishment of their people. Influenced, in part, by 'modernist' as well as Islamist understandings of Islam, helped, ironically, by their first exposure to Islamic scripturalism by the TJ, some Meo youth regard what they see as the TJ's indifference towards the this-worldly concerns of the community as wholly 'un-Islamic'. As they see it, the TJ's obsessive concern with the ritual minutiae of the *shariah*, and its silence on the social, economic, and political affairs of the community, have only contributed to their further backwardness. Comparisons are often drawn with their Hindu Jat neighbours, who are, for the most part, associated with the Hindu revivalist Arya Samaj, which took off in the region at almost the same time as the TJ. The Jats, like the Meos, were traditionally a peasant community, but in recent years, owing in part to the work of the Arya Samaj which has set up a number of schools, hospitals, orphanages, and training centres in Jat territory, they have made impressive strides in education and economic development, and are today a powerful political force to reckon with. In contrasting the TJ with the Arya Samaj, it is often lamented that the former has done little to improve the actual conditions of Meos, being almost 'completely blind', as a Meo informant puts it, to their real-world concerns. This is said to be profoundly 'un-Islamic', for in Islam, it is claimed, there is no distinction between religion (*din*) and worldly affairs (*duniya*). In appearing to make such a distinction to the point of insisting, as some Meos see it, that the two realms are mutually opposed to each other, the TJ is said to be propagating an 'un-Islamic Sufism' (*ghayr islami tasawwuf*) or 'monasticism' (*rahbaniyat*) that has no legitimacy in Islam itself. A Meo student makes the following comment in this regard:

> The division that Tablighi activists make between *din* and *duniya* is itself un-Islamic, for in Islam the world is part of the *din*. They see the *din* as lying simply in prayers and fasting and going on *tabligh* tours, the rest being *duniya*, and these two are perceived as fundamentally opposed to each other. That is why they do not pay any attention to the worldly concerns of the Meos, dismissing them as *duniyavi*, and hence of little worth. In fact, I have often heard Tablighi *maulvis* in Mewat lament in their lectures the little economic progress that we have experienced, saying that when we were poor and nearly starving we were very pious Muslims, but that today some of us are a little more comfortably off we have forgotten God. This attitude of the *maulvis* is something that many educated Meos resent today. Undoubtedly, this has caused a growing disillusionment with the movement on their part.

The perceived indifference of the TJ to the worldly concerns of the Meos is interpreted variously, both as a consequence of an 'un-Islamic' Sufism that encourages flight from this world as well as a distinctly this-worldly concern of TJ leaders and *ulama* to enhance their own authority and access to (and control over) community resources. Thus it is often alleged that while TJ leaders preach the virtues of poverty and exhort Muslims to remain content with the bare minimum of worldly goods, some as a Meo respondent puts it, run 'large religious rackets of their own' through the institutions that they manage, financed by donations from the Meo community as well as from Muslims elsewhere in India and some even from abroad. They are also often accused of preaching against modern education, which their critics claim to be a fundamental Islamic duty, for fear that educated Meos might challenge their own claims to leadership of the community.

Yet, despite its apparent lack of concern with the worldly affairs of its followers, which has made for a growing indifference to its message on the part of some Meos, the TJ has been able to accommodate itself, to an extent, to some of the challenges that modernity is bringing to Mewat today. Indeed, some of the values that it sees as central to

Islam bear a striking resemblance to a Protestant ethic that ties in with the spirit of modernity described by Weber in his classic work on the evolution of capitalism.[22] In effect, then, and similar to the Protestant case, in some respects the TJ might be said to be promoting an inadvertent modernization, albeit with a suitable 'Islamic' gloss. As the TJ sees it, the individual believer is armed with an instrumentality in realizing the Islamic mission in this world. The fortunes of Islam thus come to be seen as determined not by the presence of a Muslim ruler, as in the past, but rather by the active and conscious involvement of every Muslim individual, who is charged with a new sense of agency and mission to change the world, working to implement God's will on earth. Some of the values that the movement stresses, such as punctuality, the value of time, cleanliness, the equality of all believers and a concern for others, while derived from in certain strands of Sufism, have powerful echoes in modernity, and tie in with what the TJ sees as its 'civilizing' mission, rescuing Muslims from superstition and corrupt and wasteful practices. Its attack on the mediational cults of popular Sufism, and in the case of the Meos, of the widespread belief in spirits, ghosts and local deities, represents a distinct, albeit limited, rationalization of the world that modernity also seeks to promote. Its stress on Islamic scripturalism and the universal Muslim *ummah* works to undermine locally rooted identities, predicated in Mewat and in much of the rest of India, on caste and sect, and which are also seen as major hurdles that modernity has to contend with. Travelling outside one's own locality, to other villages and towns and even to other countries on Tabligh work, promotes a new sense of shared Muslim identity that transcends the local. It thereby promotes what could be called a 'transportable Islam', one that is at home all over the world, since TJ practices and methods are carefully sought to be made uniform and standardized wherever its missionaries are active. This represents a standardization of Islam that brings together Muslims from different regions in a shared universe of discourse and a common commitment to the Tablighi project, undermining local forms of Islam that are seen to divide the universal *ummah*. In this sense, then, the movement represents a novel form of Islamic modernity.

The TJ's ability to come to terms with some of the most pressing challenges that modernity poses in its wake is facilitated by the movement's lack of a centralized organizational structure and by the nature of its missionary strategy, that seeks to steer clear of *ikhtilafi* issues, and focusing on the *fazail* instead of the *masail*. Since the TJ issues no official statements and has no official publications of its own, at the local level TJ activists are somewhat free to interpret the TJ message in their own ways, albeit within certain broad limits. Thus, today, while some TJ activists might lament the growing enthusiasm on the part of many Meos to send their children to modern schools, the movement as such does not explicitly condemn this. Rather, some TJ leaders actually welcome this development, although they insist on the primacy of Islamic education, and argue that Meo children studying at modern schools must also receive traditional Islamic knowledge so that their faith in Islam is not diluted in general schools that often betray a distinct Hindu bias. Indeed, today some TJ activists might go so far as to insist that Muslim children must acquire modern education, for only then can Muslims establish their supremacy over others. Likewise, they argue that if pious Muslims, armed with knowledge of the world, were to excel in various fields of worldly activity, the non-Muslims with whom they would interact might be suitably impressed and might even consider embracing Islam. Thus modern education is grudgingly accepted by some TJ activists, and warmly embraced by others, but both regard it as a means for promoting what are regarded as the interests of Islam, and not as an end in itself.

Likewise, in matters of politics, the TJ displays a remarkable flexibility despite its apparent rigidity. In this, it follows in the general Deobandi tradition. The elders of the Deoband *madrasa*, rigid in matters of religion, were flexible pragmatists in matters of politics. While they stood for strict conformity to the *shariah* (as they understood it), condemning Muslim 'modernists' as veritable apostates, and seeing all religions other than Islam as pathways to hell, most of them were enthusiastic supporters of the Hindu-dominated Indian National Congress and its project of a united India. Numerous Deobandis were in the forefront of the Indian independence movement, and were among the most bitter critics of the Muslim League and its demand for a separate Muslim state of Pakistan. The rector of the Deoband *madrasa*, Maulana Hussain Ahmad Madni, went so far as to insist that nationality (*qaumiyat*) was determined not by religion but rather by the land of birth. The Hindus and Muslims of India, he insisted, arguing against the claims of the Muslim League, were members of one national community.[23] On the other hand, a minority among the Deobandis, led by Maulana Ashraf Ali Thanwi, lent their support to the Pakistan demand, insisting that Muslims and Hindus were indeed two separate nations. Ilyas was influenced by both groups among the Deobandis, counting among both several of his teachers and mentors. Yet, even at the height of the Pakistan movement in the mid-1940s, Ilyas stayed clear of overt political involvement, preferring instead to focus simply on strengthening and reinforcing Muslim commitment to Islam. This, he believed, was the only way in which Muslims could regain God's favour and establish their political supremacy over others in the future, as the people charged with spreading God's chosen faith.

In Mewat today, the TJ's silence on political affairs enables its followers to make pragmatic political decisions, thereby accommodating themselves to a non-Islamic and non-Muslim state, thus implicitly accepting the principle of secularism and the personalization of religion. Since the TJ steers completely away from *ikhtilafi masail*, seemingly unconcerned with what it regards as *duniyavi* or worldly affairs, it allows for its followers to conduct their political affairs as they choose, these being generally guided by pragmatic considerations. Since the TJ authorities do not issue any guidelines on politics, the Meos are free to decide which political parties to vote for and with whom to enter into alliances. Thus most Meos vote for parties that have no commitment to an Islamic state, which is what Ilyas himself believed to be a central component of an ideal Islamic society. For the TJ, this accommodation to practical politics and acceptance of secularism is justified in terms of what it regards as a necessary step in the path of ultimately establishing an Islamic state in the distant future. TJ leaders and activists believe that Muslims are today living in a state similar to that of the Prophet at Mecca (*makki daur*). This was a period when Muslims were learning their faith in the face of active persecution by their enemies, and when the Prophet lacked political power. The culmination of the Prophet's life was the establishment of an Islamic state at Medina, ruled according to the *shariah*. The Medinan period (*madni daur*) is thus the ultimate state that Muslim societies should aspire to establish. However, to reach that goal, they must first eschew all concern with politics, focusing, as the Muslims in the Meccan period are said to have done, on cultivating their faith in and knowledge of Islam, for only then would they win God's pleasure. Political power, as represented by the Medinan phase of the Prophet's life, is not something to be actively struggled for. Rather, it is a gift that would given by God to Muslims if they strictly abide by the commandments of the faith. Contemporary Muslims the world over, being seen as still in the Meccan phase, having 'strayed' from the path of Islam, must therefore concern themselves with the strengthening of their faith. In effect, the establishment of an Islamic state, the ushering in of the Medinan phase, is postponed into the indefinite future, for, as the TJ sees it, the cultivation of faith, the defining feature of the Meccan phase, is a long drawn-out process that, given the constant presence of worldly temptations and distractions, has virtually no end. This thus enables the followers of the movement in Mewat, and elsewhere, to conduct their politics on pragmatic, as opposed to ideological, lines and to come to terms with the absence of Muslim or Islamic rule and the presence of a theoretically secular polity. In this the TJ stands in marked contrast to Islamist movements that see their primary and immediate goal as the establishment of an Islamic state, ruled in accordance with the laws of the *shariah*.

CONCLUSION

As this general survey of the TJ in Mewat suggests, the emergence and development of the TJ in Mewat is a distinctly modern, although not quite modernist, phenomenon. The launching of the movement by Maulana Ilyas in the 1920s in Mewat was prompted largely by distinctly modern developments—the obtrusive presence of the British colonial state and competition between Hindu and Muslim elites for numbers, leading to new understandings of community identities and confessional boundaries. While not opposed to Sufism as such, the TJ, following in the general Deobandi tradition in which it is rooted, sought to redefine Sufism, bitterly critiquing what it saw as 'un-Islamic' influences, and insisting that on the need to conform to the commandments of the *shariah*. In turn, this *shariah*-centred scripturalist form of Sufism helped further galvanize the process of redefining Muslim identity, seeking to clearly demarcate Muslims from their Hindu neighbours, in part to meet the grave threat of Hindu missionaries working among *nau*-Muslim groups.

The TJ's reformed Sufism has had important consequences for religious authority and how it comes to be imagined and articulated, and this ties in with certain distinctly modern concerns. In challenging the claims of the custodians of the shrines of the Sufis as religious intermediaries, in insisting on the need for every Muslim to be armed with a knowledge of the faith and in stressing the duty of all believers in the work of *tabligh*, the TJ promotes a de-centring of authority, or what could be called the priesthood of all believers. Consequently, the role of the Sufi *shaikh* comes to be imagined differently—from a spiritual guide who leads his disciple on the mystical path or *tariqat* he is transformed into a teacher who instructs his followers on the path of the *shariah*. The ideal Sufi is no longer one who escapes the world into mystical, transcendental states. Rather, he is one who actively works in this world for the realization of God's will on earth. The charisma of the medieval Sufi *shaikh* and the *silsilah* or Sufi brotherhood is now sought to be endowed upon the charismatic community of Tablighi activists as a whole, although within the community those with more knowledge or experience of Tabligh work are accorded a special status and respect.

Along with this, the TJ's message of scripturalist reform, which it sees as a civilizing mission, promotes certain values that bear a distinct resemblance to those associated with the project of contemporary modernity. Further, while not uncritically embracing all that modern life brings in its trail, its conscious refusal to address *ikhtilafi masail* enables its followers to make pragmatic adjustments to the challenges and prospects of living under a non-Muslim state, including accepting, in practical terms, the principle of secularism. Given the loose organizational structure of the movement, its activists are able, albeit within broad limits, to adjust to what might otherwise be seen as 'un-Islamic' institutions free from rigid controls from a central authority, unlike in the case of most Islamist movements. All this then helps promote a distinctly Tablighi approach to modernity, one that while not fully approving of all or even most of what that dominant contemporary forms of modernity entail, is willing to accept aspects of them, suitably reinterpreted, as an integral part of what it sees as its own divine mission.

NOTES

1. For a detailed study of the Tablighi Jamaat, see Yoginder Sikand, *The Origins and Development of the Tablighi Jamaat (1920s-1990): A Cross-Country Comparative Study*, Delhi: Orient Longman, 2002.
2. Zia ur-Rahman Faruqi, *Ulama-i Deoband: Kaun Hain, Kya Hain*? Deoband: Dar ul-Kitab, 1992, p. 43.
3. For biographical details, see Sayyed Abul Hasan, *Ali Nadwi, Life and Mission of Maulana Muhammad Ilyas* (translated by Mohammad Asif Kidwai), Lucknow: Academy of Islamic Research and Publications, Nadwat ul-Ulama, 1983. Also, S. Anwar ul-Haq, *The Faith Movement of Mawlana Muhammad Ilyas*, London: George Allen & Unwin, 1972.
4. Barbara Daly Metcalf, *Islamic Revival in British India: Deoband, 1860-1900*, Delhi: Oxford University Press, 2002.
5. Sikand, op. cit., p. 127.
6. See, for instance, Manzur Numani (ed.), *Malfuzat-i Hazrat Maulana Muhammad Ilyas*, Delhi: Idara-i Ishaat-i Diniyat, 1991. Also, Rahim Bakhsh, *Tablighi Jama'at ke Tarikhi Halat, Malfuzat-o Makatibat-i Bani-i Tabligh, Muhsin-i Mewat, Muballigh-i Islam al-Haj Shah Hazrat Maulana Muhammad Ilyas*, Roodpa: Muhammad Hasan, 1995.
7. Sikand, op. cit., pp. 64-71.
8. Muhammad Ilyas, 'A Call to Muslims', in *The Teachings of Tabligh*, Delhi: Idara-i Ishaat-i Diniyat, 1989.
9. Barbara Daly Metcalf, 'Travelers' Tales in the Tablighi Jama'at', *ANNALES*, no. 588, July 2003, p. 145.
10. A *chillah* consists of 40 days. The practice of spending *chillahs* in spiritual retreat and meditation is of clearly Sufi provenance.
11. For detailed discussion of the *chhe batein*, see Ashiq Ilahi Bulandshahri, *Aqsi Chhe Batein*, Delhi: Jaseem Book Depot, n.d.. Also, Muhammad Khalid Nizami (ed.), *Paigham-i Falah*, Dhanbad: Dini Talimi Board, 1993.
12. Kelley Pemberton, 'Islamic and Islamicizing Discourses: Ritual Performance, Didactic Texts, and the Reformist Challenge in the South Asian Sufi Milieu', *The Annual Journal of Urdu Studies*, vol. 17, 2002, p. 72.
13. P.W. Powlett, *Gazeteer of Ulwar*, London: Trubner, 1878, p. 38.
14. P.C. Aggarwal, quoted in Sikand, op. cit., p. 113.
15. For details, see Sikand, op. cit., pp. 115-24.
16. Sikand, op. cit., pp. 147-56.

17. Ibid., pp. 83-9.
18. Ibid., p. 121.
19. Ibid., p. 164.
20. Ibid., p. 165.
21. For details, see Yoginder Sikand, 'Women and the Tablighi Jama'at', *Islam and Christian-Muslim Relations*, vol. 10, no. 9, March 1999.
22. Max Weber, *The Protestant Ethic and the Spirit of Capitalism* (translated by Talcott Parsons), London: Allen & Unwin, 1930.
23. For details, see Peter Hardy, *Partners in Freedom—and True Muslims: The Political Thought of Some Muslim Scholars in British India*, Westport: Greenwood Press, 1980.

3

Investing in the Future

Education in the Social and Cultural Reproduction of Muslims in UP

PATRICIA JEFFERY, ROGER JEFFERY
AND CRAIG JEFFREY

An Urdu poster printed by the Aligarh-based Jamia Urdu Committee, which we saw pinned on the veranda of the village *pradhan*, a Muslim peasant farmer and part-time road contractor, in one of the Bijnor villages stated.[1]

REMEMBER

- *ignorance is darkness and education is enlightenment*
- *the understanding of religion and the world comes only from education*
- *education gives us a peaceful life*
- *education helps us to get ahead and develop*
- *education makes us capable of helping our country and our people*
- *do not deprive your children of education*
- *enrol the people close to you in a* madrasah *or school and turn them into good human beings and good urbane people*

This poster encapsulates the main ideas about modernity that have been circulating in India since colonial times: that education is beneficial for individuals and the nation alike, because the educated person attains the status of an enlightened and civilized human being.

Such perceptions are part of general understandings of the significance of education in contemporary India. Indeed, more than half of President Abdul Kalam's address to the nation on 14 August 2004 was devoted to the role of the education system 'in creating an enlightened, dynamic and prosperous society' and transforming 'a human being into a wholesome whole, a noble soul and an asset to the universe'.[2]

In line with these very widespread assumptions, the President sees illiteracy as one of the root causes of poverty. This view is not so much wrong as partial, for poverty itself is a major reason for illiteracy and low levels of educational attainment. This has never been more so than in today's rapidly changing economic and global situation—and it applies as forcefully to Indian Muslims as to the rest of the Indian population. The commonplace trope of the 'backward Muslim' (and especially the uneducated Muslim woman) tends to 'blame the victims' for their own backwardness. Using our research among Hindus and Muslims in Bijnor district, in western Uttar Pradesh (UP), we want to challenge such assumptions by confronting the role played by systemic social, economic, and political processes in the educational careers and prospects of Muslim children in India.

Today in India everyone has to contend with economic liberalization, globalization and the competitive scramble for employment and economic security. Formal education is becoming increasingly important in people's attempts to maintain if not improve, the social and economic positions of their households. Children may have to spend several years of their childhood notching up examination successes and imbibing the 'General Knowledge' and social polish on which social and economic success rests. But people rise to these challenges in rather different ways, and it is important to be clear how religious group membership reinforces or cuts across the other characteristics of children and households.

Like their neighbours following other religions, Muslims occupy a range of occupational and class positions; they live in towns or in the countryside, and they are distributed unevenly throughout the country. It is therefore important not to over-generalize about Muslims and education: structural elements such as class, region, residence, and gender are also important influences on educational outcomes. Not only are the experiences of Muslims varied, but even within households the experiences of siblings may be very different, sometimes taking radically different trajectories, both in quantity and kind of formal education. Individual children may experience different kinds of schooling (say, a Hindi-medium school as against a *madrasa*) in unexpected ways. We can, however, be clear about the extremes: the prospects of wealthy urbanites (with the means to enable their children to obtain educational credentials and the social networks to facilitate their children's transition to adulthood) and poor rural households (unable to pay for extensive schooling or to access lucrative and secure 'modern' jobs or 'good' marriages) are radically different. Poverty and rural residence affect a person's ability to navigate changing educational markets, much as they do for Hindus. But communal politics play an additional and pernicious role for Muslims, whatever their class or regional location, a role that emerges more clearly through a case study. We focus on Muslims in western UP, to provide a detailed discussion of local realities. The picture cannot, of course, be generalized for the rest of India.

Muslims in independent India have been economically marginalized and, particularly in north India, they are disproportionately located towards the lower end of the socio-economic hierarchy (Shariff 1995). Muslims in western UP, for instance, suffered a general decline in their relative economic and political position after 1947, in part because of excess migration of the urban and rural élites to Pakistan (Brass 1974: 182ff.). Today, Muslim children are significantly less likely to be enrolled in so-called secular schools than children from other communities. Once registered, Muslim boys are disproportionately more likely to drop out before completing primary schooling. The few Muslim girls who enrol are as likely to complete their schooling as are Hindu girls (Siddiqui 2004: 94-8). Many Muslim children—especially from poor rural households—receive formal education only briefly, if at all. Muslim literacy rates are probably lower than among caste Hindus, especially in the rural areas. Many Muslim children continue to be educated informally, often learning by watching their parents at work. Urban Muslims, in particular, are likely to be artisans, many of whom are largely educated through apprenticeships (Hameed 2005; Kumar 1988). Somewhat higher up the economic scale, families may struggle to educate their children in a range of educational institutions. The low recruitment of Muslims into the IAS and the professions since 1947, however, reflects the relatively small numbers of urban middle class Muslims who have been able to provide their children with lengthy formal schooling.

The future of the education of Muslim children, then, must be viewed in a framework that accommodates the diversity of social and economic positions at the same time as it encompasses overarching processes. First we shall lay out some general features of the political economy of schooling in UP. Secondary schooling, in particular, is crucial for obtaining the cultural capital and credentials that give boys (and a few girls) entry into the higher reaches of the employment market, and that provide advantages for girls and boys alike in marriage markets. Briefly, the story of secondary schooling in UP is one of the rise and fall of state provision: since 1991, there has been privatization 'by stealth' and this creates the changing context in which Muslim household strategies are unfolding. We then consider the implications of the saffronization of educational cultures—a process that long predates the rise of the BJP in the state and nationally, and that seems unlikely to disappear with the BJP's electoral eclipse. We consider the emerging trends in school attendance in rural and urban Bijnor, and then place the role of *madrasas* in a wider context. In the final section we discuss the implications of the diversifying schooling patterns for the transitions of Muslim children to adulthood.

POLITICAL ECONOMY OF EDUCATION IN UP

UP, relative to other states, has consistently accorded education a low budget, but its educational policy (particularly with respect to secondary schooling) shows a marked break around 1990. In the early period, the state spread schooling through the countryside, opening schools and taking over most of the schools opened by local notables. While there was some effort to use schooling as a tool of social policy to improve the position of Scheduled Caste children, no comparable efforts were made to reduce inequalities based on religion or class.[3] Decisions about where to build government schools or which private schools to take over were not based simply on population size and 'need', but tended to reinforce existing patterns of exclusion and privilege. In the 1950s and 1960s, the Hindu urban middle classes and dominant landowning castes manipulated their political and personal connections (often through relatives) in the educational officialdom, dominated at the time and still today by upper-caste Hindus. Like the lower Hindu castes and the Scheduled Castes, Muslims had little leverage over this establishment. Rural schools were more likely to be constructed first in villages or sections of villages dominated by Hindu upper castes than near Muslim or SC-majority villages and neighbourhoods. These decisions provided children from the Hindu upper castes with a starting advantage.

In the 1990s, evidence accumulated of the state's abject failure to provide comprehensive, accessible, affordable, and good quality schools for the mass of the population, especially villagers and the urban poor (Govinda 2002; The Probe Team 1999). Generally, the fabric of rural school buildings is poor and the teaching materials are more inadequate than in urban schools. High levels of teacher absenteeism and shirking of duties compound the general problem of recruiting staff for rural posts. These inadequacies are even more glaring in schools located in Muslim-dominated villages or *muhallas*. Schools near Muslim or SC areas are still less well equipped and in poorer physical condition than those serving more mixed or caste-Hindu dominated villages. In practice, government schools rarely provide free education and regular attendance by pupils is often significantly lower than enrolment. In the context of rural India as a whole Drèze and Kingdon consider that low attendance rates among rural Muslims in India as a whole are due more to 'tangible disadvantages such as poverty and low levels of parental education' than to parental opposition to schooling (Drèze and Kingdon 1998: 14). This picture is confirmed for UP by Srivastava, who also notes that Muslim pupils are rarely entitled to the benefits—problematic though they are—of government scholarships, which probably do enhance SC enrolments in comparison with others from similar economic backgrounds (Srivastava 2001: 280). Our data from Bijnor suggest additional barriers to Muslim enrolment in primary school: a more limited physical access to schools, and the fact that those schools have also been of a poorer physical standard than those available to equivalent Hindus.

Between 1960 and 1990, teachers' unions pressurized the state government to nationalize almost all the secondary schools in the state. Basically, this was a move to improve the salaries and conditions of the teachers, and to give them the job security of other civil servants. As a result, the salaries of the teachers on the government payroll absorbed the lion's share of the UP education budget. This skewing has subsidized the urban middle classes at the expense of expanding educational provisions serving the rural population and the poor (Kingdon and Muzammil 2001). With growing number of school age children, there were too few government schools and teachers to meet the potential demand, especially in the rural areas. Since the state of UP was unwilling to tax rural incomes or to limit the subsidies that go to the relatively affluent urban classes, it became increasingly obvious that its educational policies were unsustainable.

With UP fiscal crisis during the 1990s, the numbers of teachers per capita and real per capita expenditures on education declined (Drèze and Gazdar 1997; Drèze and Kingdon 1998; Drèze and Sen 2002; Srivastava 2001; The Probe Team 1999). Meanwhile, there has been a remarkable growth of non-state schools and colleges not in receipt of government aid, primarily in response to the government's failure to provide minimally adequate schooling for the majority of its population. The process of privatization has accelerated during the 1990s and may compensate somewhat for the shortfall in state provision. It does not redress inequities in access, however (R. Jeffery et al. 2005a and b). Indeed, the educational market reflects (and tends to accentuate) the pre-existing inequalities. The new educational institutions normally rely on fees and other levies from parents (e.g. 'donations' to obtain admission). Generally, the founders locate their institutions—particularly secondary schools—where they can benefit from the growing demand for schooling from concentrations of moderately wealthy families: in other words, near urban centres or neighbourhoods in small towns dominated by upper-caste Hindus (Drèze and Gazdar 1997: 71; NCERT 1997: Tables V. 17, and V. 41). The rural poor, in particular, have very few options, especially for young children who cannot travel far alone: their school attendance rates are generally the lowest (Drèze and Gazdar 1997: 80; Srivastava 2001). Moreover, aside from fees, providing transport or arranging for children to board with urban relatives poses severe problems, even for relatively wealthy villagers. Most non-state educational institutions, then, actually exclude the poor, including most Muslims, rural and urban.

Girls are additionally disadvantaged, and Muslim girls even more so. In the UP education sector, gender differentials in school attendance, literacy and educational attainment remain wide (Drèze & Sen 2002: 143-88, 229-74; Karlekar 2000; The Probe Team 1999; Wazir 2000).[4] General problems of access to education are exacerbated for Muslim girls because schools are unlikely to be located in Muslim dominated villages or *muhallas*. In education, as in other fields, there is a general problem of recruiting and retaining women for rural posts, whether in the government or private sector (Drèze and Gazdar 1997: 61, 68-9; Nayar 2001: 43). Unless there are compelling financial difficulties, women's employment outside the home is still widely frowned upon—especially if it entails working with men, or travelling to villages (which are believed to be dangerous for unaccompanied women). Employed women must usually continue to perform their domestic duties, whilst the time and cost of travelling to work are further disincentives. Not surprisingly, most women teachers work in urban or large village schools, mainly in the primary sector. Like many other parents, Muslim parents may hesitate to enrol their daughters if perceptibly few local girls are attending school, if the school is too distant, or if there are no women teachers (The Probe Team 1999: 18ff.). Rural schools often fail to provide girl-friendly environments (such as separate toilet facilities), and there is evidence of gender bias by teachers as well as in the curriculum (Karlekar 2000). Parents are also often worried about sexual harassment on the way to school (Srivastava 2001: 305). For the poor, for villagers and for Muslims, the most acceptable—as well as affordable—option is to curtail their daughters' education once they reach puberty. Indeed, Muslim girls were all but absent even in the primary schools in our research villages. Not surprisingly, efforts by donor agencies to increase girl enrolment (e.g. through supporting the District Primary Education Programme or the Sarva Shiksha Abhiyan, its successor) have had to address these issues. Midday meals and the creation of feeder classes in small villages have begun to make a difference in some parts of UP, but it is too soon to say whether these initiatives are likely to be sustained.

In sum, the education sector in UP (and north India as a whole) is characterized by long-standing class and residence biases that have been especially (though not exclusively) disadvantageous to most Muslims. Simply put, however strongly Muslim parents in UP want to provide for their children's education, most have inadequate opportunities to do so.

SAFFRONIZED EDUCATIONAL CULTURES

In general, north Indian Muslims confront much the same systematic exclusionary processes as their poor neighbours from other castes and communities. Another layer needs unwrapping here, though: communal politics. The role of the dominant classes and castes in determining the location of schools by no means exhausts the issue. Thus, we turn now to the ambience of schools in north India, particularly focusing on the medium of instruction, aspects of curriculum, and the domination of teaching by upper-caste Hindus.

Urdu in the Persian script occupied a prime position among the vernacular languages in official business and in publications well into the twentieth century. But the 'Hindi establishment' (many of whom were employed in the colonial education administration) gradually facilitated the development of a curriculum and teaching in Hindi in Devanagari script in schools and colleges (Orsini 2002).[5] Urdu and Hindi became 'symbolic links among members of the same ethnic group, barriers to communication between members of different ethnic groups, and additional marks of identity and separateness for such groups' (Brass 1991: 85). Since 1947, Urdu has been widely seen as an alien language and a threat to national unity. Its decline has been precipitate.[6] It ceased to be an official language of UP in 1951 and was relegated to 'minority language' status: repeated efforts to get Urdu recognized as the second official language of UP have failed. Given the Constitutional guarantees to provide 'mother tongue' teaching for minorities at primary school level and the 'three language formula' as applied to UP (Hindi, English and another Indian language), Urdu might have achieved some prominence in school curricula. It is, however, marginal. As a medium of instruction, Urdu has been relegated to the *madrasa* sector (see below). Most schools are Hindi-medium, where a highly Sanskritized version of Hindi is valorized, and Sanskrit is generally taken as the third language. Few secondary schools offer Urdu even as an optional literary subject, although it became an optional subject in some government primary schools in the 1990s.[7] Hence, the schools tends to marginalize and denigrate the vernacular non-élite forms of Hindi spoken by most villagers and the poor (Kumar 1991; 1993; Orsini 2002; Rai 2001). For the Muslims among them, problems of script compound those of vocabulary and grammar: Urdu facilitates children's access to Islam, including reading the Koran Sharif, whereas Hindi in the Devanagari script does not.

Inevitably, English complicates the linguistic contest. In the immediate post-Independence period, English was to occupy the position of a national language only as an interim measure (Brass 1990: 135ff.). As an international language, however, English has stronger currency than Hindi in the employment market, in India and abroad (Deshpande 2000; Mohan 2000; Srivastava 2000). English language schooling is, however, socially and politically divisive (Faust and Nagar 2001). The higher fees charged in English-medium schools not only indicate the greater prestige of English in comparison with Hindi but put competence in English out of the reach of most Hindus, leave aside most Muslims. In the language stakes, then, Urdu has been doubly marginalized, by English as well as by Sanskritized Hindi.

Most UP schools are also characterized by curricula—formal and hidden—that presume that the pupils are Hindu and that tend to marginalize and even demean Muslims. This largely pre-dates the overt and official saffronizing of curricula under the auspices of the BJP government in the late 1990s. The 'institutional stranglehold' (Orsini 2002: 382) of the Hindi establishment over education had ossified the UP Education Board Hindi literature courses, which still contain narratives of history, mythology, and literature in which Muslims are portrayed in a negative light. Sanskrit itself is associated with the Hindu scriptures. The Hindu bias of the Hindi syllabus has long been a matter of concern to Muslim commentators (see Brass 1974). Yet the recent debates about NCERT textbooks and school syllabi more generally have focused on history, social science, and 'Vedic mathematics and astrology' rather than Hindi (Sahmat 2001; 2002a; 2002b).

The continuing domination of school teaching in general by upper-caste Hindus is crucial here. Most schools—government schools included—exhibit 'banal Hinduism' (see Billig 1995), the taken-for-granted yet insidious practices that tend to construct an upper-caste Hindu ambience. There is no formal schedule of religious instruction in most schools, but textbooks and lessons are not the only medium through which religion is 'taught': daily assemblies and other functions, such as Founders' Days and 26 January celebrations, are replete with Hindu iconography and Sanskritized Hindi (Bénéï 2000). Muslim children also often allege that teachers are unsympathetic (if not overtly unpleasant) to Muslim pupils, that they display favouritism in marking schoolwork or accepting pupils for tuitions. Such tendencies are clear, even if they are not as extreme in government or aided schools as in Arya Samaj or RSS schools with overt anti-Muslim agendas (Balagopalan and Subrahmanian 2003; Kumar 1989: 59-77; 1993; Thapar 2005). Furthermore, teachers in RSS schools are not a separate cadre and teachers may work in RSS schools before moving seamlessly into a better-paid job in another school. Some teachers in apparently 'secular' schools are involved in or at least approve of the activities of the RSS or its associated organizations.

The government elected in 2004 committed itself to removing the most explicitly saffronized elements from school curricula. But this will be insufficient. Teachers do not need to be actively committed to the worldviews of the RSS to influence the ambience of the schools where they teach: because much Hinduism is 'banal', even well-meaning teachers may peddle it without consciously appreciating how the existing systems tend to denigrate and marginalize Muslims.

EDUCATIONAL OPTIONS, EDUCATIONAL OUTCOMES

Most Muslims in north India, then, face numerous obstacles to obtaining satisfactory education for their children, in the government or non-state sector. They share some of these hurdles—relative poverty, rural residence—with their non-Muslim neighbours. Others—e.g. the Sanskritized Hindi, upper caste Hindu educational culture—particularly affect them as Muslims. How, then, do Muslim parents deal with the challenges of providing their children with education?

Here, we want to stress the diversity of the educational careers of Muslim children in Bijnor. We start with rural Muslims, for whom *madrasas* have become the dominant mode of education for girls and boys alike, before considering the schooling of urban boys and girls and that of the richer rural children able to travel to Bijnor town. But we should remember that, for the vast majority—the urban poor and most villagers—lengthy education is simply not an affordable or feasible option.

In the villages, and in some poor urban neighbourhoods too, Muslim children are now attending *madrasas*. Unfortunately, neither Drèze and Gazdar (1997: 72) nor Srivastava (2001: 267) included 'non-profit' or 'informal' schooling in their accounts, so we cannot gauge the extent to which the experiences of Bijnor's Muslims parallel those of Muslims elsewhere in UP. Nevertheless, in Bijnor, *madrasas* are best understood within the wider political and administrative context.

Madrasas share many features with other educational institutions (Jeffery et al. 2004 and 2005). Schools and *madrasas* are not hermetically sealed from one another: individuals or even entire management committees are sometimes involved in simultaneously managing schools and *madrasas*. As with non-state schools, *madrasa* managers are usually prominent and relatively wealthy members of their locality. School and *madrasa* teachers alike come from middle to poor peasant rural backgrounds or from middle-ranking urban backgrounds. Most of the male teachers we interviewed had spent two or more years at one of the large seminaries (such as Dar ul-Ulum in Deoband) whilst the small number of women teachers had mainly been educated informally. Teaching in a *madrasa*—like teaching in most non-state schools—is poorly paid, although it is respectable white-collar work and gives religious merit. Teachers in schools and—*madrasas* have similar educational philosophies. They all tend, for instance, to be preoccupied with 'discipline' and the need for 'moral education', and they share understandings of how children learn and the importance of the teacher's civilizing role. *Madrasa* and school pupils alike are punished if they do not practise bodily self-control in the classroom, fail to sit still in correct posture, display disobedience or disrespect for their instructors, do not memorize their lessons assiduously, or fail to pick up their instructors' linguistic styles and manners. Schoolteachers and *madrasa* staff also share the same range of views towards the form of that punishment. Some consider the threat of physical punishment the only reliable way of maintaining classroom discipline and ensuring that children study diligently, while others vehemently oppose corporal punishment and consider that pupils' misdemeanours should be dealt with only through verbal chastisement and shaming.

A growing number of Muslim children of school age, an increasing demand for formal education during the 1980s and 1990s and a state system incapable of responding to these demands resulted in a rapid expansion in the *madrasa* sector in Bijnor. Essentially, *madrasas* are primarily a response to the failures of the state and of the market alike, and in any case go only some way to address the lack of access to formal education. Around Bijnor town there are large *madrasas* on the main roads, and smaller *madrasas* are located further into the rural areas or in the Muslim *muhallas*. A minority of *madrasas* have extensive premises and hundreds of students, some of whom are boarders. Most, however, have only one or two teachers and a handful of pupils, and they would more usually be termed *maktab*, since they cater almost exclusively to young children from poor backgrounds.

The expansion of *madrasas* has been possible only because of the growing affluence of some sectors of the Muslim population (for instance, those who have benefited from agricultural developments, or from migration to the Gulf). Unlike non-state schools that rely on fees, *madrasas* are funded by subscriptions collected through networks of traders, landowners, and others within the locality or in more distant places, such as Mumbai and Surat. By contrast, SCs and other poor communities, Lacking social networks across regions, cannot readily fund educational institutions comparable to *madrasas*. Nevertheless, given their relative poverty, Muslim fund raising remains erratic and unpredictable. Most *madrasas* are poorly resourced—a quality they share with government schools and smaller non-state schools, but not with the exclusive and expensive private schools in towns.

Largely because of these funding issues, most *madrasas* provide a limited curriculum, with Urdu and recitation of the Koran Sharif occupying prominent positions.[8] Most cannot offer instruction in Arabic and Persian and other advanced Islamic subjects. Yet *madrasa* teachers are rarely opposed to 'this-worldly' education. Indeed, some *madrasas* have UP state recognition to teach Hindi and other subjects in the UP curriculum up to Class 5, although the employment of Hindi and English teachers is constrained by finances. Usually, *madrasas* charge no fees for instruction in Urdu and the Islamic curriculum, but they might require parents to buy books and other resources for Hindi, English, and other 'secular' subjects—a serious deterrent for poor parents. Few *madrasas*, though, can contemplate extending and 'modernizing' their curricula by introducing subjects such as science and computing, purchasing equipment and teaching materials, and employing well-trained staff on attractive salaries and conditions.

The larger *madrasas* tend to provide no more than five or six years of schooling for children from several surrounding villages, and their pupils are mainly young children. Most boys who attend *madrasas* do so for only a few years, and often irregularly. They usually discontinue their studies by the age of ten or so, before becoming functionally literate in Urdu, let alone in Hindi. The enrolment of Muslim village girls in formal education in *madrasas* increased particularly strikingly in the 1990s, indicating parental response to changes in the accessibility of educational facilities. Many rural *madrasas* teach as many or more girls than boys, teaching them in either different buildings or separate classrooms. Occasionally, small boys and girls are taught in the same rooms but at separate benches. Girls are likely to be more regular attenders and to continue studying until they are about twelve, or when they reach puberty. Other children—often boys from wealthier rural households—attend a *madrasa* for only a few years before moving on to secular schooling. A few rural children bypass the *madrasa* completely, and receive their Islamic education from the *imam* of the local mosque, or with a visiting tutor. Relatively few older boys are full-time students in a *madrasa*. Many of these on scholarship, as orphans or because of extreme poverty, and some come from Bihar or similar distances away. In Bijnor town, few children are solely educated in a *madrasa*; more commonly, pupils attend secular schools as well as attending a *madrasa* to learn Urdu and Arabic before or after regular school timings. *Madrasa* education (and Urdu) have, then, largely become a fallback option for poor Muslims—a remarkable change from the earlier prestige of those learned in Urdu (and Persian and

Arabic), the religious scholars and lawyers, the urban élites and literati.

Some urban English-educated Muslims have accused—*madrasas* of obscurantism and of failing to equip Muslim children with the credentials and skills necessary in today's labour market, in which Urdu is no longer a strong currency.[9] For most Muslim parents, however, their preferences for *madrasas* over schools rest on their accessibility and low cost, their safe, user-friendly environment and conscientious teaching, as well as 'moral education' from an Islamic perspective (Engineer 2001; Sikand 2001a). Poor and rural Muslim parents complain that government schools are characterized by poor facilities, inaccessibility, a lack of committed teachers, and a failure to teach their pupils, and that non-state schools are too costly or too distant. Many Muslims also say that government and non-state schools alike emphasize knowledge and examinations, but that their teaching is devoid of ethical content and their ambience is unsympathetic to Islam. Yet Muslim parents are keenly aware of the costs of illiteracy and want their children to be educated. Better, they say, a *madrasa*

TABLE 1: DISTRIBUTION OF MUSLIM PUPILS BY SCHOOL TYPE, BIJNOR TOWN, 2001-2

Pupils	Hindu and others	SC	Muslim	Total
Government and Government aided schools (percentage)				
Girls	2970 (50)	888 (15)	2084 (35)	5942 (100)
Boys	3499 (57)	1249 (20)	1369 (22)	6117 (100)
Unaided English-medium schools (percentage)				
Girls	284 (87)		43 (13)	327 (100)
Boys	581 (83)		123 (17)	704 (100)
Unaided Hindi-medium schools (percentage)				
Muslim-run: Girls	0 (0)	11 (10)	104 (90)	115 (100)
Boys	1 (1)	7 (9)	74 (90)	82 (100)
SC-run: Girls	1 (8)	10 (77)	2 (15)	13 (100)
Boys	3 (21)	9 (64)	2 (14)	14 (100)
Hindu-run: Girls	178 (77)	39 (17)	14 (6)	231 (100)
Boys	281 (71)	71 (18)	43 (11)	395 (100)

Note: Communal breakdown was not provided of 199 pupils in four Hindi-medium schools, and of 924 pupils in two English-medium schools.

Source: Survey of secondary schools, October-January 2001-2.

education than no education at all; better one that imparts Islamic values than one that marginalizes Muslims.

Yet *madrasas* are only a part of the story of Muslim education in Bijnor—and by the secondary stage they are relatively insignificant, mostly providing just out-of-hours Islamic education for children who have not already learned to read Arabic and the Koran Sharif. Supposedly 'secular' schools provide schooling for substantial numbers of Muslim children who live in towns or are accessible to them. The vast majority of secondary-age Muslim children who are still in formal education are following the UP Board Hindi-medium curriculum, which means that these children must put at least some aspects of their Muslim identities in cold storage whilst at school.

In Bijnor town, few of the schools teaching secondary classes—basically, only the two run as minority institutions (a boys' inter-college and a girls' middle school) and those non-state schools with a Muslim management committee—have more than one or two Muslim teachers.[10] Taking all secondary schools together, our survey of 2001–2 found that fewer than one in five teachers is Muslim: in the English-medium schools, the figure is one in eight. In the Hindi-medium schools, 15 per cent of the teachers are Muslim, but almost all of them teach in the two schools run by Muslims. Out of the 102 teachers employed by Hindu managers in private Hindi-medium schools, only three are Muslim.[11] We do not know, unfortunately, how far these figures reflect the distribution of the qualified population, but it seems surprising that the number of Muslim teachers is so low in a town that is about 50 per cent Muslim.

In Bijnor, the schools and colleges established by local Muslims not only cater for Muslim children but also recruit a fair number of Scheduled Caste children. The Muslim-run schools—in the towns or in the larger villages—are as reliant on having enough people able to pay the fees as are other non-state schools.[12] As yet there are no fully English-medium schools in Bijnor under Muslim management, but one has struggled to establish an English-language stream. The other Muslim schools offer educational facilities on a par with those provided in other schools in the same price bracket. In the Bijnor area, at any rate, these schools all teach in Hindi and follow the UP curriculum.

The three largest Muslim-run institutions all offer Urdu as an optional subject, perhaps resulting in less erasure of Muslim identity.

Significantly, urban Muslim children who go to other schools—the majority of those still undergoing formal education by the ages of 11 or 12—are disproportionately lower in quality institutions. Our data from Bijnor show that secondary school enrolment varies by religion in significant ways. Until 1991 almost all secondary schools in UP (outside the metropolitan areas) were Hindi-medium and either fully- or part-funded by the government. The major change since 1991 has been the rise in non-state schooling, both English- and Hindi-medium. The government or government-aided Hindi schools are of two kinds: relatively poorly-funded middle schools (teaching only up to Class VIII) and relatively well-funded government and aided schools that continue up to Class X or XII (the latter known as intermediate colleges). Muslim children are over-represented in the former—schools that, like most government primary schools, are best described as 'failing'—with Muslims making up 96 per cent of the enrolment in the girls' junior and middle schools, and 52 per cent of the enrolment in the boys' middle school. Muslim children are under-represented in the better-funded (and increasingly expensive, competitive-entry) government and aided intermediate colleges. In the boys' intermediate colleges, about 22 per cent of the pupils are Muslim; in the girls' colleges, the figure is about 21 per cent (whereas the population of the catchment area is probably over 50 per cent Muslim).

There are marked differences between the experiences of boys and girls at school. Muslim girls attend schools in large numbers, not only in single-sex institutions (like the government girls' junior and middle schools, and the government and aided intermediate colleges) but also in some apparently co-educational schools, where girls are often taught separately from boys. In the rapidly-growing co-educational English-language schools, much the most expensive and highest status, Muslims form only 13 per cent of girl pupils, but 20 per cent of boys. Although boys of all religious communities outnumber girls in this form of schooling, for Muslims the disparity is more marked, with nearly three times as many Muslim boys as Muslim girls getting English-medium schooling.[13] In private Hindi-medium schools, the second-fastest growing category, there are almost exactly the same number of Muslim boys and Muslim girls, but they constitute less than 30 per cent of the pupils. Almost all the girls of secondary age still at school (87 per cent) are in Muslim-run schools, but the boys are more widely spread, with 62 per cent in Muslim-run schools, and 36 per cent in those run by Hindus. The remainder are in the one school managed by an SC couple.

If these trends continue, and if government and aided schools continue to be privatized and charge higher admission and tuition fees, we suspect both that the total numbers of Muslim pupils will not grow as fast as the numbers from other religious communities, and that there will be an increasing segregation of pupils. Already, hardly any caste Hindu children attend schools with Muslim or SC managers. We predict that this will become the norm, and schooling will be increasingly separated by religious community. One exception to this emerging pattern is an English-medium school that has a mixed management committee: although the principal is Hindu, the school teaches Urdu to those children who want to learn it, as part of a clear strategy to recruit more Muslim pupils.

TRANSITIONS TO ADULTHOODS

As with many other aspects of Muslim Indian lives, schooling experiences are diverse and fragmented, varying dramatically by class, and for urban and rural populations. Urban middle class Muslim children generally have very different experiences of education from rural and poor children, experiences that are like those of Hindus from comparable backgrounds. These similarities should be borne in mind in what follows.

For girls the transition to adulthood is still largely a matter of marriage. Girls in all classes and communities are being educated—albeit in different ways—primarily because having some education is an important currency in the marriage market. Boys are said to want educated brides, even if they are not highly educated themselves (Hasan and Menon 2004; Jeffery et al. 2005). For Muslim girls from poor households, *madrasa* education provides basic knowledge of Islamic practice and belief, and tries to inculcate the demure behaviour required of a bride. The girls of richer families will probably have attended school, though not necessarily for as long as their brothers have. Additionally, many middle-class parents, Muslim and Hindu alike, advocate girls' education as a means of ensuring that their daughters can 'stand on their own feet' in the event of problems in their married lives, such as widowhood or divorce. Very few parents prioritize employment prospects when considering a girl's schooling.

For middle-class Muslim boys, and especially for those living in urban areas, there is a wide range of occupational options. Like some boys from moderately wealthy rural backgrounds, they are much more likely to have attended a school than a *madrasa*, and to have continued in formal education at least through secondary schooling, and possibly at degree colleges. For these boys, attending school, gaining the skills and credentials relevant for moving into white-collar employment and maintaining and even improving one's life style are aspirations that they might realistically share with others from similar class backgrounds. On the face of it, these Muslim boys seem the most likely to become successfully integrated into the Indian 'mainstream'. This might be too facile a conclusion, however, because there are limitations on the extent to which Muslim boys are able to enter the labour market on equal terms with Hindus of comparable economic standing. Their aim for mainstream incorporation is not always successful: secure jobs in the 'modern' sector are highly competitive, and most (from all backgrounds) fail. Moreover, Muslims face additional hurdles, especially if they are trying to enter employment markets for which there are few family or community precedents.[14] New job-seekers need 'pioneers' who can sponsor young men into jobs, and Muslims often do not have kinship- and trust-based networks that they can mobilize in order to enter such work. They are more likely to follow established links and kinship networks, for example to work in cities elsewhere in India or in the Gulf States (where they may be exploited, separated from their families and discontented with their civil status).[15]

In any case, most Muslim families do not have the economic, social, or cultural capital necessary to get their children into 'good' schools (whether government or aided schools, or expensive, private schools) in the first place. Poor Muslim parents consider it futile to spend their scarce resources on educating their children in inadequate or failing schools, because their children will fail to obtain credentials and they themselves lack the social contacts and financial resources necessary to facilitate a successful transition into employment (Jeffery and Jeffery 1997: 179ff.). And their children have little incentive to stay the course in these inferior schools to the end of upper primary (Class VIII), let alone to complete secondary (Class X or XII) schooling. Their level of literacy will leave them at a distinct disadvantage in getting well-paid jobs or dealing with the public sphere of newspapers, government offices, and officialdom. Indeed, in most respects, Muslim boys leaving school and those leaving *madrasas* are in very similar circumstances. *Madrasa* education is a positive choice for only a tiny minority, and most parents know that *madrasa* education does little to enhance one's skills in the employment markets in which Hindi and English dominate, or to access non-Muslim networks that might open up routes into a wider range of jobs.

Like boys with five or eight years of 'secular' schooling, boys with four or five years of *madrasa* schooling usually move straight into the occupations of their fathers (farming, small business, or artisanal positions such as butchery). Increasingly, however, competition is limiting the income they are able to earn in this way, and a younger son may find that there is enough work only for his elder brother. Other options are to take up an apprenticeship for a craft skill such as carpentry or car maintenance, or unskilled work in agriculture or transport (rickshaw pulling, head-loading, etc.). Some boys move to towns and cities, usually following existing migration chains to places such as Delhi, Surat, and Kashmir. In the case of boys we know in rural Bijnor, one growing area of employment is the export-oriented machine embroidery in Delhi (at least while the government clamp-down on polluting industries is in abeyance). Such work may be relatively well paid, and does not depend on academic qualifications: but it is not clear for how long young men can continue with such work before their eyesight or manual dexterity deteriorates. Here at least, however, Muslims seem to operate at a relative advantage compared to young SC men.

The minority of those who take advanced Islamic training in the Bijnor *madrasas* often compete to gain admission to one of the larger

Islamic seminaries, in Deoband, Saharanpur, Lucknow, or Delhi. For them, higher training in Islamic subjects may open the way to posts such as *maulvi* or *imam*, to lead prayers and to teach, using their education directly and in a respected (though not lucrative) fashion. These positions are not always regarded as second best to white-collar secular occupations: we were often told that the ability to memorize so much, and in Arabic, is an accomplishment few boys can manage, and a certain prestige attaches itself to such achievement. But not all these young men feel a vocation to a religious position, and some with a higher Islamic qualification gain alternative credentials or become involved in family enterprises, whether as traders, landlords, or artisans. In general, though, the Islamic seminaries offer a learned and genteel Muslim identity that provides, for some, an appealing alternative to 'secular' alternatives—it involves a public commitment to Islam, an implicit critique of Westernization and, sometimes, consumerism and modern jobs. This is, perhaps, one reason why *madrasas* provoke such hostility.

CONCLUSION

Recent public debate in India has tended to exoticize *madrasas* as primarily 'Islamic' institutions, and they have become crucial ciphers in communal politics. They are often represented as evidence of supposed Muslim introversion, conservatism, and lack of patriotism. The Sangh Parivar has vilified them as training grounds for Islamic fundamentalists and terrorists, or as hideouts for the banned SIMI (Students Islamic Movement of India), for Pakistani spies, and for arms stashes (Godbole 2001; Kumar 2000b; Sikand 2001a).[16] At various times in the past decade or so, several kinds of state intervention have been proposed to regulate and inspect *madrasas*, to oversee or dictate their curricula, to insist that they are registered with the government, even to close them down. Such proposals to control (but not fund) *madrasas* often reflect an anti-democratic and communal political agenda, rather than a concern with educational standards.

Nevertheless, *madrasas* in UP are performing an important educational role for Muslims, especially for the urban poor and for villagers. Given the other alternatives that are available to Muslims in

UP, it is far from clear that *madrasas* are an especially poor educational option. On the other hand, as educational institutions, they certainly are problematic. Most of their pupils will remain illiterate in Hindi, and possibly barely literate in Urdu. Their poor resourcing and their continuing emphasis on Urdu and Islamic subjects limit the scope for change. They also involve a segregation of schooling along religious lines that is not a healthy sign. *Madrasa* education—involving only Muslims, particularly poor and rural ones—provides all too few opportunities for inter-faith dialogue and friendship and all too many for Muslims and *madrasas* to be demonized (Sikand 2001b). Further, the development of *madrasas* may have exacerbated the processes of economic, social and political exclusion and separation of Muslims in UP and limited the intra-class and cross-community mobilization needed to improve schooling for all.

The *madrasa* issue, however, should not distract attention from the more pressing issues for Muslims in UP: the widespread and established processes of social and economic exclusion, to which *madrasas* themselves have been one response. The expansion of the *madrasa* sector in UP would probably not have been so rapid if enough schools had met the perfectly reasonable expectations of Muslim parents. Evidence from around the country indicates that Muslim parents enrol their children in schools, if they can afford to, if those schools are accessible and non-threatening to their children, and if the schooling offers realistic chances of leading to good jobs (Hasan and Menon 2004). Muslim-friendly schools—schools in the right places, with sufficient facilities and committed staff, and with the worst excesses of saffronization removed—would draw in Muslim children.

Yet sufficient Muslim-friendly schools are unlikely to materialize, since the private sector responds only to market forces. Unfortunately, more schools will not necessarily be a panacea, because processes of segregation and separation are also visible in—'secular' schooling just as they are in *madrasas*. Schools—whether government funded, government aided or not—seem to be increasingly the preserve of Hindu children taught by Hindu staff. Where there is no critical mass of Muslims, there would probably be nothing at all or only—*maktabs*, masquerading as *madrasas*; where there is a critical mass, including a relatively affluent middle class sector, there will be *madrasas* and private schools. But these Muslim-run schools will also tend to have teachers and a pupil body mainly Muslim, and thus do nothing to undermine patterns of communal separation.

Although the direct threat to minority schooling has retreated, now that the BJP has lost power both at the UP and national levels, the state is unlikely to act to remedy this situation. Because of the fiscal crisis in UP, the state education system is collapsing. Alongside the liberalization of the economy, the inequalities of the market are untrammelled and on the rise. The general privatization of social provisions leads to élitism, diversification, and the fragmentation of schooling, with further emphasis on social distinction. Increasingly, government schooling is serving only those groups who cannot get access to better, more expensive, non-state alternatives. Because the new non-state institutions are beyond the means of most north-Indian Muslim parents, their children seem likely to be left behind in the race to be part of a new India. The schooling and educational patterns we have described suggest that the future for Muslims in India is not bright: most Muslim children are unlikely to be able to overcome the established processes of social and economic exclusion that perpetuate inequalities through the generations. In the face of consumerism and with problematic access to employment, young Muslims are likely to be increasingly disaffected as they see the prizes of modernity and money eluding them.

NOTES

1. We are grateful to the Ford Foundation and the Royal Geographical Society for funding the research in Bijnor district (UP) on which this paper is based, and to the Institute of Economic Growth, New Delhi, for our attachment there in 2000-2. None bears any responsibility for what we have written here. We also thank our research assistants, Swaleha Begum, Shaila Rais, Chhaya Sharma, and Manjula Sharma, the people of Qaziwala and Nangal Jat, the school and *madrasa* staff, and the many others who so readily answered our questions.
2. Full details of his address to the nation on 14 August 2004 can be found at http://presidentofindia.nic.in/scripts/independencedetail. jsp?id=5
3. The term 'Dalit' is not commonly used in western UP.
4. Using data from the 1991 national census and the 1992-3 National Family Health Survey, Drèze and Sen estimate that rural enrolment rates in UP in the early 1990s were 43 per cent of girls and 70 per cent of boys aged 6-14; the

urban rates were 70 and 77 per cent respectively. Some 44 per cent of girls never enrolled in school, compared to 19 per cent of boys. Only 30 per cent of girls aged 15-19 had completed 8th class, compared with 55 per cent of boys (Drèze & Sen 2002: 147). Data from 1997-8 (Nayar 2001) and from the 2001 Census (supplied in electronic format File ST2001RU, Table 1) show little material change in the differentials. Girls' chances of enrolling at school and becoming literate are closely related to their mothers' education, which in part explains the low levels of their school enrolment in areas—like Bijnor—with low levels of adult female literacy (Drèze and Kingdon 2001; Srivastava 2001: 271).

5. See also King 1994; Rai 2001.
6. For more on the contemporary position of Urdu in UP, see Abdullah 2002; Ahmad 2002; Brass 1974: 119-274; 1990; 1991: 69-108; Farouqui 1994; Latifi 1999; Pai 2002; Rahman 2002: 198-262; Russell 1999; Venkatachaliah 1999.
7. Many Muslims in Bijnor expressed cynicism about the qualifications of staff appointed to teach Urdu, and considered the move a political ploy by Mayawati and Mulayam Singh Yadav in their competition for Muslim votes, rather than a commitment to Urdu.
8. For more details on the girls' Islamic course, a staple of Bijnor *madrasa* teaching for girls up to the ages of 11 or 12, see Jeffery et al., 2004.
9. See Ahmad 2002. There have also been numerous articles to this effect in *Times of India*, *Hindustan Times*, *Milli Gazette* and *Muslim India*.
10. 'Minority' institutions can select their own staff, and are not subject to requirements to meet reservations quotas for SC or ST pupils or staff.
11. SC teachers are also under-represented, with only 7 per cent of all secondary teachers in Bijnor, and only 5 per cent of those teaching in English-medium schools.
12. In recent years (when the BJP was in power in UP) Muslim private school managers claim to have faced problems in getting government recognition, or in being allowed to refill posts that have become vacant. Almost all school managers—Hindu or Muslim—told the same kinds of stories, however, so we do not know if there were more difficulties for Muslim-run institutions.
13. Two of the five English-medium schools did not provide a breakdown of pupils by religion, so we base these figures on the other three schools, with about half the total pupils in this sector.
14. This point also applies to other historically marginalized groups such as the Scheduled Castes.
15. Men in such circumstances are often regarded as particularly vulnerable to recruitment to fundamentalist movements, but we have no evidence of this for young Muslim men from Bijnor.
16. In addition, *Times of India*, *Hindustan Times*, *Amar Ujala*, and the RSS weekly *Organiser* have carried numerous articles on this subject, especially since 2001.

REFERENCES

Abdullah, H., 2002, 'Minorities, Education and Language: The Case of Urdu', *Economic and Political Weekly* 37, 24: 2288–92.

Ahmad, I, 2002, 'Urdu and Madrasa Education', *Economic and Political Weekly* 37, 24: 2285-87.

Balagopalan, S. and R. Subrahmanian, 2003, '*Dalit* and *Adivasi* Children in Schools: Some Preliminary Research Themes and Findings', *IDS Bulletin* 34, 1: 43-54.

Bénéï, V., 2000, 'Teaching Nationalism in Maharashtra Schools', in *The Everyday State and Society in Modern India*, ed. C.J. Fuller and V. Bénéï, pp. 194-221, Delhi: Social Science Press.

Billig, M., 1995, *Banal Nationalism*, London: Sage.

Brass, P.R., 1974, *Language, Religion and Politics in North India*, London: Cambridge University Press.

———, 1990, *The Politics of India since Independence* (The New Cambridge History of India IV-1), Cambridge: Cambridge University Press.

———, 1991, *Ethnicity and Nationalism: Theory and Comparison*, Delhi: Sage.

Deshpande, A., 2000, 'Hindustani in India', *Economic and Political Weekly* 35, 15: 1240-2.

Drèze, J. and H. Gazdar, 1997, 'Uttar Pradesh: The Burden of Inertia', in *Indian Development: Selected Regional Perspectives*, ed. J. Drèze and A. Sen, pp. 33-128, Delhi: Oxford University Press.

Drèze, J. and G. Kingdon, 1998, *School Participation in Rural India* (Development Economics Discussion Paper 18), London: STICERD, London School of Economics.

———, 2001, School Participation in Rural India, *Review of Development Economics* 5, 1: 1-33.

Drèze, J. and A. Sen, 2002, *India: Development and Participation*, Delhi: Oxford University Press.

Engineer, A.A., 2001, 'Muslims and Education', *Economic and Political Weekly* 36, 34: 3221-2.

Farouqui, A., 1994, 'Urdu Education in India: Four Representative States', *Economic and Political Weekly* 29, 14: 782-5.

Faust, D. and R. Nagar, 2001, 'Politics of Development in Postcolonial India: English-Medium Education and Social Fracturing', *Economic and Political Weekly* 36, 30: 2878-83.

Godbole, M., 2001, 'Madarsas: Need for a Fresh Look', *Economic and Political Weekly* 36, 41: 3889-90.

Govinda, R. (ed.), 2002, *India Education Report: A Profile of Basic Education*, Delhi: Oxford University Press.

Hameed, R., 2005, 'Learning Processes within the *Ustad-Shagird* Relationship', in *Educational Regimes in Contemporary India* (eds.) R. Chopra and P. Jeffery, pp. 197-215, Delhi: Sage.

Hasan, Z. and R. Menon, 2004, *Unequal Citizens: A Study of Muslim Women in India*, Delhi: Oxford University Press.

Jeffery, P.M., R. Jeffery and C. Jeffrey, 2004, 'Islamisation, Gentrification and Domestication: 'A Girls' Islamic Course' and Rural Muslims in Western Uttar Pradesh', *Modern Asian Studies* 38, 1: 1-53.

———, 2005, 'The Mother's Lap and the Civilising Mission: *Madrasah* education and Rural Muslim girls in Western Uttar Pradesh', in *In a Minority: Essays on Muslim Women in India*, ed. Z. Hasan and R. Menon, pp. 108-48, Delhi: Oxford University Press.

Jeffery, R. and P.M. Jeffery, 1997, *Population, Gender and Politics: Demographic Change in Rural North India*, Cambridge: Cambridge University Press.

Jeffery, R., P.M. Jeffery and C. Jeffrey, 2005a, 'Social Inequalities and the Privatisation of Secondary Schooling in North India', in *Educational Regimes in Contemporary India*, ed. R. Chopra and P. Jeffery, pp. 41-61, Delhi: Sage.

———, 2005b, 'Patterns and Discourses of the Privatisation of Secondary Schooling in Bijnor, UP', in *Education in Modern South Asia—Social and Political Implications*, ed. K. Kumar and J. Oesterheld, Delhi: Orient Longman.

Karlekar, M., 2000, 'Girls Access to Schooling: An Assessment', in *The Gender Gap in Basic Education: NGOs as Change Agents*, ed. R. Wazir, pp. 80-114, Delhi: Sage.

King, C.R., 1994, *One Language, Two Scripts: The Hindi Movement in Nineteenth Century North India*, Delhi: Oxford University Press.

Kingdon, G. and M. Muzammil, 2001, 'A Political Economy of Education in India', *Economic and Political Weekly* 36, 32–33: 3052-62, 3178-85.

Kumar, K., 1989, *Social Character of Learning*, Delhi: Sage.

———, 1991, *Political Agenda of Education: A Study of Colonialist and Nationalist Ideas*, Delhi: Sage.

———, 1993, 'Hindu Revivalism and Education in North-Central India', in *Fundamentalisms and Society: Reclaiming the Sciences, the Family and Education*, ed. M. Marty and R.S. Appleby, pp. 536-57, Chicago: University of Chicago.

Kumar, N., 1988, *The Artisans of Banaras: Popular Culture and Identity, 1880-1986*, Princeton: Princeton University.

Kumar, P., 2000, 'UP: Religious Places Bill', *Economic and Political Weekly* 35, 12: 977-8.

Latifi, D., 1999, 'Preserving Urdu through Self-help', *Economic and Political Weekly* 34, 22: 1321-3.

Mohan, P., 2000, 'Hindustani, Hindi and English in India', *Economic and Political Weekly* 35, 19: 1672-3.

Nayar, U., 2001, 'Education of Girls in India: an Assessment', in *India Education Report: A Profile of Basic Education*, ed. R. Govinda, pp. 35-46, Delhi: National Institute of Educational Planning and Administration.

NCERT, 1997, *Sixth All India Educational Survey: National Tables*, Vol. 1 *(Educational Facilities in Rural and Urban Areas)*, Delhi: National Council of Educational Research and Training.

Orsini, F., 2002, *The Hindi Public Sphere, 1920-1940: Language and Literature in an Age of Nationalism*, Delhi: Oxford University Press.

Pai, S., 2002, 'Politics of Language: Decline of Urdu in Uttar Pradesh', *Economic and Political Weekly* 37, 27: 2705-8.

Rahman, T., 2002, *Language, Ideology and Power: Language-learning among the Muslims of Pakistan and North India*, Karachi: Oxford University Press.

Rai, A., 2001, *Hindi Nationalism*, Delhi: Orient Longman.

Russell, R., 1999, 'Urdu in India since Independence', *Economic and Political Weekly* 34, 1-2: 44-8.

Sahmat, 2001, *The Saffron Agenda in Education: an Exposé*, Delhi: Safdar Hashmi Memorial Trust.

———, 2002a, *Against Communalisation of Education: Essays, Press Coverage, Reportage*, Delhi: Safdar Hashmi Memorial Trust.

———, 2002b, *Communalisation of Education: The Assault on History (Press Reportage, Editorials and Articles)*, Delhi: Safdar Hashmi Memorial Trust.

Shariff, A., 1995, 'Socio-Economic and Demographic Differentials between Hindus and Muslims in India', *Economic and Political Weekly* 30, 46: 2947-53.

Siddiqui, M.A., 2004, *Empowerment of Muslims Through Education*, Delhi: Institute of Objective Studies.

Sikand, Y., 2001a, 'Countering Fundamentalism: Beyond the Ban on SIMI', *Economic and Political Weekly* 36, 37: 3803.

———, 2001b, 'Targeting Muslim Religious Schools', *Economic and Political Weekly* 36, 35: 3342-3.

Srivastava, R., 2001, 'Access to Basic Education in Rural Uttar Pradesh', in *Elementary Education in Rural India: A Grassroots View*, ed. A. Vaidyanathan and P.R. Gopinathan Nair, pp. 257-319, Delhi: Sage.

Srivastava, S., 2000, 'The Farce that is Hindi', *Economic and Political Weekly* 35, 43-4: 3898-9.

Thapar, R., 2005, 'Knowledge and Education', *Frontline* 22, 2: Internet edition.

The Probe Team, 1999, *Public Report on Basic Education in India*, Delhi: Oxford University Press.

Venkatachaliah, M.N., 1999, 'Language and Politics: Status of Urdu in India', *Economic and Political Weekly* 34, 26: 1659-60.

Wazir, R. (ed.), 2000, *The Gender Gap in Basic Education: NGOs as Change Agents*, Delhi: Sage.

4

Tamil Muslims and the Self-Respect Movement

S.M.A.K. FAKHRI

The Tamil Muslim relationship with the Self-Respect movement provides an ideal vantage point from which to examine questions of political identity raised by both Tamils and Muslims in India. It is for the recovery of the self-worth of the Dalits that Islam and the Muslim communities of India acquired their relevance to the Self-Respect movement. The movement absorbed Muslims as part of the Dravidian/Tamil community. Muslims reciprocated such an incorporation by upholding Tamil as their liturgical language and even participated in the anti-Hindi agitations. It is within a discourse between caste and language that a Tamil Muslim matrix was produced.

Political developments in the period between the collapse of the Khilafat movement and the moment of Indian independence were crucial to the formation of the cultural and political identities of Muslims in Tamil Nadu. These developments determined the shape of Tamil politics in independent India. The *Suyamariyathai Iyakkam* or Self-Respect movement was initiated in 1925, and it transformed the political and social landscape of Tamil Nadu. The objective of the Self-Respect movement was to destroy Brahmin dominance and the caste system. Meanwhile, by the 1930s, Dravidian/Tamil resistance to the cultural imposition of all-India nationalism emerged. The first anti-Hindi agitations occurred in 1937-8. They also gave rise to the politics of regionalism in the late 1930s and 1940s.

The Dravidian umbrella generated a political space in which diverse and multiple identities could be combined and asserted. It explicitly sought to include Tamil Muslims within its fold. Dravidianism was a matter of caste and language.[1] The ideology and programme of the Self-Respect movement both in terms of its non-Brahminism and its affinity with the Tamil language presupposed the inclusion of Muslims. On the contrary, and significantly, its political vocabulary did not distinguish between Tamil Muslims and Dravidians. As Tamil speakers and non-Brahmins, the region's Muslims were obviously Dravidian. For Tamil Muslims, this meant that they were not perceived or treated as a separate or a monolithic community. Being Dravidian and Tamil did not foreclose the options for Muslims to pursue interests, aspirations and purposes which may be identified with Islamic politics and culture.

This paper discusses the relationship vis-à-vis Tamil Muslims and the Self-Respect movement between 1925 and 1947. The politics of the Self-Respect movement had an impact on the manner in which Islam was perceived among the general Tamil population. The movement ensured that Islam was relevant in the Tamil context. It enabled Muslims to enjoy a political space of their own and yet not be set aside as a separate community. Thus, Muslims of the Tamil region could be treated as yet another caste and considered autonomously as well—in both senses they were clearly an integral component of Tamil society.

The language of the politics of the Self-Respect movement included Muslims as part of the Dravidian/Tamil *inam* or community. Tamil terms most frequently used in the propaganda of this movement to convey the meaning of caste and community were *jati*, *kulam*, and *inam*. The word *inam* has often been misread as meaning race. As M.S.S. Pandian has pointed out, the tendency to attribute a 'race theory' to Dravidian polemic has arisen from precisely such mistranslation. In fact, '*inam* is a dexterous Tamil word which can signify different forms of community'.[2] Further, in the discourse of Dravidianism, 'Aryan' and 'Dravidian' categories were used to denote 'different cultural complexes, the relationship between them mediated by power and powerlessness'.[3]

The first section of this paper investigates how Muslims related to the Self-Respect movement, especially in the context of its politics of caste and social reform. In particular, I sketch the endeavour to promote a certain construct of Muslimness as an alternative to caste-oppression especially among Dalits. I will then examine how the Tamil language offered an important base for Tamil Muslim identity. By participating in anti-Hindi agitations, developing a Muslim press in Tamil, and by opting for Tamil over Hindi/Hindustani as their day-to-day and even liturgical language, Muslims addressed themselves as Tamils and asserted their presence within the Dravidian/Tamil community.

In 1916 the colonial regime encouraged the founding of the Justice Party to challenge the growing power of the Brahmin-dominated Congress in the Madras Presidency.[4] The Justice Party with non-Brahmin elites at its helm introduced a new political vocabulary of non-Brahminism in south India.[5] Nevertheless, this party had a limited impact on caste politics in the region until E.V. Ramasamy (popularly known as 'Periyar', the great one), a former Congressman, assumed its leadership in 1938. He merged it with the Self-Respect movement in 1944 and formed the Dravida Kazhagam (D.K.). Ramasamy's political biography[6] could even be considered co-terminus with the history of twentieth-century Tamil Nadu. Hence, his ideas assume primacy for an understanding of the Self-Respect movement.

Ramasamy was active in the Congress until 1925. Disillusioned with the social and political attitudes of the nationalist elite, represented mainly by the Brahmins of south India, he left it. The congress leaders were reluctant to accommodate the concerns of non-Brahmins on communal representation and on vital social issues such as untouchability. M.S.S. Pandian has argued that the arrival of the nation for Ramasamy, meant solving the 'problem' of subordinate social groups such as the Sudras, Dalits and women. In this sense, the concept of the nation in his political discourse was disengaged from its classical Indian/Tamil past and envisaged fully in the future.[7] It is within Ramasamy's political outlook and the wider programme which placed at its centre equality for the lower castes, that the relationship between Muslims and the Self-Respect movement must be situated.

Ramasamy perceived religion as an instrument of power in the hands of the dominant upper castes and thus a source of oppression of the lower castes and women. He propagated atheism and spoke highly of certain religions in the context of Dalit emancipation. Religion generally, and Buddhism, Christianity, and Islam specifically, occupied a significant and relational position within Ramasamy's political discourse.[8] It is within such a relational understanding of religion that we need to consider Ramasamy's position on Islam and Muslims, and corresponding Muslim responses to his ideology.

ISLAM AS REPRESENTED BY THE SELF-RESPECT MOVEMENT

The significant threads of Ramasamy's political discourse in understanding his approach to Islam were: first, the liberation of subordinate social groups such as Dalits, women, and the poor were crucial to the development of the nation; second, these subordinate social groups must find their own voices and speak for themselves; third, it was politically strategic to blur the boundaries between oppressed groups; finally, the all-India national movement was led by upper-caste elites and could lead to all power accruing to them and had to be opposed.

Broadly, Ramasamy's position on Islam has to be contextualized in the light of his problematization of the Hindu caste system. Hinduism for him not only represented entrenched caste relations but also multiple relations of power over subordinate groups such as Dalits, women, and the poor.[9] If Islam was useful to the Self-Respect movement, it did not mean that Ramasamy's was a blanket endorsement of Muslims and their attitudes. On the contrary his engagement with Islam involved a critique of the cultural and religious practices of the Muslims. His discourse on Islam had space for a multiplicity of positions and reflected an ambivalence, at times deliberate, to suit his political needs and ends. This depended on whether he was addressing Muslims or Dalits. He perceived Indian Muslims as former Dalits who over the centuries, converted to Islam, to escape what he saw as caste oppression in the Hindu social system. Ramasamy worked consistently within a framework of pan-Islam and pan-Indian Islam and repeatedly cited these as sources of strength for Muslims across the world and in India.

The Self-Respect movement was intended to restore to Dravidians the self-respect that the caste system had denied them. Islam, for the purposes of this movement, would help Tamils achieve a caste-free, egalitarian society. The Self-Respect movement made Islam a significant part of its propaganda: the principles of unity, rationality, freedom, and self-respect which it was said to espouse were presented as those which differentiated it from Hinduism and its oppressive caste system.[10]

The prime reason for the conversion of Dalits to Islam, Ramasamy argued, was the problem of untouchability and pollution taboos. Often when Ramasamy addressed Dalits, he presented Islam as a kind of panacea for all the ills plaguing them. This needs to be juxtaposed with his critical attitude to Islam. When he addressed Muslims, he constantly compared Muslims in India with their co-religionists elsewhere and criticized Islam in India for its conservatism as compared to Turkey. His favoured frame of reference, thus, for 'ideal Islam' was Turkey.[11] Ramasamy frequently cited how Muslim women in Turkey were treated progressively by Muslim men there. He was disturbed by the attitude of the Muslim men in India regarding their approach to women as well as their religious conservativeness.[12] It must also be noted that the gender question transcended religious boundaries. Ramasamy's critique of patriarchy within Muslim society was an extension of his general reading of history on gender issues.[13] The Muslim priesthood, for Ramasamy, performed the function that Brahmins performed in the Hindu social system. He was severely critical of the hold of the *mullas* on the Muslims and the manner in which they impeded the progress of their community.[14]

Ramasamy placed Islam under the lens of his rationalism just as he did Hindu religious practices. Islam, he firmly believed, was not just what the Koran said, but what the Muslims did—Islamic principles could only be gauged only by the way Muslims conducted themselves in practical life. The idea of pilgrimages, for instance, came in for scathing criticism[15] because similar customs existed among Hindus. Festivals too came in for severe censure. Working within a purist and orthodox framework himself, Ramasamy held that Muslim festivals should not be patterned after Hindu festivals and was critical of non-Muslim Tamils calling Muharram the 'Allah-Sami' festival.[16]

Within the discourse of the Self-Respect movement, syncretic practices such as *dargah*-worship and all the rituals that accompanied them were viewed with the same attitude as the upper-caste practice of Hinduism's attempt to dilute the 'rational' elements of Islam.[17] This emphasis on rationality or *pakutharivu* was central to Ramasamy's attempts to challenge the caste system. The sayings of the Prophet of Islam on the pursuit of knowledge and the use of reason were often cited to impress on Tamil Muslims the importance of rationality.[18]

The need to differentiate Islam from the Hindu religious and social systems was important for the movement, enabling it to negotiate the power structures of caste within Tamil society. In doing so, the protagonists of Self-Respect movement had to present Islam as an 'ideal' faith which they could recommend to the untouchables as a solution to their problems. While the movement made no attempt to gloss over the problems in Muslim practices, it was keen to present the Muslim communities as homogeneous and lacking in hierarchy and the 'ideal' faith of Islam as inherently 'pure and rational'. In this interpretation, the practices of 'syncretism' were undesirable accretions from Hinduism.

MUSLIM RESPONSES TO THE SELF-RESPECT MOVEMENT

The manner in which the propaganda of the Self-Respect movement affected the politics of the Muslims of Tamil Nadu could be understood by their ideological statements and the political processes between 1925 and 1947. The most significant response to its propaganda was the manner in which Tamil Muslim writers represented Islamic ideology. The discourse on Islam by Ramasamy and the Self-Respect movement was appropriated by Islamic ideologues to show that Islam was the most 'rational' and 'natural' religion. These ideologues argued that Islam gave its women and lower social orders as much equality, dignity, and comfort as any other religion could offer.[19] The response of Muslim ideologues to the rhetoric of the Self-Respect movement shows that Islamic ideology of the time borrowed concepts from Dravidianist discourse to present Islam as 'natural' and an 'ideal' path. This was a response to the contentious ideological milieu of the time: Islamic ideology had to adapt itself to Dravidianist discourse as well as respond to Indian nationalism and the growth of socialist and trade-union movements.

Even though Tamil Muslims recognized non-Muslim Tamils as 'Hindus', their knowledge and recognition that the latter did not constitute a single community, but were fragmented into various castes, meant that there was no 'other' for them in Tamil Nadu. This implied that Tamil Muslims did not have to confront an organized 'Hindu' arrayed against them. More evidence that Tamils did not lend themselves to a politics invoking religions as monolithic communities is found in the positions taken by the colonial administrators. H.M. Hood, the District Magistrate of Thanjavur, for instance, argued against a scheme proposed at an all-India level to set up district conciliation boards to resolve Hindu-Muslim disputes. In a letter dated 16 November 1924, he told the Government of Madras, 'I know of no instance in which the Muslims *as a body* have pitted themselves against the Hindus as such'[20] (emphasis mine). As a result, there was no need for Tamil Muslims to sharply assert their Muslimness at the regional and local levels. Moreover, their self-perception as Dravidians/Tamils subsumed an affirmation of Islam. Significantly, this was not to be the case when Tamil Muslims participated in all-India politics. They needed to differentiate themselves *as* Muslims while responding to the politics of the Congress, the Hindu Mahasabha, and the Arya Samaj. In the all-India context, Tamil Muslims demonstrated their affiliation with pan-Islam.

As was the case with the rest of Indian society, the social and political reality was that Muslims too were stratified along *quasi*-caste and doctrinaire lines. V.M. Shamsuddin, a sympathizer of P. Daud Shah, the editor of *Darul Islam*, appealed to the Tamil Muslims to project a picture of unity. He recommended: 'Say that you are a Muslim when you are asked about your caste. Do not reply that you are Pathan, Labbai, Turk, Rowther, or Maraikkayar'(Shamsuddin 1929:96). M. Ibrahim, a Tamil Muslim from Sri Lanka, complained of the 'religious fanaticism that was tearing humankind' and enumerated the following divisions within Islam: 'Sunni, Shiah, Wahabi, Ahmadiyya, Hanafi, Shafi, Hanbali, Maaliki, Qadiriya, Sadiriya, Chistiya, Ribaiya, and Naqshabandhi sects'.[21]

The leaders of the Self-Respect movement were aware of the fragmentation occurring among Muslims in various ways. There was the constant reference to class-divisions among them and the distinction between Muslim *mullas* and the Muslim lay-population, was said to correspond to the *purohit*—lower caste division among Hindus. Publicists of the movement were also aware that the concept of Muslim brotherhood, though an important part of Islamic scripture and worship, was fractured into sectarian and doctrinaire divisions. It was not in the interests of the Dravidian movement to stress these internal schisms among Muslims—the movement portrayed Muslims as a community with 'unity', 'brotherhood', and 'pan-Islamic solidarities'. The movement ignored the stratification within Tamil Muslim communities as it wished to retain the prescriptive value of Islam in the Tamil context. The movement absorbed Muslims as part of the Dravidian community which was, in turn, confirmed by Muslim self-perception as Dravidians.

Muslim ideologues sought to persuade Dalits that Islam provided an egalitarian social order that would benefit them. Presenting Hindu society as a series of divisions and hierarchies, one writer asked Dalits, if the upper castes amongst them had distinctions of high and low, how would they achieve real brotherhood with lower castes?[22] Dalits did not need to protest or perform *satyagraha* in order to enter Islamic places of worship.[23] This was a clear reference to the temple-entry campaign that gained momentum in Madras Presidency in the late 1920s. Ramasamy earned his political spurs through his temple entry campaign in the Travancore state.[24] Ramasamy drew a clear link between the rights of 'untouchables' (temple-entry) and conversion to Islam. Addressing the anti-untouchability conference in 1943 at Madras, he said:

> Converting to Islam is the solution because it offers social unity and self-respect . . . *Adi-Dravidas* ought to leave Hinduism and join Islam . . . I am not referring to God, *Nabi* or the *Quran* when I refer to Islam. I am speaking of Islam of the *lungi* and the cap. Wear the red lungi and the Turkish cap and then see what happens. You acquire dignity and courage. The Travancore temple was opened for *Adi-Dravidas* because 200-300 of them had chosen Islam. Alternatively, if you remained in Hinduism, even if you get *swaraj* in 2000 AD, nothing would have changed for you.[25]

Such polemical statements by Ramasamy were an expression of solidarity with Dalits. For Ramasamy recommending conversions to Islam had an added advantage besides enabling Dalits to escape the physical reality of caste oppressions. The advantage was in the form of a constant threat to upper-caste Hindu politicians or those among them who were reluctant to grant Dalits their rights, despite considering them 'Hindu'.[26] Ramasamy emphatically posited:

My preaching of Islam would be to the extent that it is not enough to grant temple entry (to the depressed castes). I am not going to stop preaching about Islam until lower castes are allowed into the temple in the place where the Brahmin rings the bell (and the depressed castes gain their rights).[27]

This was echoed by Dalits themselves, as when the Adi-Dravida Progressive Association at Seerkai warned 'the Government and capitalists that it would resort to conversions to Islam to escape harassment'.[28] Apart from being a kind of relief from the immediate social environment, conversion or the threat of it, was clearly a bargaining tool in the hands of the Self-Respect movement. In a sense, Dalit conversion to Islam was not a necessary precondition for the Self-Respect movement to move towards a caste-free society. At a practical level, it was just as important to sustain the propaganda for, and the threat of, conversion to Islam. This would pressurize some upper-caste Hindu elites to concede the demands of Dalits.

Significantly, the ideas of the Self-Respect movement gained ground among local leaders of depressed castes. M. Saminathan, an Adi-Dravida, requested Muslim leaders to help people of his caste who wished to escape untouchability by converting to Islam.[29] The secretary of the United Adi-Dravida Youth Association of Tiruvannamalai expressed the willingness of 200 Adi-Dravidas to convert to Islam to save their self-respect. These people were motivated to change their religion by listening to Janaka Sankara Kannapar, an important Dalit leader of the region, an associate of Ramasamy and member of the Madras Legislative Assembly. Kannapar was also the editor of the Self-Respect newspaper, *Dravidian*. Adi-Dravida's constituted one-third of the population of Tiruvannamalai, a town in south Arcot district. The secretary added that among these Adi-Dravidas, those belonging to Seelaimpatti, a part of Tiruvannamalai, had already set the example by converting to Islam.[30]

Another significant appeal to the Dalits came from Munisamy Pillai, M.L.A., who, at a meeting of the Madras Adi-Dravida Mahajana Sabha, wondered how Hindus would treat Adi-Dravidas after obtaining *swaraj* if they were mistreating them under British rule. Consequently, Pillai deemed *swaraj* undesirable. He then advised Adi-Dravidas to achieve their goals by joining 'their Muslim brothers'.[31] As for Muhammad Ibrahim, he was worried that *varnashrama dharma* might be the real intention of upper-caste elites who were struggling for *swaraj*.[32] Such prescriptions to convert to Islam benefitted Muslims as much as Adi-Dravidas. Islam earned added relevance with lower-caste Tamils because of the politics of the Self-Respect movement.

How did this ideological justification and related propaganda translate itself into actual conversion to Islam by Dalits? Available information indicates cycles of conversion between 1925 and 1935, followed again in the period 1940 to 1945.[33] Cumbum town in Madurai district manifested the first major wave of conversions in 1934. The Muslim proselytising association, Ishat-ul-Islam, founded in 1929, appears to have contributed to the conversion of at least 1,100 persons in Cumbum town and its neighbourhood and 400 others from different regions of Tamil Nadu and Travancore. C. Abdul Hakeem, a leading leather merchant in north Arcot, was a major patron of this association.[34]

Another cycle of conversions were reported in Tirunelveli district in 1945, involving about 2000 people. This led to a counter-mobilization by the Hindu Mahasabha and the formation of the Hindu Mission Society to step up an anti-untouchability campaign and to prevent lower castes from joining other faiths.[35] There were then the sporadic conversions of individuals and families in places as far apart as Tiruvannamalai and Dinidvanam (south Arcot), Namakkal, Tiruchirapalli, and Madras city.[36]

Muslim responses to Ramasamy's propaganda differed in each locality. While there were many places where the Muslim elite and *ulama* delighted in it, and often invited Ramasamy to address the Prophet's Birthday celebration meetings, others opposed it. At Nagalnagar, in Dindigul for example, Muslim youth faced the threat of ostracization if they followed the Self-Respect line. This resulted in their undertaking to cease all connection with the Self-Respect movement.[37] However, in Attur, in Salem district, a Muslim couple volunteered to conduct a Self-Respect marriage. Such marriages, a clear manifestation of Ramasamy's concern for women's emancipation, differed significantly from the usual Hindu marriages in the absence of the conventional *tali* (or the yellow-thread necklace tied by the groom on the bride), Brahmin priests, and Sanskritic rituals.[38] At Attur, the Self-Respect marriage between Haji Ghulam Mohideen and

Khadijah Begum was marked by the absence of the *karuppu mani* or the black-beaded necklace, the south Indian Muslim equivalent of the *tali*.[39]

Muslim elite resistance to gender reform[40] butressed by the *ulama* and concomitant resistance to the involvement of Muslim youth in the Self-Respect movement, clearly held back the democratization of Muslim society. If Ramasamy found Islam egalitarian on questions of caste, he was more critical of the role of *mullas*, the treatment of women, and the various class and sectarian differences. References to the 'absence' of caste in Islam flattered Muslims, though their responses were quite contrary in the case of these other issues. Their attitude to Self-Respect ideology seemed to say, 'this far and no further'. Self-Respecters noticed this partial acceptance of their line, among both Muslim priests and youth. One such report noted that none of the Muslims spoken to had anything to say about God.[41] This meant that Muslims either ignored the atheist ideology in the Self-Respect movement or rejected it as unacceptable.

For Ramasamy, the power-structures, differences and debates within Muslim society had to resolve themselves: this involved different issues, sects, *ulama*, and leaders, depending on the occasion and the political context. While independently empathizing with issues concerning the democratization of Muslim society, Ramasamy's engagements with Muslims have to be viewed in strategic relation to his political challenges to upper-caste Hindus and the politicians amongst them. However, this did not mean that Ramasamy ignored problems in Muslim society.[42] He was clear in his criticism of the structures of power within Muslim society. He did not accept the Muslim priests as the sole interpreters of the religion and presented a nuanced pan-Islam. Further, he reinforced a favourable representation of Islam, validating it as a religion to be adopted in his vision of the Dravidian community. In such a vision, Ramasamy did not give Islam and the local Muslim communities blanket endorsement: his was a contextual affirmation depending on the forum that he addressed. For the Muslim elite and the *ulama*, the Self-Respect movement could only be met half-way. The acceptance of their anti-caste programme and conversion episodes did not mean consent to Self-Respect ideology on atheism, socialism and gender. For elite, male and pious Muslims to concede these issues was tantamount to rejecting their identity as Muslims. They drew sustenance from the Self-Respect movement, but clearly did not merge with it. It suited the Self-Respect movement and the Muslim ideologues to negotiate their positions on these lines to achieve a place for their respective groups within their vision of a Dravidian/Tamil community. Like caste, language was another area where Muslims defined themselves as part of the Tamil community.

MUSLIMS AND THE TAMIL LANGUAGE

The Tamil language was crucial for the overall development of a Dravidian/Tamil political identity in twentieth-century India.[43] It emerged as a site for a 'national-popular' project by encompassing a range of democratic concerns connected with caste, gender, and region, and involving different social groups.[44] Tamil was significant for the Self-Respect movement because it provided a means for non-Brahmins and Dalits to negotiate the power structures of Sanskrit and English, which Brahmins used to reinforce their dominance over Tamil society. In other words, it was not important for the movement and its leaders that the Tamil language had a 'glorious past' but that it derived its significance in serving as a useful egalitarian basis for different social groups to build a 'Dravidian/Tamil community'. [45]

If the Self-Respect movement incorporated Islam within its definition of Dravidianness and Tamilness, Muslims reciprocated by an increased identification with the Tamil language. Muslims used Tamil as the medium for understanding and propagating Islam. Daud Shah laboured to make Tamil the liturgical language of Muslims and P. Khalifullah led the anti-Hindi agitations. Recently, Sumathi Ramaswamy argued that in the 'process of producing the *tamilan* (Tamil), pre-existing allegiances are recognized and set aside . . . in favour of declaring one's primary loyalty to Tamil'.[46] As far as Tamil Muslims were concerned, this was not the case. On the contrary, the Self-Respect movement promoted a Dravidian Tamil identity containing within it a strong affirmation of Islam. It is within a discourse between caste and language that a *Tamil Muslim* matrix was produced. The propaganda of the Self-Respect movement included Muslims among the lower-caste groups who could be part of the struggle to recover the Tamil language from what it feared as the dominance of Sanskrit and Hindi. During the anti-Hindi agitations in 1938, Ramasamy underlined the inclusion of Muslims as Tamils. For Ramasamy, Muslims were Tamils who had converted to a different religion to escape upper-caste oppression. He suggested that Muslims were originally Dravidians who had converted to Islam fearing religious persecution.[47] He pointed out how terms such as *tulukkan* (a popular Tamil version of the word 'Turk', categorizing all Muslims as Turks or outsiders) were used pejoratively for Muslims. The *tulukkan* for Ramasamy was a *mleccha* in brahmanical pollution taboos.[48] To the Self-Respect movement's conscious incorporation of Muslims within the Dravidian fold, the latter responded by asserting their 'Tamilness'. Muslims thus began to contend with groups among them who pressed for Arabi-Tamil as the social and religious languages of choice. They preferred Tamil (over Arabi-Tamil) as the language of their political, social and religious lives.

MUSLIM PREFERENCE FOR TAMIL OVER ARABI-TAMIL

Arabi-Tamil (or *arwi*), a tradition of writing Tamil in Arabic characters, was said to have parallels in Malayalam, Bengali, and Malaysian Jawi. Arabi-Tamil is said to still prevail as a live language form among Sri Lankan Muslims.[49] It originated with Arabs who visited ancient Tamil Nadu and the earliest Tamil Muslims, who spoke Tamil but *wrote* the language in the Arabic script. M.M. Uwise holds religious reasons as primarily responsible for the evolution of Arabi-Tamil. Tamil's association with Arabic enhanced its religious associations. Further, Tamil was at times perceived as inadequate to convey the complete meanings or full significance of Islamic or Koranic terms. Therefore Tamil was written in Arabic script.[50] Another consideration was that Muslim women, who could only speak Tamil but could not read or write it, could do so through Arabic. This was possible because Muslim women were said to be more familiar with the Arabic script as their ritual reading of the Koran was more often than that of the men. In fact, women were said to be more familiar with Arabi-Tamil than men.[51]

Arabi-Tamil was considered to be the major medium of religious and cultural expression for Tamil Muslims between the eighth and nineteenth centuries. It was also a medium of communication: letters were then written in Arabi-Tamil. In fact, the nineteenth century was seen as the high point for Arabi-Tamil when it flourished in Kayalapattinam and Kilakkarai. These towns had a distinct history of contact with Arabs and the Indian Ocean maritime trade. Similar developments in Arabi-Tamil occurred in Sri Lanka, Malaysia, Singapore, and Burma. The first Tamil Muslim journals were in Arabi-Tamil: the *Pudina Lankari* (1876) was started in Colombo, the *Muslim Nesan* (1883) in Malaya, and the *Asanbey Charitram* (1885).[52]

If the nineteenth century represented the high point of Arabi-Tamil, the twentieth century saw its decline. As we shall see, Tamil Muslim writers and social reformers in the early twentieth century criticized Arabi-Tamil. The result of such criticism of Arabi-Tamil was that even Arabic *madrasas* now began excluding the language from their curriculum. This led to its decline among the general Muslim populace, especially its women.[53]

P. Daud Shah, editor of *Darul Islam* and 'father of Tamil Muslim journalism', led the opposition against Arabi-Tamil as a language for Muslims. His efforts were aimed at lessening the hold of the *mullas* on Muslim society by denying them their main source of power, knowledge of Arabi-Tamil and Arabic. These were languages used for conducting clerical functions and for interpreting religion. Shah met with condemnation during and after his lifetime for his efforts to challenge the position of the *ulama*. An example of a viewpoint which continues to attack Daud Shah even today is provided by Takya Shu'ayb who regrets that such a vicious political campaign was conducted against Arabi-Tamil. He suggests that such an anti-Arabi-Tamil movement resulted in the Muslim community ' . . . drifting along the revivalist Tamil movement and with it tragically away from religion'.[54] Actually Shu'ayb's position is untenable because what the Muslims did was to use the medium of the Tamil to express their Islamic religious beliefs. Further, the preference for Tamil over Arabi-Tamil was an expression of their Tamilness. The reality was therefore that Muslims moved simultaneously closer towards Islam and Tamil. Daud Shah's promotion of Tamil and the opposition to Arabi-Tamil was to earn Tamil Muslims a place in what he saw as the emerging modern Dravidian-Tamil community.

Shah's programme of reforming Muslim society went beyond Arabi-Tamil, though language was its mainstay. He had a six-point agenda which comprised the following: the end of purohit rule; the use of Tamil, the mother-tongue (of Muslims) as the medium for understanding their religion, Islam; the conduct of *Qutba* or sermons in Friday prayers in Tamil; the education of all Muslims in Tamil; the teaching of English and Tamil to all Muslim women to help them secure their rights; the avoidance of brahmanical positions on 'national' matters.[55]

Daud Shah campaigned in favour of Islamic preaching that was intelligible to the Muslim masses. He argued, 'If the *Qutba* is preached in the Arabic language, which most of us do not understand, what else does one expect but ignorance on the part of the Muslims of Tamil Nadu?'[56] To Shah, Arabic was an esoteric language often unintelligible to the Muslim laity. He opposed the *Qutba* being in Arabic because he saw in it the equivalence of Sanskrit and brahmanism among Muslims. He used the term *mullatanmai*, meaning brahmanism, to convey his disappointment and anger at the *ulama.* [57] He had faced severe criticism all his life from them and other Muslim elites for his efforts to earn a place for his co-religionists in the emerging modern Tamil community. Muslims opposed to Shah's politics dismissed him as a heretic, calling him a proponent of the Ahmadiyya sect. This was the position taken mainly by the *ulama* and other elite among Sunni Muslims. The *ulama* so feared Shah's growing influence and the popularity of his journal *Darul Islam*, that they passed a *fatwa* which forbade Muslims to read the journal.[58] In fact, his opponents went to the extent of saying, '. . . the four journals *Saiful Islam*, *Al-Kalam*, *Mussalman* (from Tenkasi), *Tajul Islam* (from Erode) are working for Islamic social reform and . . . [*Darul Islam*] is working towards the growth of the Tamil language and for the Qadiani movement'.[59]

The journals *Al-Kalam*, *Tajul Islam*, and *Hifazathul Islam* opposed *Darul Islam* (Sami 1994: 236, 395). *Hifazathul Islam* literally meant the 'protection of Islam'. Many *ulama* opposed Shah's efforts to democratize Muslim society so as to defend their own powers. Shah's endeavours to propagate Islam in Tamil to enable it to reach the masses would have made the *ulama* more vulnerable in the presence of a more awakened, literate and knowledgeable Muslim society. Besides Daud Shah, Ghulam, a resident of Attur (Salem district) was also opposed to Arabi-Tamil. Ghulam was said to be a relation of Shah and conducted his own publishing and printing house.[60]

There were other factors peculiar to the linguistic tradition of Arabi-Tamil that contributed to its decline besides the opposition of Daud Shah. In the first place, it was not considered a popular language.[61] Second, it did not have a grammar of its own to be considered a separate language.[62] Finally, Muslims preferred to print their religious books in Tamil as Arabi-Tamil involved a more complicated and tedious process. This was the technological factor that contributed to the decline of Arabi-Tamil.[63]

In the final analysis, the ensured popularity of Tamil as the medium of the religious, social, and political life of Tamil Muslims over Arabi-Tamil was among the clearest testimonials to, and an affirmation of, Tamil identity.

DEVELOPMENT OF TAMIL MUSLIM LITERATURE AND PRESS

Muslim preference for the Tamil language for religious instruction and expression was accompanied by a proliferation of Muslim literature in Tamil and an increase in the number of Tamil journals. The first complete translation of the Koran into Tamil was concluded in 1943 and published in 1949, by Maulana Hameed. This was a major landmark in the development of a modern Tamil identity among Muslims.[64] They configured their Muslimness and to this day continue to do so through Tamil in their oft-used slogan, *Islam engal vazhi, inba-Tamil engal mozhi* (Islam is our path, sweet Tamil is our language).[65]

A duality of religion and language was built into Muslim identity. The institutions and rituals of Islam in Tamil Nadu were coloured and conditioned by local Tamil cultural practices.[66] Such influences clearly indicated the long tradition that identified Muslims of the region as Tamils who shared a culture, belief-system, and language.

The early part of the twentieth century saw the development of modern Tamil prose among Muslims. Religious subjects were among the most popular themes covered by this prolific literature, broadly be classified as biographies (of important Islamic personalities such as Muslim mystics, leaders and philanthropists, the most frequent and popular biography being that of the Prophet. Islamic history, social reform, theology, commentaries on the Koran and philosophical speculations, pamphlets and tracts on the political movements of the time (such as Indian nationalism, Khilafat, the Muslim League and the Dravidian movement). Most significantly, Tamil Muslim mystics in the fashion of Nyanmars, Alwars, and Siddhars encouraged devotionalism through their contribution to the development of Tamil literature.[67]

The First World War and the Khilafat movement gave an impetus to the rapid and extensive development of a Muslim press with different doctrinaire, ideological, and political positions as well as varied locations, patrons, and audiences. While *Al-Islam*, *Al-Kalam*, *Tajul Islam* and *Hifazathul Islam* were pre-occupied with confronting *Darul Islam*, others such as *Sudandara Nadu*, *Vande Mataram*, and *Pakistan* were engaged with the crucial issues of colonialism, nationalism, and partition.[68] Other popular journals included the *Samarasam* for the propagation of Islam and *Balyan* for Muslim children.[69]

The emergence and development of such a press among the Muslims was significant in building a modern Tamil identity and generating a capacity to imagine the wider Tamil, Indian, and Islamic communities of which they formed part. In places as far away as Malaysia, Singapore, Myanmar, and Vietnam, Tamil Muslims articulated the Tamil and Muslim character of their cultural inheritance through the promotion of journalism.[70] The most popular among Tamil Muslim newspapers and periodicals were *Saiphul Is'lam* (1890s/Rangoon), *Malaya Nanban* (1943/Malaysia) and *Tamil Murasu* (Malaysia). The significant feature of the South-East Asian press was that general Tamil newspapers were also edited and published by Muslims.[71] The manner in which Muslims related to the Tamil language presents us with an occasion to consider their response to all-India Congress and Muslim League politics.

MUSLIMS AND THE ANTI-HINDI AGITATIONS

The Congress adopted the policy of obtaining a single language for the entire sub-continent and sought, from 1918 onwards, to introduce Hindi in south India, even though it employed Tamil for propaganda and mobilization. The effort to popularize Hindi among south Indians (the 'Hindi movement' as it was called in Congress circles) was inaugurated by M.K. Gandhi. In June 1918, the Dakshin Bharat Hindi Prachar Sabha was founded in Madras to spread the knowledge of Hindi in the four linguistic regions of south India.[72] Through the late 1920s and 1930s, the Congress pursued a self-assured policy of Hindi popularization, C. Rajagopalachari, S. Satyamurti, and K. Santhanam designating it the *lingua franca* of the India-to-come, and advising Tamils to adopt it.[73] This propaganda was funded by north Indian sources and attempts were made to raise money in the south as well.[74]

The work of the Hindi Prachar Sabha had been effective for more than a decade. In 1931 Kaka Saheb of the Gujarat Vidyapith, Ahmedabad, declared that the Hindi Prachar movement had done 'splendid work' and that he was 'highly impressed with the enthusiasm and response for Hindi' among south Indians.[75] Further, within south India, certain areas were more enthusiastic than others, 'Andhra seems to have taken a great fancy for the Hindi tongue. Everyone there seems to make a heroic attempt to learn Hindi'.[76] The all-India nationalist movement propagated Hindi as the language that would bind all Indians. Incidentally this militates against Sumathi Ramaswamy's contention that Indianism placed its hopes in Tamil as the bond that would tie together all Tamil speakers, Hindu, Muslim, and Christian.[77] But Tamils opposed it strongly. Resistance to Congress initiatives for the spread of Hindi from the late 1930s to the 1960s formed the cornerstone of Dravidian-Tamil nationalism. The Dravidian movement for its part voiced its fear that 'Aryan culture' would be imposed in the south to the neglect of Tamil.

For Ramasamy, one of the means by which Tamils could recover their self-respect was opposition to Hindi as the Sanskritic imposition of Brahmins. He was consistently opposed to Hindi propaganda in the south even as early as 1924-5.[78] This resentment against Hindi was transformed into a mass agitation when the Congress government in July 1937 made Hindi a compulsory subject for the first three classes in 125 identified secondary schools.[79]

Ramasamy consciously incorporated Muslims within the Dravidian movement against Hindi by affirming that Muslims were Tamil. Muslims in turn responded through a significant participation in the anti-Hindi agitations. This clearly reflected their aspiration to be part of a Dravidian/Tamil 'community'. Tamil Muslim leaders were central figures in the anti-Hindi agitations and the meetings of the Tamil Nadu Muslim League between 1937 and 1940 provided a forum for protesting against Hindi. In fact, P. Khalifullah, a Muslim Leaguer and member of the Legislative Assembly, enjoys the distinction of being the first Tamil to raise his voice against the imposition of Hindi.[80]

Susbsequently when P. Khalifullah became a minister in the Interim Congress Ministry in Madras, he endorsed Urdu in the Hindi-Urdu controversy in north India. In 1937 he maintained that Urdu was a finely developed, majestic, and beautiful language. He argued that the Congress, in promoting Hindi, was trying to give life to a dying language and Urdu should instead be the *lingua franca* in order to give real significance to Hindu-Muslim unity.[81]

Other Tamil Muslims echoed Khalifullah's perspectives. K.M. Hanif of Coimbatore stated, 'If Hindi becomes compulsory, Muslim culture and civilisation would surely be affected . . . for if Hindi becomes compulsory, then Muslim students would find it difficult to learn Arabic, Persian, and Urdu'.[82] Sultan Baghdadi, the editor of the Tamil Muslim journal *Samarasam*, along with C.N. Annadurai and Navalar Somasundara Bharathiar, participated in a meeting in Madras on 5 September 1937, to plan the first anti-Hindi agitation.[83] Sharfudeen from Vellore and Mohideen from Tiruppur were the other Muslim personalities who accompanied Khalifullah.[84]

Muslim participation in the anti-Hindi agitations took different forms. S.K. Mohammed Haneef composed a song asking Muslims to protect Tamil by taking part in the anti-Hindi agitation, reminding his people that they belonged to a heroic community.[85] Khaja Mian Rowther provided support to Ramasamy in August 1939 at Trichy.[86] More than 2,000 Muslims turned up at a public meeting in Vaniyambadi to protest against Hindi.[87] Moulvi S. Mohideen Baqawi, a Muslim Leaguer joined in the black flag protest at Poraiyar in connection with the anti-Hindi agitation.[88] At one anti-Hindi meeting on the Madras Triplicane Beach Muslims turned to face west to offer *namaz*, and then turned east to listen to the speeches of the meeting. Vellore Sharfudeen of the North Arcot Muslim League had spoken at this meeting in praise of Ramasamy and the agitation.[89]

The dynamic and reciprocal nature of the interaction between Islam and the Self-Respect movement was exemplified by the manner in which Ramasamy were invited to speak at the Prophet's Birthday celebrations and Daud Shah and Khalifullah were invited to speak at the Self-Respect conferences. P. Khalifullah proved to be a unique presence at these conferences: he presided over the second north Arcot district Self-Respect conference at Ambur in November 1937 and hoisted the Tamil flag at the Coimbatore district Muslim League conference, and also spoke at the commencement of the anti-Hindi procession which left Trichy for Madras in August 1938. Khalifullah presided over a mammoth meeting of 50,000 Tamils in June 1938 on Madras Beach, and later in October 1938 condemned the arrest of the editor of the Dravidian paper *Viduthalai*.[90]

The Tamil Nadu Muslim League's opposition to Hindi was both an opportunity for it to follow the central League leadership's policy on the Hindi-Urdu issue as well as to maintain a local alliance with the Self-Respect movement. Significantly, while Jinnah used the term 'Hindu' elsewhere, in the context of Madras, he likened Congress attempts to introduce Hindi for Muslim children in schools to thrusting a compulsory 'Aryan religion' on them.[91] The Self-Respect movement and the Muslim League had valuable allies in each other on the Hindi issue. The Congress argued that the propagation of Hindi/Hindustani would promote Hindu-Muslim unity.[92] Through such an argument, the Congress sought to wean Muslims away from participation in the anti-Hindi agitations. It presented 'Hindi' to Tamil Muslims as 'Hindustani', and suggested that since Hindustani was, in its perception, a language of the 'Indian Muslims', Tamil Muslims could have no objection to it. In this manner, Congress policy treated Tamil Muslims primarily as an all-India religious community.

Tamil Muslims were not persuaded by Congress propaganda and continued their agitation. M.A. Rahman, a Muslim Leaguer from Coimbatore, was unambiguous in his criticism of Rajagopalachari's claim that Muslims were in favour of Hindi. Rahman was critical of Muslims who endorsed the positions of Rajagopalachari in favour of Hindi.[93]

Congress assumptions regarding Indian religious communities was most visibly demonstrated in the nature of its propaganda material for the Muslim Mass Contact Campaign of 1939. It did not arrange its propaganda material in Tamil for mass contact in south India. M.K. Kader, Secretary of the Kayalpattinam Town Congress Committee in Tirunelveli, was told by the All-India Congress Committee office in Allahabad that they did not possess this literature in English, but they did have some pamphlets in Urdu.[94] It appeared that the Congress took Muslim mass contact rather more seriously in the north than other parts of India. M.K. Syed Ahmed, also from Kayalpattinam, wrote to the AICC compalining that the Tamil Nadu Congress Committee (henceforth TNCC) was indifferent to the Muslim mass contact campaign.[95] The latter responded by informing the Central leadership that it was enrolling Muslims briskly.[96]

Another factor played a not insignificant role. If Tamil Muslims rejected the Congress contention that the adoption of Hindi would promote Hindu-Muslim unity, Dakhni Muslims, whose mother tongue was Urdu, accepted it more readily. The Tamil Muslim rejection of Hindi/Hindustani was not just a rejoinder to Congress policy but simultaneously challenged the power of Dakhni Muslims who were part of the Congress party in Tamil Nadu.[97]

When the subject of Hindi being introduced in the Madras Presidency was debated in the Urdu Press, Nehru as AICC President enquired from Rajagopalachari, the Chief Minister of Madras, about the facilities available for those preferred to learn Hindustani in the Urdu rather than the Hindi script.[98] In response Rajagopalachari hurried through a public statement, to make the position of his government and that of the Provincial Congress clear on the choice of script:

> We have no such intention of forcing either the Devanagari or the Urdu script, but have definitely decided on leaving it as a matter for option. It will be open to Mussalman children or others who prefer the Urdu script, to use and to be taught through it and it would be equally open to those who prefer the Devanagari character to use it for learning the language. . . . *No one need imagine that we shall rob the people of the choice of their script with reference into the national language*[99](emphasis mine)

Rajagopalachari issued orders to the Madras Education Department to prepare and publish Hindustani books in both Devanagari and Urdu scripts. To approve these manuscripts, he also sought the help of a respected Muslim academic, Mohammed Abdul Haq, of the

Government Muslim College, Madras.[100] The Education Department voiced Rajagopalachari's concern regarding the recruitment of Hindustani teachers capable of handling the subject in the Urdu script.[101] The reality was that many Hindustani teachers did not know the Urdu script. This seemed to justify the fears of Tamil and Dakhni Muslims that learning Hindustani would mean doing so in Devanagari. This was proved by a departmental survey which showed that Muslim students learning Hindustani in the Urdu script were only 325 in number, or one-third of all Muslim students enrolled in the compulsory introduction scheme in the Madras Presidency.[102]

This offer of a 'choice' on the question of the script appeared to prove attractive to Dakhni Muslims. However, Tamil Muslims found such a 'choice' over script meaningless when Hindi was made compulsory. The very idea of Hindi was abhorrent, it was perceived as a means of brahmanization. Tamil Muslims rejected the communal harmony argument for promoting Hindi. Khalifullah, Jamal Mohammed, and C. Abdul Hakeem gave expression to this position. Consequently, the attempt of the Congress to make Tamil Muslims adhere to its language policy hardly made any headway.

CONCLUSION

The communal harmony argument or the nationalist ideas regarding Hindu-Muslim unity was not relevant to Tamil Muslims, because through Ramasamy's leadership, community-formation in Tamil Nadu did not proceed along the lines of 'Hindu' or 'Muslim' but was subsumed under Dravidian and lower-caste solidarities.

The Self-Respect movement accepted a multiplicity of identities as part of its Dravidian community-formation process, and Muslims were beneficiaries of such a process. The nature of the interaction between Muslims and the Self-Respect movement was dynamic and reciprocal. If the movement provided an occasion for Ramasamy to endorse Islam in Tamil society, the anti-Hindi agitations gave Muslims an opportunity to assert their Tamilness. The relationship between the Self-Respect movement and the Muslims in Tamil Nadu showed the latter's aspirations to be Dravidian and Tamil.

Muslim identification with the Tamil language and Dravidian politics continued well into the 1960s with an endorsement of, and participation in, the DMK movement. Over the years the rump version of the Muslim League needed the support of either of the Dravidian parties, the DMK and the AIADMK, to win national and state elections. However, Muslim involvement with Dravidian politics underwent a transformation in due course. The demolition of the Babri Masjid at Ayodhya in 1992 and the violence against Muslims in Gujarat in 2002 saw the spread of a pan-Indian Muslim consciousness. The language and politics of Hindu-Muslim relations that prevailed in the north of the country permeated Tamil Nadu. The Self-Respect movement and its legacy has a 'profound edge' (Hooks 1990: 145-53) to it which historically afforded the space for Muslims to be firmly embedded in a regional society. In the post-Gujarat and post-9/11 world these come across as rare political spaces that belonged to a bygone era.

NOTES

1. See Hardgrave 1965; Irschick 1969; Barnett: 1976; Ram 1979; J. Pandian 1987; Ryerson 1988; S. Ramasamy 1997; Washbrook 1989.
2. Pandian 1993: 2287.
3. Ibid.
4. Washbrook 1976: 288-304; Baker 1976: 22-39; Pandian 1995: 385-91.
5. Irshick 1969: 36-54; Venkatachalapathy 1995: 761-8.
6. Diehl 1977; Visswanathan 1983.
7. Pandian 1993: 2282-87.
8. *S.F.* 839 dated 28 September 1933; *S.F.* 896 dated 16 October 1934, TNSA.
9. Pandian 1994: 98-9.
10. *Kudiarasu*, 9 August 1931, 28 June 1943.
11. Ibid., 4 December 1927.
12. As cited in Veeramani 1994: 46-7.
13. Ibid.: 30-1; Anandhi 1991: 25-7.
14. *Kudiarasu*, 25 August 1929, 9 August 1931.
15. Ibid., 9 August 1931.
16. Ibid., 9 August 1931, 2 February 1936.
17. Ibid., 7 September 1930, 14 June 1931, 1 November 1931, 25 February 1934.
18. Ibid., 28 June 1931, 20 November 1931.
19. See Baqawi 1930.
20. G.O. 546 (Judicial Magisterial), 30 December 1924, TNSA.
21. *Kudiarasu*, 14 January 1934, 30 September 1934.
22. Baqawi 1930:15.
23. Ibid.: 21.
24. Mankaiyarkkaraci 1980: 90-100.

25. *Viduthalai*, 28 June 1943.
26. For the positions of upper-castes opposed to the temple-entry campaign, see letter from N.R.N. Ayyar, Tuticorin to Jawaharlal Nehru, 23 October 1931, AICC papers file G-86 of 1931 NMML and the correspondence between Jawaharlal Nehru, C. Rajagopalachari, and T.S. Ramasamy Iyer, Secretary, Madras Provincial Varnashrama Swarajya Sangha 9, 19 and 26 June 1937, AICC papers file P-19 of 1937 NMML.
27. *Viduthalai*, 11 April 1947.
28. Ibid., 28 July 1947.
29. *Kudiarasu*, 1 September 1929.
30. Ibid., 27 September 1929.
31. Ibid., 26 April 1931.
32. Ibrahim 1939:11.
33. Rifayee 1988: 240.
34. Hifazathul Islam, May 1934, as cited in More 1993: 93.
35. *Kudiarasu*, 4 August 1945; *FR* July(1), August(1), September(1), 1945, TNSA.
36. See *Kudiarasu*, 9 August 1925, 27 September 1929, 25 January 1931, 8 March 1936.
37. *Hindu*, 19 March 1930.
38. Anandhi 1991: 28-30.
39. *Kudiarasu*, 16 February 1936.
40. Ibrahim 1939: 19-25.
41. *Kudiarasu*, 15 December 1931.
42. Ibid., 22 March 1947.
43. Barnett 1974a.
44. Pandian 1996: 3323.
45. Ibid., 3324-5.
46. S. Ramaswamy 1997: 252.
47. *Viduthalai*, 20 October 1938.
48. *Kudiarasu*, 7 February 1937.
49. Azeez 1966: 6-10.
50. M.M. Uwise cited in Sami 1994: 53-5.
51. Shu'ayb 1993: 89; Raheem(I) 1981: 415.
52. Raheem(I) 1981: 415; Sami 1994: 34-6.
53. Raheem(I) 1981: 415.
54. Shu'ayb 1993: 117.
55. *Darul Islam*, December 1925; Sami 1994: 229.
56. Sami 1994: 235.
57. *Darul Islam*, February 1927; March 1927.
58. Sami 1994: 236.
59. *Tajul Islam*, 1925 August as cited in Sami 1994: 235.
60. Shu'ayb 1993: 118.
61. Nafeesa Kaleem as cited in Shu'ayb 1993: 90.

62. Maulana P.M. Mohammed Baqawi as cited in Sami 1994: 53.
63. Raheem(I) 1981: 415; Shu'ayb 1993: 120-2; Sami 1994: 60.
64. Raheem(I) 1981: 148; Sami 1994: 64.
65. Karim 1982: 251; Also, see A.K.A. Abdus Samad's foreword to Sheriff 1981: iii.
66. Raheem 1980: vii; S. Bayly 1989: 104-50; Sulaiman and Ismail 1977: 11-27.
67. See, for instance, Basheer 1983: 78-85.
68. See Jamil 1948: 417-19.
69. Sami 1994: 181, 284-90.
70. Fakhri 2002.
71. Ibid.
72. C. Rajagopalachari papers, file 57, NMML.
73. Ibid.
74. C. Rajagopalachari to Seth Jamnalal Bajaj, 16 March 1930, C. Rajagopalachari papers, file 56, NMML.
75. Kaka Saheb to C. Rajagopalachari, 7 October 1931, C. Rajagopalachari papers, file 56, NMML; M. Satyanarayana to C. Rajagopalachari, 20 September 1931, C. Rajagopalachari papers, file 56, NMML.
76. Kaka Saheb to C. Rajagopalachari, 7 October 1931, C. Rajagopalachari papers, file 56, NMML.
77. Ramaswamy 1997: 53.
78. *Kudiarasu*, 10 May 1931 as reproduced in Anaimuthu(III) 1974: 1764 and *Viduthalai*, 8 August 1948 as reproduced in Anaimuthu(III) 1974: 1766.
79. AICC paper, PL-3(i) of 1937, NMML; Arooran 1980: 195-6.
80. *Kudiarasu*, 26 June 1938.
81. C. Rajagopalachari to P.D. Tandon, 4 June 1937, C. Rajagopalachari papers (microfilm roll I), file 1 of May-August 1937, NMML; Arooran 1980: 199-200.
82. *Viduthalai*, 26 October 1938.
83. Sami 1994: 181-4.
84. *Viduthalai*, 10 and 24 September 1938.
85. *Kudiarasu*, 3 July 1938.
86. Ilanchezhian 1986: 190.
87. *Viduthalai*, 10 September 1938.
88. Ibid., 4 November 1938.
89. Ilanchezhian 1986: 168-9.
90. *Viduthalai*, 28 October 1938; also see Ilanchezian 1986.
91. *Kudiarasu*, 26 June 1938; Ilanchezhian 1986:70.
92. Arooran 1980: 199.
93. *Viduthalai*, 3 September 1938, 1 October 1938, 3 December 1938.
94. Secretary, AICC office, Allahabad to M.K. Kader, 9 August 1939, AICC papers, file G19(Kwi) of 1939, NMML.
95. See letter from J.B. Kriplani to M.K. Syed Ahmed, 11 September 1937, AICC papers, file P19(ii) of 1937, NMML.

96. See telegram from Shafi Mohammed to Nehru, 28 September 1937, AICC papers, file P19(ii) of 1937, NMML.
97. *Viduthalai*, 3 September 1938, 1 October 1938, 21 October 1938, 3 December 1938.
98. Jawaharlal Nehru to C. Rajagopalachari, 2 September 1937, C. Rajagopalachari papers (microform roll 2), file 4 of 1937-45, NMML.
99. C. Rajagopalachari to Jawaharlal Nehru, 7 September 1937, AICC papers, file PL3(ii) of 1937, NMML.
100. G.O. 1402 (Education and Public Health), 21 June 1939, TNSA.
101. Ibid., 2084 (Education and Public Health), 19 September 1939, TNSA.
102. Ibid., 1364 (Education), 16 June 1939, TNSA.

REFERENCES

Arooran, Nambi K., 1980, *Tamil Renaissance and Dravidian Nationalism, 1905-1944* (Madurai: Koodal Publishers).

Azeez, A.M.A., 1966, *Arabu-Tamil Engal Anbu Tamil* (Colombo: [pub. n/a]).

Baker, Christopher John, 1976, *The Politics of South India, 1920-1937*, Cambridge: Cambridge University Press.

Baqawi, Maulana A.K. Abdul Hameed, 1930, *Iyarkkai Matham*, Trichy: Islamic Prachar Sabha.

Barnett, Marguerite Ross, 1974a, 'Creating Political Identity - The Emergent South Indian Tamils', *Ethnicity*, vol. 1, 237-65.

______, 1974b, 'Contemporary Peasant and Post-peasant Alternatives in South India: The Ideas of a Militant Untouchable', *Annals of the New York Academy of Sciences*, vol. 220, 385-410.

______, 1976, *The Politics of Cultural Nationalism in South India*, Princeton: Princeton University Press.

Basheer, Takkalai M.S., 1983, 'Islamiya Sufikalin Tamil Thondu', in Manavai Mustafa (comp.) *Tamizhil Islamia Meigana Ilakkiankal*, Madras: Meera Publications.

Bayly, Susan, 1989, *Saints, Goddesses and Kings: Muslims and Christians of South Indian Society 1700-1900*, Cambridge: Cambridge University Press.

Chandavarkar, Rajnarayan, 1997, 'The Making of the Working Class: E.P. Thompson and Indian History', *History Workshop Journal*, Issue 43, 177-96.

Devadasan, E.D., 1982, *A Study on Conversion and its Aftermath*, Madras: Christian Literature Society.

Diehl, Anita, 1977, *Periyar E. V. Ramasami: A Study of the Influence of a Personality in Contemporary South India*, Lund: University of Lund.

Divan, S., 1994, *Viduthalai Poril Tamizhaka Muslimkal*, Palayamkottai; Suhaina Pathipakkam.

Fakhri, S.M.A.K., 1998, Caste, Ethnicity and Nation in the Politics of the Muslims of Tamil Nadu, *1930-1967*, Ph.D. thesis, University of Cambridge.

———, 2002, *Print Culture amongst Tamils and Tamil Muslims in Southeast Asia, c. 1860-1960*. Working Paper No. 167 at the Madras Institute of Development Studies, Chennai.

Hooks, Bell, 1990, *Yearning: Race, Gender and Cultural Politics*, Boston, MA: South End Press.

Ibrahim, T.A. Muhammad, 1939, *Naveena Muslim* Madras: Naveen Muslim Book Depot.

Ilanchezian, M., 1986, *Tamizhan Thodutha Por: Mudal Hindi Poratta Varalaru*, 2nd edn., Madras: Periyar Self-Respect Propaganda Association.

Irshick, Eugene F., 1969, *Politics and Social Conflict in South India: The Non-Brahman Movement and Tamil Separatism, 1916-1929*, Berkeley: University of California Press.

Jamil, S.M. comp., 1948, *The Muslim Year Book of India and Who's Who with Complete Information on Pakistan 1948-49*, Bombay: Bombay Newspaper Company.

Kamal, S.M., 1990, *Muslimkalum Tamizhakamum*, Madras: Islamic Studies and Cultural Centre.

Karim, Abdul M., 1982, *Islamum Tamizhum*, Tirunelveli: Saiva Siddhanta Publishing Society.

Mankaiyarkkaci, 1980, *Varalaru Kanta Vaikkam Veerar*, Madras: Maruthamalaiyan Pathipakkam.

Mohideen, Fazulu S., 1977, *Modern Tamil Prose of the Muslims*, Nagercoil: [pub. n/a].

Nagata, Judith, 1993, 'Religion and Ethnicity among the Indian Muslims of Malaysia', in K.S. Sandhu and A. Mani (ed.), *Indian Communities in Southeast Asia*, Singapore: Institute of Southeast Asian Studies, 513-40.

Pandian, M.S.S., 1993, 'Denationalising the Past: "Nation", in E.V. Ramasamy's Political Discourse', *Economic and Political Weekly*, vol. 28, n. 42, 2282-7.

———, 1995, 'Beyond Colonial Crumbs: Cambridge School, Identity Politics and Dravidian Movement(s)', *Economic and Political Weekly*, vol. 30, nos. 7-8, 385-91.

———, 1996, 'Towards National: Popular Notes on Self-Respectors' Tamil' *Economic and Political Weekly*, vol. 31, no. 51, 3323-29.

Ram, N., 1979, 'Dravidian Movement in Its Pre-Independence Phases', *Economic and Political Weekly*, vol. 14, nos. 7-8, 377-402.

Rifayee, A.K., 1988, *Tamizhakathil Islamiar Varalaru* (Tenkasi: author).

Raheem, M. Abdur, 1981, *Islamia Kalai Kalanjiam*, 3 vols., Madras: Universal Publishers.

Ramaswamy, Sumathi, 1997, *Passions of the Tongue: Language Devotion in Tamil Nadu 1891-1970*, Berkeley: University of California Press.

Sami, A.M., 1994, *Tamizhil Islamiya Ithazkal*, Madras: Navmani Pathipakkam.

Sheriff, Muhammad, N., 1976, *Tamizhaka Muhammadiyar Varalaru*, Manamadurai: Munnetram.

Shu'ayb, Takya, 1993, *Arabic, Arwi and Persian in Sarandib and Tamil Nadu: A Study of the Contributions of Sri Lanka and Tamil Nadu to Arabic, Arwi, Persian and Urdu Languages Literature and Education*, Madras: Imamul Arus Trust.

Sheriff, Kavika Mu., 1981, *Vallal Sithakathi Varalaru*, Madras: Seethakathi Book Publications.

Sulaiman, S.M. and M.M. Ismail, 1977, *Islam, Indian Religions and Tamil Culture*, Madras: University of Madras.

Lakshmi, C.S., 1997, 'Bodies Called Women: Some Thoughts on Gender, Ethnicity and Nation', *Economic and Political Weekly*, vol. 32, no. 46, 2953-62.

Venkatachalapathy, A.R., 1995, 'Dravidian Movement and Saivites: 1927-1944', *Economic and Political Weekly*, vol. 30, no. 14, 761-8.

Veeramani, K. comp., 1994, *Religion and Society: Selections from Periyar's Speeches and Writings*, Madras: Emerald Publishers.

Visswanathan, E. Sa., 1983, *The Political Career of E V Ramasami Naickar*, Madras: Ravi and Vasantha Publishers.

Washbrook, David Anthony, 1976, *The Emergence of Provincial Politics: the Madras Presidency, 1870-1920*, Cambridge: Cambridge University Press.

———, 1989, 'Caste, Class and Dominance in Modern Tamil Nadu: Non-Brahminism, Dravidianism and Tamil Nationalism', in Francine R. Frankel and M.S.A. Rao (eds.), *Dominance and State Power in Modern India: Decline of a Social Order*, I, Delhi: Oxford University Press, 204-64.

5

The Hindutva Gameplan to Checkmate Muslims

AMIR ALI

The title of this paper has been taken from the game of chess and refers to the systematic efforts of Hindutva forces to hem in and checkmate the minorities, especially Muslims. The idea of describing Muslims as checkmated occurred to me when I was having a conversation with an extremely worried Muslim gentleman who felt that the Muslims had been systematically and brutally targeted in the Gujarat pogroms and that afterwards they had been unfairly accused of being potential terrorists. The perceptive gentleman described the condition as typically 'Catch-22'. The man went on to describe how in the aftermath of the Godhra incident and the Gujarat carnage he suffered from what he termed a 'double fear'. What he meant was that in an era of increasing terrorist violence he was afraid of their random character, the fact that he among many others could be killed if he was unfortunate enough to be near the site of such an act. He explained to me that while global discourse had thoroughly equated Islam and Muslims with terrorism, the typical terrorist attack itself did not target particular victims and could as much affect Muslims as non-Muslims. What was worse was the second aspect of the double fear that the man was referring to. This arose from the fact that in the aftermath of a terrorist act, there were the immediate accusatory finger pointed at Muslims, and there was a high degree of likelihood that if one had a Muslim name, then one could be targeted and detained under the draconian anti-terror laws that had been put in place by the governments of various countries after 11 September 2001.

Thus, it was the randomness of the terrorist attack and the often unfair targeting of the Muslims as a whole after the attack that constituted the double fear of this man. He went on to explain how the Muslims had been put in a state of siege by the brutal genocide unleashed on them by Narendra Modi's government and how this injury was followed by the insulting accusation that terrorists are Muslims. He referred despairingly to the ways in which Muslims were expected to speak up and condemn every terrorist attack that took place. Referring to the surprisingly widespread sentiment among large sections that if the Muslims had sufficiently condemned the Godhra incident, the subsequent riots in Gujarat might have been a little less harsh, he threw up his arms in resignation, saying that you were damned if you did condemn and damned if you didn't.

The hostility towards the Muslim and the idea of checkmating has been used in this essay to argue that this hostility specifically arises from the different discourses of nationalism. Further, the particularly bad situation that Indian Muslims have recently faced arises from the fact that in the last two decades or so the dominant discourse on nationalism has been a vicious right wing nationalism in the form of Hindutva. It will further be argued that the way out of the predicament is not to appeal to nationalisms other than Hindu (Nehruvian, Ambedkarite, or Gandhian) which Hindutva has effectively sidelined and consigned to the margins. An important point that Sumit Sarkar makes is that nationalism during the freedom movement was multi-stranded and that this multiplicity has often been overlooked, with the result that Hindutva forces have been able to portray themselves as the sole nationalists, all others inevitably being anti-national. While there were sharp differences between the alternative nationalisms of Nehru, Gandhi, the Left, and Ambedkar, there remained an underlying commonality, which was 'a basic concern with the fate of the most numerous and most poor'. Sarkar goes on to note that an important exception was constituted by communal forces, notably the Hindutva formation, in whose writings and activities the questions of mass poverty and exploitation 'hardly ever figured' (Sarkar 2002: 212).

What is being suggested in this paper is that rather than attempting to bring the other nationalisms into the centre to create a discursive space that can contend with and outflank Hindu nationalism, it might be better to go beyond and transcend nationalism—to seek a post-national solution to the problem. The reason is a 'structural bias' inherent in the idea of nationalism—it is inherently weighted against a minority (see Misra 2004). A post-national solution that immediately springs to mind is the kind of appeal to a constitutional patriotism to which the German social theorist Jurgen Habermas has referred.

The reason, then, for a disillusionment, with nationalism lies in the problems of nationalism itself. A larger point that this paper is attempting to make is that while it was certainly a good idea in its anti-colonial and anti-imperialist phase, it may have outlived its political uses. This can be seen in the fact that extreme violence in the form of ethnic cleansing and genocide witnessed in the Balkans in the decade of the 1990s, is the product of the recrudescence of an extremely vicious form of nationalism. The larger point, then, to put a twist to Eric Hobsbawm's observation on the end of nationalism, is that while the owl of Minerva has flown at dusk and brought with it wisdom (Hobsbawm 1990), the dusk of nationalism was witness to enormous atrocities in the form of pogroms and massacres and ethnical cleansing. This paper is then hinting at an understanding of issues by going 'Beyond Nationalist Frames' to use the title of Sumit Sarkar's recent collection of essays (Sarkar 2002).

HINDU NATIONALISM AND THE MUSLIM 'OTHER'

Amalendu Misra has pertinently noted that 'part of the continuing resentment against both the Muslim rule and Islam has to do with the development of Indian nationalist thought' (Misra 2004: 12). It is nationalist thought itself that has constituted the Muslim as some kind of problematic 'other'. There are of course some streams of thought such as Savarkar's and Bankim Chandra Chattopadhyay's that have done this more vehemently than others and indeed are characterized wholly by hostility towards Muslims. However, there also seems to lie embedded deep within the idea of nationalism a proclivity that makes it easy to constitute a minority group like the Muslims as the 'other'. Thus, even the most inclusive kinds of nationalism like the Nehruvian variant are unable to fully integrate the Muslim within the nationalist fold. Misra thus argues that the 'Indian nationalist tradition had a structural bias. At its worst it was hostile to Muslim rule and Islam, and at its best ambivalent towards them' (ibid.: 23).

Misra has incisively taken the example of Nehru to show that someone as secular as him, someone as 'secure in his cosmopolitan identity' as him, could also be 'shackled by his own Brahmanic inheritance'. It is important to look more closely at this seemingly over-critical view of Nehru, especially after the BJP's years of domination at the centre of Indian politics have done much to destroy and harm the Nehruvian consensus around which India as a modern state was sought to be created anew, even after the trauma of Partition. Misra clarifies, 'This is not to suggest that Nehru was either wholly pro- or anti-Islam. My attempt is to highlight the tensions prevalent in Nehru's own line of thinking. As is common with many leaders, Nehru's programmes, policies and attitudes on a variety of issues were ambivalent. Because of this ambiguity, I would term Nehru a "soft secularist" . . .' (ibid.: 16).

As progressive, liberal, and secular a nationalism as Nehru's was unable to prevent the Muslim being made into a problematic 'other'. This is what prompts the arguments made here. During the freedom struggle, the enemy of an anti-colonial nationalism was the British; however, the Muslim could very easily lapse into the enemy position. Consider the ideas of Bankim in *Anand Math*, and its portrayal of the Muslim as the outsider.

The creation of the Muslim 'other' in nationalist thought was a long drawn out process. Following Misra's analysis in which he closely studies the views of Vivekananda, Gandhi, Nehru, and Savarkar, it can be argued that this process began with nationalism in its early formative stages. Vivekananda as one of the earlier thinkers on nationalism made his contribution to this creation of the other. It is in the writings and thought of Vivekananda that one finds an inquiry into why the nationalist sentiment has not found a stirring among Hindus. This is further reinforced in the writings of Savarkar in the early twentieth century where one finds a growing antipathy to the Muslims.

In the case of Vivekananda, Gandhi, and Nehru, Misra notes that their responses to the Muslim presence in India ranged 'from equality to assimilation'. In contrast to this range of responses to be found in the case of these three thinkers, which are characterized by their ambiguity and the need to assimilate Muslims, there is in the thought of Savarkar an unambiguous element of exclusion of the Muslims (ibid.: 149). Misra further argues that the nationalism of the Indian National Congress was territorial; that of the Muslim League was cultural, attempting to forge a distinct Islamic identity; and that the nationalism of the Hindu Right was a combination of the two (ibid.: 150). Misra's analysis of Savarkar and his thought reveals the manner in which until the late nineteenth and early twentieth centuries the British were considered outsiders and how the 'concept of "otherness" was invariably attributed to the British colonialists in this period' (ibid.: 150). Savarkar's importance lies in the way in which he created the Muslim as the 'other', which underlines the point about the replacement of enemies mentioned earlier.

Interestingly, while Savarkar's ideas may have been understood by the majority of the Hindus, they were simply overshadowed by the dominance of Gandhi. The strength and importance of Savarkar's thought lies then in the fact that even though his ideas may have been relatively neglected when they emerged, they have been picked up and revived by the current Hindu right (ibid.: 150). Would it be correct to link Savarkar to the currently virulent phase that Hindutva has manifested, for example, in the pogroms against Muslims in Gujarat? Misra has noted that many secularists, especially of a leftist persuasion, have equated Savarkar with extreme forms of racism on the line of Fascism and Nazism. Misra clearly argues (ibid.: 162) that Savarkar never mapped out plans to ethnically cleanse in the manner of the Nazi final solution in order to establish Hindu domination.

The dangers inherent within this strain of nationalist thought cannot be countered by Gandhian thought on nationalism, which was characterized by its greater catholicity and inclusiveness. Misra would argue that Gandhian nationalism would actually be complicit in suppressing the Muslim 'other' and subordinating it in a larger Hindu synthesis. Gandhi's excessive use of the religious idiom has been vehemently criticized for its effects of desecularizing the national movement and ultimately the domain of Indian politics (see Vanaik 1997). Misra himself is unsparing of Gandhi in his criticism, and feels that the Hindu-Muslim harmony espoused by him 'was primarily a Hindu concept' and that in his emphasis on 'inclusivism' the result would be the 'gradual elimination of "the other"' (Misra 2004: 65). Paradoxically Gandhi was also the leader responsible for perhaps the most concerted effort to bring Muslims into the national movement by means of the Khilafat, a movement that relied on a heavy dose of pan-Islamic religious symbolism, where again Misra argues that 'Gandhi himself is to be blamed for raising separatist aspirations among Indian Muslims' (ibid.: 65).

The situation of checkmate on the Muslims has also stalled the possibility of much needed and much talked about reform among them. The majority of Muslims score very badly on most social indicators. Further, in the preoccupation with majoritarian communalism throughout the decade of the 1990s, minority communalism, which arguably is a lesser breed and much less dangerous, has been largely neglected. Indeed, being checkmated has ironically worked to the advantage of those vested minority communal interests opposed to reform and social uplift.

Here one must also move back a little to analyse the moves immediately before the checkmate. These were the moves made by a section of Muslim orthodoxy in the 1980s, during the Shah Bano controversy, over the issue of Muslim personal law. The Rajiv Gandhi led Congress government pandered to these orthodox sentiments. Remarkably these very moves made by conservative and orthodox sections of the Muslims were to provide the opportunity for Hindutva forces to launch their aggressive campaign that would ultimately checkmate the Muslims.[1]

THE THREE PHASES OF HINDUTVA'S TRAJECTORY

The trajectory that Hindutva has taken can be divided into three distinct phases. Mapping this particular trajectory provides us with a clear understanding of the advance of Hindu nationalism from the 1980s. One can understand how the conceptual resources of Hindu nationalism that it drew from its thinkers like Savarkar were translated into political actuality. Before such a mapping is done it would be pertinent to point out that the point of departure for Hindu nationalism lies in the ideas of thinkers like Vivekananda. Further, the creation of the Muslim 'other', which is not so pronounced in Vivekananda's writings, finds greater expression in the writings of Savarkar. Hindutva or the movement for Hindu nationalism draws on these conceptual resources to culminate in a situation in which the 'other' is finally demarcated and earmarked for elimination. By the time this stage has been reached, Hindu nationalism has graduated to the stage of attempting a physical elimination, which could be seen in its most gruesome form in the genocide in Gujarat in 2002 (see van der Veer 1996).

Let me first reiterate how bad the situation has been for those at the receiving end of Hindu nationalism and its violence. While speaking in terms of liberal niceties like equal opportunities and minority rights, we have been forced to speak in terms, not of greater employment opportunities, or uplift in terms of better social indicators, but the basic and fundamental right to life and dignity, issues which one would have thought are resolved beyond contention in a liberal democracy. We have not been debating how the plight of Muslim women should be improved or the percentage of Muslims receiving employment in the state sector. Interestingly enough, the issue of Urdu and the means to make it a more self-sustaining language, which has in many ways been the pet subject whenever discussions on the improvement of the situation of Muslims cropped up, has not been raised over the last few years. This gives us in many ways a sense or an indication of where we stand today and the strength of the Hindutva forces that has resulted in things reaching such a sorry state.

The First Phase: 1986-1992

1986 is taken here as the starting point on account of the Congress government's decision to open the gates of the Babri Masjid, and with the mammoth majority that the Congress used to enjoy in those days, to pass the Muslims Women's Protection of Rights on Divorce Bill. (The scale of such a majority actually makes one shudder at the consequences of what would have happened if the BJP had ever gained such a following). The first period starts with this political lift-off and ends in 1992 with the demolition of the Babri Masjid. This is the first rabble-rousing phase of Hindutva, in which it does not have a significant presence in parliament, just a couple of BJP seats. It therefore relies on a frenzied, high decibel campaign on the streets for the Ram Temple at Ayodhya. This period was to bring electoral dividends for the BJP when it managed to garner first 88, and subsequently 119, seats in the 1989 and 1991 elections respectively. The rabble-rousing phase, then, paid handsomely in terms of giving strength to the BJP as a political force. The highlight of this period was L.K. Advani's Rath Yatra and the most spectacular achievement in terms of sheer visual impact was the demolition of the Babri Masjid.

The Second Phase: 1992-1998

The next period begins in December 1992 and ends in the year 1998 when the BJP, in order to project itself as a responsible political party with the maturity and responsibility of forming a government, begins to mellow a little. Increasingly the 'liberal' Vajpayee is foregrounded over the more strident, hardline and raucous tones of Advani. This period of maturing from wild adolescence into an uneasy, hesitating, and often tentative adulthood that attempts to assume and shoulder the responsibilities of affairs of state, does culminate in catapulting the BJP into power at the centre, but only just. It leaves it tantalizingly short of the majority that is needed to form a government on its own and this compels the BJP to enter into troublesome coalitions often described by its spokespersons, especially women like Sushma Swaraj in terms of the inevitable pulls and pressures of the great Indian institution of marriage and ultimate marital bliss.

The Third Phase: 1998-2002

The third period of greater adulthood and maturity begins with the year 1998 and takes us to 2002, the year of the Gujarat incidents, which, to state the obvious is something of a landmark in the evolution and development of Hindutva. In this last stage the Hindutva movement is actually able to use its privileged position of power in government to manipulate the ideological state apparatus seen for example in the form of redrawing history syllabi and rewriting school history. This is also the phase in which the Hindutva movement can be seen using the repressive state apparatus to suppress and bring the minorities in line as seen in the Gujarat incidents.

It is now important to understand what the post 2002 phase with the Gujarat incidents mean in the development of Hindutva. In many ways Gujarat 2002, coming ten years after the December 1992 incidents, represents a complete turn of the wheel. The Hindutva movement has reintroduced and unleashed its forceful and powerful hardline Hindutva project, about which it feels that it does not have to be too apologetic. Gujarat 2002, then, represents a new level of force and brutalization that has come to characterize the movement for Hindu nationalism. As a global phenomenon it represents the recrudescence of intense nationalistic feelings—if nationalist at all—expressed in frenzied, psychopathic, and indeed savage forms on the street. Its closest and most remarkable parallels can be found in the levels and intensity of hatred whipped up by Serb nationalism in the mid to late 1990s. It is then an especially virulent and malignant form of nationalism. Its butchery and the levels of human misery that it can cause are ascertainable not merely from the numbers killed in Gujarat, which from most accounts ranged anywhere between 2,000 and 5,000, but the nature of the violence that was perpetrated and carried out. This is especially true of the kind of sexual violence that was unleashed against women and horrendous stories in the media of rape and slitting of foetuses, which defy imagination and indeed logic.[2]

The responses of the Left and other secular liberal democratic sections of society were extremely impoverished. The poverty of such strategies can be seen in the fact that repeatedy evasive steps taken to check the Sangh's onslaught have had a boomerang effect working to the advantage of the Sangh. There are other instances like the manner in which secular forces reacted to the demolition of the Babri Masjid, calling it an attack on secularism. The point is that secular forces have tended to respond to the Hindutva threat in terms of binary opposites like secularism-communalism and nationalism-communalism. Such reactions have not worked. In the case of the secularism-communalism binary, the Sangh has successfully redefined secularism to cast itself as secular and its opponents as pseudo-secular. Similarly in the case of the nationalism-communalism binary, even sections of the Left have been trying to outwit and outdo the Sangh in their holier-than-thou/ more nationalist-than-thou efforts, thereby falling in the Sangh's trap of defining the nation in a narrowly territorial fashion.

The political agenda has increasingly been set by the Hindu Right in the past few years. The Congress sets a pathetic example whenever it plays the soft-Hindutva card. Until recently it had not learnt the lesson that the only way it could gain a distinct advantage over the BJP was not by placing itself on the Right through a soft Hindutva stance, but by moving back to the centre and by upholding a more robust variety of secularism. There has been a tendency especially among sections of the English media to celebrate the electoral reverses that the BJP periodically suffers in state assembly elections as evidence that Hindutva is not making headway. The decisive verdict against the NDA government in the Lok Sabha elections of 2004 has similarly been celebrated as a final blow to Hindutva. Yet the Sangh is too persistent to be disappointed by a few electoral reverses.

The electoral defeats that the BJP has periodically suffered, reverses which have become more regular of late, should be viewed with a certain degree of equanimity. The Congress, in spite of its present position of strength, must display a principled commitment to end communalism of all sorts. This would mean a principled commitment to secularism and not the kind of waffling it has displayed especially on Muslim minority issues in the 1980s. It must also completely and totally abandon its soft Hindutva card, which is both tactically disastrous, as it works to the advantage of the far-right BJP, and just wrong on principle. Broadly, this means that the Congress must continue to occupy the Centre-Left of the political spectrum. It must also display a greater commitment to issues of social justice, which, it needs to be remembered, was one of the issues that brought it to power at the centre. Thus the Congress must take a stronger position on economic neo-liberalism, which is something that it has not done since coming to power. An inability to counter the effects of economic neo-liberalism would only provide fertile ground for the resurgence of the BJP, which, it must be remembered, was partly due to its ability to rise to the demands and imperatives of big business and the capitalist sector.

HINDUTVA ON THE RETREAT?

One of the most astounding things to happen was the resounding defeat suffered by the ruling NDA in 2004. The defeat was all the more surprising because in the run up to the elections there was a general apprehension among many of us that we were in for another five-year spell of BJP rule. That was indeed frightening: it spelled was doom for the future of a secular, liberal, and open India. Around the time of January 2004 a book aptly titled *Will Secular India Survive?* was published. The book (ed. Mushirul Hasan) raised a particularly apt question. Its timing was again perfect, just a few months before the general elections. The interesting thing was that the very title of the book displayed minimal optimism, the seeds of which have again begun to sprout in the aftermath of the general elections. It reminded one at the time of a couplet by Faiz: *Thahri hui hai shab ki sayahahi wahin magar/ kuch kuch sahar ke rang parafshaan hue to hain* (The darkness of the night still prevails/ Even then, the faint glimmer of dawn is slowly spreading).

In the run up to the elections the majority of comments and analyses appearing in the media seemed to be indicating in the direction of another NDA victory. After the results most of them have changed tune. Many have appeared to be exultant in their celebration of the resilience and increasing maturity of the Indian electorate. The more skeptical and cautious have felt inclined to believe that too many may be reading too much into the significance of the verdict. There is a general feeling that the overall rejection of the NDA can be interpreted under two counts. The first is the rejection of the kind of anti-secularism that the BJP was vigorously pushing through. The second is a rejection of the anti-people neo-liberal economic reforms that the BJP-led NDA had been vigorously advocating with its blatantly urban, upper middle-class slant. This was what led the BJP to float its 'India shining' campaign blitzkrieg, which, as we all know, so famously misfired. On both these counts progressive Left liberal circles have been marveling at the remarkably progressive nature of the verdict delivered by the electorate.[3]

While the more exultant analyses may be brimming with too much optimism, there is at the same time a need to appreciate the significance of the NDA's defeat. There is in this verdict a confirmation of the strength and institutionalization of Indian democracy. At the same time the fabric of Indian social life, variously defined as a composite culture, a multicultural mosaic, and a syncretistic tapestry, is in need of urgent mending: it has frayed at the edges during the NDA's years in power. It is here that one needs to exercise some degree of caution. The Congress victory in this election should not necessarily be interpreted to mean that a secular and liberal India is secure. No open society can ever be safe and there is always a need to be on the vigil and lookout against tendencies that have the potential to subvert, undermine, and undo the gains of democracy. It is further important to add that it was not just during the six years of the NDA rule that the communalization of the Indian polity was in progress. The four decades of Congress dominance in the post-Independence period are equally to blame. Indeed it needs to be realized that the Congress itself paved the way and set the stage for the vicious communalization of the polity witnessed in the 1990s.

To get a grip on this connection between Congress and BJP policies it is important to realize that the rise of the BJP occurred in the very political space that was vacated by the shrinking Congress in its years of decline. As the Congress shrank, that part of the polity that was occupied by its Right wing was taken up by the expanding and ballooning BJP. It is again precisely this connection that brings out why it makes so much sense for the Congress party to occupy the Centre-Left of the political spectrum, as the swing to the Left in these elections itself has shown. It again goes to underline the futility of the Congress taking up the soft-Hindutva line by trying to pander to majoritarian Hindu communalism.

Stepping back into the four post-Independence decades (1950 to 1990) to understand the roots of communalization will not be enough. Indeed it is important to go further back into the very decades of the high tide of the Indian national movement, the 1920s, 1930s and 1940s, to realize that the Indian polity was being communalized in its very heyday when the great figures of the Indian national movement themselves were at the helm of affairs. This brings about a need for a critical look at the role of such leaders as Gandhi and their response to communalism during the decades of the national movement (see Vanaik 1997). It is also important to add that the history of communalism and the consequent communalization of the Indian polity does not go back there. There is also a history of communalism in the nascent period of the national movement, there are the many revivalist movements of the late nineteenth and early twentieth centuries. The development of communalism in the early part of the twentieth century under the influence of events like the partition of Bengal and the separate electorates awarded under the Morley-Minto Reforms of 1909 is also significant. However, for the analysis in this article the rapid communalization of the Indian polity that took place after the mass movement phase of the national movement needs to be considered. This outright communalization began in the 1920s with the adverse fallout of the collapse of the conjoined Non-Cooperation and Khilafat movements spearheaded by Gandhi.

We then have three phases of the communalization of the Indian polity after the mass movement phase of the Indian national movement, from 1920 onwards. This is the pre-Independence phase of the 1920s, 1930s and 1940s. There is then the second, post-Independence, phase in which the effects of communalization are more subdued in the Nehruvian era of the 1950s and 1960s but which picks up momentum in the 1970s and 1980s; this second phase, presided over by a Congress party moving continuously to the Right, first under Indira Gandhi and then Rajiv Gandhi, paves the way for the systematic and outright third phase of communalization of the 1990s and the beginning of the first decade of this century. This third was presided over by a BJP government in state power in coalition at the centre. The level and brutalization of communalism attained in this last phase was most dramatically captured by the pogrom that took place in Gujarat in 2002.

In many ways, the years of the NDA's dominance in power at the centre bought forth an outpouring of high quality intellectual debate from Left and liberal circles.[4] Historians especially, amongst other members of the social science fraternity, were perturbed by the ways in which a culturally philistine Sangh Parivar was, in the name of a cultural nationalism, wreaking havoc in centres of learning. The contribution that such intellectual outpourings of concern made to the NDA's undoing needs to be noted with a degree of satisfaction. At the same time there can be noted a certain smugness setting in within those very circles. This smugness was noted and effectively expressed by Arundhati Roy when she was spoke at the Jamia Millia Islamia in September 2004, on the issue of censorship. Roy noted how the very same people who had been up in arms against the NDA's atrocious censorship policies were now exploiting their connections with the new establishment to get themselves around difficult government regulations. Roy's observations point to an issue on which the left-liberal intelligentsia needs to do some introspection. The point is whether the intelligentsia's response came from of a genuine concern for academic freedom, or whether it was a more specific, selfish, and defensive posture against what was perceived as an attack on their own turf. Roy's observation would make it seem that much of the response, though not all of it, stemmed from the second kind, that is, a defensive guarding of one's turf. A genuine commitment to openness and secularism would demand from the intelligentsia a response closer to the more principled first concern for political, academic, and intellectual freedom.

As mentioned earlier the rather optimistic reading that some commentators have made regarding the mandate may be reading too much into the verdict of the elections. The two counts under which the elections results were understood were first an opposition to the aggressively anti-people neo-liberal economic policies that were pushed through by the NDA government; and second a decisive rejection of the anti-secularist stance of the BJP. While this may be too optimistic in its tone, this article will use these two counts as a kind of normative indicator towards which politics in India hopefully should be able to move. That is to say that an opposition to economic neo-liberalism and a commitment to secularism are two desirable goals that the India polity should move towards. The two goals are themselves intimately linked, and could possibly form the nodal points of future progressive politics. It is precisely this manner of looking at current politics that will bring in the question of the position that minorities occupy in the country.

My point is that the demand for minority rights and minority protection should form an integral part of the politics of this country. Hither to the politics of minority protection and rights, has occupied the less desirable political ground of social conservatism, religious revivalism, and outright obscurantism. This has done its bit to significantly undermine and discredit the idea of minority rights in general. Thus, what is remarkable about the whole aspect of minority rights and minority protection in this country is that it has reinforced the more conservative tendencies within communities (Ali 2000; Mahajan 1998; see also Rajan 2002).

This brings us to the responses of progressive, Left, and liberal circles to the rise and dominance of Hindutva in the 1990s. Many a brave stand has been taken by academic commentators against the intolerant majoritarian tendencies exhibited by Hindutva. Progressive circles wrote their hearts out on the horrors of Narendra Modi's genocide in Gujarat. The extensive documenting of those atrocities probably contributed to the resounding election defeat of the BJP. What is needed, then, is a changed perspective on minority rights in this country. The whole minorities question needs to be placed within part of a progressive politics for it to be made effective and perhaps more crucially, credible. This would be a significant change in the manner in which the minorities question has been debated in this country. It needs to be made part of a larger progressive politics that can bring about a more energized 'radical democracy'. Chantal Mouffe talks about setting an agenda for the Left that involves learning from the mistakes that social democracy made during the second half of the twentieth century; accepting and acknowledging the crucial achievements made by the political side of liberalism; bringing together the traditional concerns of the Left such as the ecological movement, the movement against the oppression of religious minorities and other marginalized sections, and the campaign for nuclear disarmament. Crucially all these aspects which Mouffe mentions as important in the sense that they need to be acknowledged and brought close to its centre of concern, need to be addressed in opposition to the larger issue of economic neo-liberalism (Mouffe 1992).

It is this point that brings into sharper focus the two guiding normative concerns that were made earlier. The first was the opposition to economic neo-liberalism, which links directly to the point being made by Mouffe. The second point is related to the commitment to secularism. One shudders to think what the BJP would have done if it had remained in power for another five years. The judiciary, referring to the higher judiciary and more specifically the Supreme Court, was one of the last remaining bastions that had been battling valiantly to defend secularism. Other institutions like the National Human Rights Commission (NHRC) also did their bit. Indeed it was increasingly becoming a battle for the soul of India, a battle over who would get to define the idea of India. Other institutions such as the Election Commission, with bright and resolute bureaucrats like J.M. Lyngdoh have all given us a sense of pride in being Indian.

It is precisely because constitutional bodies like the Election Commission have worked so well that there is to be found in this paper an emphasis on 'constitutional patriotism'. Over the past few years we have been witness to some of the most vulgar displays of patriotism by the BJP. The sheer crassness of its patriotism was exhibited some years ago by an urban middle class caught in the frenzy of jingoistic fever during the Kargil war. This war, very much in the manner of that Falkland factor that gave Margaret Thatcher victory, rewarded the BJP with five years of uninterrupted rule at the centre. The new BJP led NDA government set up a Constitutional Review Commission at a very early stage of its tenure. Obviously, the Constitution was acting as something of an obstruction to the BJP's plans. The patriotic fervour of the BJP's variant of nationalism, which led it to undermine the Constitution, needs to be appreciated. Interestingly, the word 'patriotism' has, contained within it, a connotation of a backward regressive movement, a going back to a paternalistic and patriarchal state of the forefathers. A principled commitment to country and Constitution can hopefully bring about a sober and progressive influence that would counter the vicissitudes that a frenzied nationalism has brought about.

NOTES

1. For a useful documentation of the issues concerning Muslims in this period see A.G. Noorani, 2003.
2. The violence in Gujarat was certainly not a spontaneous reaction as portrayed by many Hindutva proponents. Far from such a state of affairs it was a cold, calculated form of violence that was aimed at terrorizing and physically eliminating the 'other', in this case the Muslim. See van der Veer, 1996.
3. For an analysis of the mandate and what it meant, see the *Seminar*, May 2004, no. 539, 'A Mandate for Change'.
4. It can be compared to the 'liveliest republic of letters in European socialism' that Perry Anderson, 1990, refers to regarding the British left intelligentsia's vibrant response to the Thatcher years.

REFERENCES

Ali, Amir, 2000, 'Case for Multiculturalism in India', *Economic and Political Weekly*, vol. XXXV, nos. 28 & 29, 15 July.

Anderson, Perry, 1990a, 'A Culture in Contraflow-I', *New Left Review*, no. 180, March/April, pp. 40-78.

———, 1990b, 'A Culture in Contraflow-II', *New Left Review*, no. 182, July August, pp. 85-137.

Hobsbawm, Eric J, 1990, *Nations and Nationalism: Programme, Myth, Reality*, Cambridge: Cambridge University Press.

Mahajan, Gurpreet, 1998, *Identities and Rights: Aspects of Liberal Democracy in India*, Delhi: Oxford University Press.

Misra, Amalendu, 2004, *Identity and Religion: Foundations of Anti-Islamism in India*, Delhi: Sage.

Mouffe, Chantal, 1992, *Dimensions of Radical Democracy*, London: Verso.

Noorani, A.G. (ed.), 2003, *The Muslims of India: A Documentary Record*, Delhi: Oxford University Press.

Rajan, Nalini, 2002, *Democracy and the Limits of Minority Rights*: Delhi: Sage.

Sarkar, Sumit, 2002, *Beyond Nationalist Frames: Relocating Postmodernism, Hindutva, History*, Delhi: Permanent Black.

Vanaik, Achin, 1997, *Communalism Contested: Religion, Modernity and Secularization*, Delhi: Vistaar.

van der Veer, Peter, 1996, 'Riots and Rituals: the Construction of Violence and Public Space in Hindu Nationalism', in Paul Brass (ed.), *Riots and Pogroms*, New York: New York University Press.

Zavos, John, 2000, *The Emergence of Hindu Nationalism in India*, Delhi: Oxford University Press.

6

Hindutva and Future of Muslims in India

ANWAR ALAM

The recurring question of the future of Muslims in the Indian republic has acquired a new urgency since the rise of Hindutva in the 1980s. It underlines the continued existence of *insecure* conditions for Muslims at large. This paper does not focus on the conventional theme of under-representation of Muslim communities in various fields of life, but attempts to unearth some emergent political trends among various Muslim segments as a response to the challenges of Hindutva, and their implications for the future. In addition, this paper, in part, reflects critically on the nature of dominant political discourse and processes within which 'Muslim politics' have been conducted and legitimized and that has, over the years, adversely affected the life situations of Muslim people. The terms 'Hindutva', 'majoritarian communalism' and 'communal fascism' are used inter-changeably throughout the text.

I

'Hindutva' refers to the 'historical process of construction of majoritarian (Hindu) communalism and its gradual transformation into a specific political-ideological creed of nation state in a given political, social and economic context. At present it is represented by the Rashtriya Swayam Sewak Sangh and its political outfit, the Bharatiya Janata Party (BJP) on the one hand and political forces such as the Shiv Sena (SS) on the other. Their ideology continues to pose the gravest challenge to the logic of pluralism, diversity, democracy, and basic rights of our country, despite the setback they received in the parliamentary elections of 2004. Despite a considerable amount of scholarly differences on the origin and dimensions of Hindutva,[1] it appears that this brand of fascism is more dangerous than its Nazi variant for the simple reason that, unlike the latter, it successfully conceals its fascist character, retains its invisible forms, combines the element of moderation and flexibility in its strategy, has organic links with the society through its hundreds of educational, cultural, and social institutions, and does not rely solely on state power for its existence and expansion. Hence only dislodging it from state power will not prove enough to put an end to it. Its hegemony and legitimacy at the political, social, and cultural levels must be challenged. It is not characterized by uni-dimensionality but is multi-faceted. The goal of Hindutva is to institutionalize the notion of the Hindu Rashtra; unfettered rule of capital over labour; the re-establishment of brahmanical hegemony to legitimize that rule; and to suppress, if necessary with violence, the rising voice of the oppressed. The anti-minority plank is but one political and ideological strategy to secure this goal.

Though all marginalized communities and groups are today under attack from the forces of Hindutva, the Muslim minority is the most vulnerable for the following reasons:

(a) Muslims are not only the largest religious minority group and but constitute the second largest Muslim population in the world. However, unlike other religious minority groups, they are geographically spread out all through the country.
(b) Muslims had been the ruling elite of this county for several hundred years and this factor has an important bearing on the Hindu-Muslim relationship.
(c) Of all the religious minorities, the Sangh Parivar considers Muslims as settler colonizers of this country.
(d) Partition and the subsequent construction of nationalism with majoritarian overtones has serious implications for Muslims. The dominant Indian discourse does not view minorities (read Muslims) from the perspective of social and economic equality, but defines them within the narrow parameters of the discourse of com-

munalism *versus* secularism and nationalism *versus* separatism.

(e) Communal riots generally involve Hindu-Muslim conflict.

(f) Anti- Muslim plank is the most specific political strategy in the hands of Sangh Parivar to unite the Hindu rank and file and to usher in a Hindu Rashtra. Hindutva consciously projects the image of 'Hindu' India under siege externally by Pakistan, Bangladesh, and Afghanistan, and internally by Indian Muslims. By highlighting the Islamic dimension of terrorism in Jammu & Kashmir, 'Politics of ISI and Bangladeshi refugees' the Hindutva brigade creates a mindset that suspects Muslims as the threat to the unity and integrity of the country.

(g) No other religious community in independent India has been subject to such systematic persecution and discrimination as the Muslims.

(h) The conception of a monolithic, communal, unified, singular, collective and cohesive community is specifically applied only to Muslims in popular perception. This image is sustained not only by various religious groups/representatives/leaders, by the very narrow upper-class political elite, and by the mainstream political parties—national or regional—on the Left, Right and Centre—but also in the larger political discourse within the 'minority framework' that lends legitimacy to a unified collective perception of otherwise diverse Muslim groups. The dominant representation of Muslims as 'monolithic entity' has some bearing on the development of Hindutva.[2]

II

Like other social groups and communities, Muslims in India are also regionally, socially, culturally and economically diverse and locating their response to Hindutva is indeed a difficult task. A glance at the statements in various Muslim newspapers, by political leaders and social and religious activists on the Gujarat carnage reveals a sense of dejection, alienation, apathy, inferiority, resignation, withdrawal, fear-psychosis, insecurity, and a total loss of faith in the state machinery and the principle of secularism. Such responses, widely prevalent, cut across caste, class, and regional variations among Muslims. Such a response is also conditioned by the way Muslims have conceived and internalized the phenomenon of Hindutva . It seems that the community hardly sees the logic of fascism being applicable to Hindutva or even if some self-styled leaders of the community use the terminology they do not use it in its class sense or its implications for the nation as a whole. They use it to refer to the aggression and brutality they suffer from Hindus. Hence Muslim responses to Hindutva are essentially coloured by the latter's threat—real or imaginary—to the faith, its culture, identity, and heritage. The response thereby becomes divorced from the national context. Muslims lament the state of affairs and demand constitutional protection from the state and political parties, but do not actively engage in any nation-wide struggle against Hindutva. It must be underlined here that the absence of wider participation of Muslim communities in the democratic struggle partly lies in the fear of upper class Muslims that such participation will be counterproductive to their own hegemony and control of community resources. This upper class political and religious elite has a vested interest in sustaining the monolithic image of an otherwise diversified community in order to project themselves as legitimate representatives of all Muslims and to bargain with successive governments, irrespective of their ideology on class interest.

Notwithstanding the singular pattern of Musilm responses to the communal fascism, one discerns a number of political trends operating among the various Muslims groups since the period of demolition of Babri Masjid. These can be summarized as follows.

First, there is a greater assertion of traditional religious identity, cutting across class, caste and regional variations. Yesterday's Muslims with a secular outlook are now increasingly asserting their religious identity, whether in terms of attending mosque, observing Ramdan, or performing other rituals. This trend is very visible at least among lower and middle class Muslims.

Second, there is a growing emphasis that Muslims should consciously withdraw from the political process and pay attention to the economic and educational development of the community. This view is more prevalent among upper middle class Muslims. Their argument is that Muslim intervention in state politics has historically proved counterproductive, giving rise to militant Hindutva, hence they should pay more attention to building schools, colleges, hospitals, professional institutions and other resources. In other words, *Muslims should become like Jews.*[3] The import of this is that once the community builds strong economic assets, it will be able to influence the decision making process of the state. This viewpoint among a well to-do Muslim section is not out of the present national context. It has emerged out of the thinking that given the resource crunch of the state and, with globalilzation, its gradual withdrawal from the social sector along with the communalization of the state sector, Muslims hardly hope to get anything from shrinking state resources. Since the cost of intervention in the political process is high it is better to stay away from the large political discourse and concentrate on economics and education so as to improve its bargaining capacity in the market economy. This has been reflected in low turn-out at times of voting. This section of the Muslim population is getting mentally prepared to live with the reality of a fascist Hindu state, provided it gives them security and stable condition to pursue their economic activities.

The absence of any alternative to Hindutva has also contributed to the sense of resignation. However such a perception is highly dangerous as it amounts to directly playing into the hands of the Hindutva forces. By terrorizing the minorities, particularly Muslims, the RSS wants them to withdraw from the political process and not claim any share in state power or resources. They must live in the space allotted by RSS, and more important, they should not play any role or have any say in the nation building process. Moreover, even if they build economic and educational assets, the security of these is not guaranteed in the absence of thoroughgoing democratization of Indian society and state. In fact, if one looks at the historical pattern of communal riots one finds that the most intensive riots have occurred in those places where the prosperity of Muslims is visible.[4] Further, withdrawal from the political process runs contrary to the interests of lower-middle- and working-class Muslims need massive intervention of the state for uplift.

A third and important trend is a communal response to the rise of Hindutva. The votaries of this belong to the dominant religious-political formations like Jamaat-e-Islami, Milli Council, Muslim Personal Law Board, Jamait-e-Ulema Hind, All India Babri Masjid Committee, traditional Islamic institutions such as the Dar-al Ulum in

Deoband, Nadwa in Luknow, Imariat-e- Sharia in Munger and leaders such as Syed Shahabuddin, Syed Bukhari of the Jama Masjid, and others. They tend to project the danger of Hindutva *exclusively* in terms of a threat to Islam, and call upon the government to 'honour' the constitutional obligation of protection of minority rights and culture, to uphold the 'principle of secularism' and the rule of the law. They also tried, without much success, to *externalize* the threat of Hindutva by projecting the demolition of the Babri Masjid as co-ordinated international conspiracy aimed at the disintegration of Muslim *Ummah* as a whole, and sought the support of the international Muslim community through such agencies as the Organization of Islamic Conference (OIC), the Mecca-based Muslim World League, and the Rabiat al- Alam-Islami (RAI).[5] Two reasons can be advanced to explain this and the stubborn resistance to democratic reform, educational and legal, within the communities. First is the genuine belief that such threats to Muslim identity actually exist. The second is the desire to protect their entrenched privilege positions.

No wonder then that the Muslim leadership have played the politics of identity, veering around a few religio-cultural issues such as the protection of Muslim personal law, the declaration of Urdu as the second official language, the minority character of the Aligarh Muslim University, the recognition of Muslim religious celebrations as national holidays, the eradication of Hindu religious mythology and anti-Muslim bias from the school books, the protection of mosques, idgahs, darghas, madrasas, and so on. Worse, these demands are projected at the all India level as if they are central to the issue of Muslim identity. It is worthwhile to point out that such upper-class Muslim politics have brought more harm than good—whether religious or secular. Take the case of Urdu. An insightful paper by Imtiaz Ahmad has clearly demonstrated how Urdu lost its market value: in the process of Muslim politics it became identified with Muslims, a marker of Muslim identity at the all-India level. It did not become marginalized by systematic discrimination of successive governments. Not only have Muslim politics failed to restore the glory of Urdu, it has diluted the syncretic tradition of Indian society and alienated the general Muslim mass from the large segment of Indian society.[6] However this does not mean that successive governments played no role in the marginalization of Urdu.[7]

Neither could their politics protect the Babri Masjid from its eventual demolition by the forces of Hindutva.

As a response to Hindutva, the communal Muslims have increasingly been toying with the idea of an independent political formation. The rationale behind this is that, given the increasing fragmentation of social and political constituencies that has resulted in coalition-politics, such a formation will play a decisive role in the formation of government and thereby increase the bargaining position of Muslims. However so far, such formulation has not been given institutional shape, probably because of the fear that it will be counterproductive and will further strengthen and consolidate the communal fascist forces. One example of this trend can be seen in creation of All India Muslim Forum by Nehal Ahmad in Uttar Pradesh (UP). So far this party has contested the local municipal elections in Lucknow with modest gains and has unsuccessfully tried to enter into an alliance with the Samajwadi Party in UP. The party remains on the fringe and without any national significance. It is worth recalling that such an attempt is bound to fail, given past Muslim experience. The MMM (Muslim Majlis-e-Mushawarat) of the 1960s collapsed within a few years of its existence without bringing any material gain or spiritual benefit to Muslims and only alienated them from national politics.[8]

Following the loss of legitimacy in the wake of the demolition of the Babri Masjid, the upper class communal segment of Muslim leadership intensified its advocacy of the introduction 'principle of proportional representation' in politics and reservations of government jobs and seats in educational institutions for Muslims at both the centre as well as state level on the ground of 'under-representation'. It also raised the issue of *sharia* court[9] in various parts of the country in order to retain their leadership over Muslim masses. In relation to their demand of introduction of proportional representation and reservation of Muslims, they are also supported and aided by a section of liberal-progressive Muslims who feel that a greater representation in government and the law enforcing agencies will provide better security. None of these measures are bound to ameliorate the pathetic conditions of the general Muslim mass; they will end up, as in the case of Urdu, in further alienating the Muslim masses from the political process, thereby increasing the process of the ghettoization and isolation of the Muslim poor. First, these demands are designed specifically to cater to the interest of a miniscule Muslim upper class at the cost of the lower class Muslims.[10] Second, while increasing representation of minority communities in governmental bodies and other law enforcing agencies is certainly desirable, such measures do not constitute a sufficient protection against a majority backlash. A study by Wilkinson has shown that rather than representation, it is the degree of 'competitiveness of political parties' and the ideological inclination of ruling governments that provide the better condition for the security of minorities. The greater the competitiveness of political parties, the greater the value of minority votes and hence the lower the chances of communal riots.[11] Third, there are a number of theoretical as well as practical constrains that work against 'Muslim representatives' to serving what are called 'Muslim interests'.[12] Further, the effectiveness of representation of Muslim interests, according to Imtiaz Ahmad, largely depends upon the foundation of trust between the majority and the political leaders of the minority. According to him,

> as far as Muslim and Christian minorities are concerned, at least until about a decade ago there appears to have been some foundation of trust. . . . Muslim and Christian community members regularly approached legislators and administrators from the majority community with requests and advice and met with significant, if not total, success. . . . In the wake of the anti-Muslim and anti-Christian sentiments that have surfaced during the recent years, their capacity to trust the members of the majority to take their concerns seriously and to address them equitably has been seriously damaged.[13]

Finally, it is questionable that in a democratic polity the representation of minorities should necessarily be measured against the number of members it has in the legislature and in the administration. It is possible that others enjoying the support and confidence of a particular minority group will act as its representatives. For example, for twenty years after Independence, Jawaharlal Nehru was a powerful spokesperson of Muslim interests even though the number of Muslims in the legislature in those days was considerably higher. Subsequently, Indira Gandhi and, particularly after the Ayodhya crisis, Mulayam Singh and Lalu Prasad Yadav in their respective states had been active spokesperson of Muslim interests.

In this context it is worthwhile to point out that the issues related with the Muslim communities can be more effectively served by the latter's participation in the government bodies through the secular process at the regional level. The experiences of Muslim politics in south India are instructive in this regard. Whether it is the Majlis-i-Ittihad al-Muslimin in Hyderabad, or Muslim League in the Malapuram area of Kerala, they have consciously eschewed national-level issues while raising the religious and cultural issue of Muslims, largely acted as a pressure group and have been successful in achieving various concessions and benefits from successive governments. The tendency to assert the Muslim politics at all India level is typical of the north Indian Muslim leadership, mostly in what is called the BIMARU states. Given the narrow social base of this leadership, they consciously indulge in the politics of religious symbols—selectively chosen to be meaningful for all strata and segments of Muslim population—such as personal law, Urdu, Aligarh Muslim University, etc., so as to assert their claim of representing all Muslims and thereby monopolize the 'political space' to negotiate with the successive governments in their class interest. By forcing the Rajiv Gandhi government to enact the retrogressive Muslim Womens Bill in 1986 in order to annul the progressive verdict of the Supreme Court on Shah Bano, the All India Muslim Personal Law Board (AIMPLB) has succeeded in claiming near-official recognition of itself as the spokesperson of Indian Muslims.[14] As a result, today it is religious-political organizations like Jamait-e-Ulema Hind and Muslim Personal Law Board that are filling the political space and asserting their claim to represent all Indian Muslims. In fact, given the increasing social, political, and economic marginalization of the community and faced with the project of Hindutva offensive, the process of consolidation of minority communalism has certainly been intensified.

However, yet another development, the fourth in our list, is discernible. This is the political assertion of subaltern Muslims, principally Dalits and OBCs. This has emerged in the last decade in the face of the failure of traditional leadership to respond to the concerns of the Muslim masses, and their inability to protect Muslim lives and interests from the menace of Hindutva. The movement gained momentum in the context of 'Mandalization' of political processes and the loss of legitimacy of the Muslim leadership in the wake of the demolition of the Babri Masjid. The organized political expression of this movement has been found in the formation of Pasmanda Muslim Mahaj led by Ali Anwar, All India Backward Muslim Morcha led by Ajaz Ali, and All India Muslim OBC Organization led by Shabir Ahmad Ansari.[15] The activity of the first two organizations is confined to the state of Bihar, while the last is mainly in Maharashtra. While sharing the perspective of social and educational reform within the communities, the basic orientation of these organizations is essentially Mandalite. They seek to undermine the social and political hegemony of the Muslim leadership by dislodging it from access to state power. Their primary concerns and demands are to include all backward caste communities among Muslims in the OBC and SC lists at state and central levels. It also seeks to pressure the mainstream political parties to give them more representation in their organizational structures and in ticket distributions at all levels of elections: municipal, assembly, and parliament. However, many factors hinder the growth of this movement. The absence of a middle class (unlike the Hindu OBCs); the 'diluted' sense of caste inequality (in contrast to Hindu society); a major section of Muslim OBCs have already been recipients of state affirmative policies for long; the process of 'Ashrafization' among lower caste Muslims; the bulk of Muslim OBC continue to receive educational instruction in the Ashraf dominated Islamic institutions of learning, *madrasas*; 'the constant threat of majoritarian communalism to Muslim identity' (whether real or perceived); and above all, the 'conscious underplay of social differentiation among Muslims by all mainstream political parties so as to ensure the block voting of Muslims'.

Notwithstanding these obstacles and their narrow and limited agendas, these organizations and their politics have a few noteworthy features. Their primary concerns are secular, with a commitment to building an equitable society. They take the stand that a secular social structure and class/caste hierarchy are more important than religious identities.[16]

Further, as Asghar Ali Engineer has noted, with the assertion of these organizations, Muslim politics will become more grass roots centric and issue oriented, and will cease to be reactionary.[17] Finally, there is a conscious effort to forge relations between Dalit and OBC Muslims on the one hand and OBC Hindus and Dalits on the other. This has the potential of helping large numbers of Muslims to break out of the 'ghetto' in which their traditional leaders and many parties have placed them.

In the interests of completeness of coverage I mention a fifth and very minor trend, reflected in the urge for social and educational reform within the Muslim communities. It is being pushed by a miniscule liberal-progressive section among the secular academia. The demand for social reform came at the time of the Shah Bano case and the demolition of Babri Masjid. Recently a reform of Muslim personal law, especially the provision of *talaaq*, has been a focus of the reform agenda. However, the offensive of Hindutva makes this task difficult.

The last development is a militant Islamic response that remains at the fringe. The regional location of Islamic militancy is an interesting dimension. It originated not in the centre of the Muslim population (north India) but from the periphery (south and north-eastern India). Thus, al-Umma in Assam, ISS (Islamik Sevak Sangh, now operating as Peoples Democratic Party) in Kerala, and al-Umma in Tamil Nadu are representative of militant Islam and is directly linked to rise of Hindutva and its attack on life, property, and religious symbols. The announcement of the formation of the Adam Sena by Bukhari in Delhi never took any root. Neither have the north Indian Muslims supported the cause of 'Islamic Jihad' in Jammu and Kashmir. One must make it clear that the Islamic militancy in Jammu and Kashmir has nothing to do with the rise of Hindutva (rather it is other way round) and it has quite different historical roots. In fact the functioning democracy in India has, to a great extent, thwarted the development of militant form of Islamic response on a wider scale.

III

Having briefly surveyed the emergence of various political trends among the different segments of Muslim communities in the context of Hindutva, let us now turn our attention to the dominant political discourse and the political events that have over the years adversely affected the Muslim situation in India. A critical examination of the national political discourse and process—conducted by mainstream political parties—reveals how it has resulted in keeping the Muslims apart, confined them into 'minoritism', and hardly encouraged them to participate in the national politics. The national consensus on the 'doctrine of secularism' has never moved beyond the recognition of secularism as *a necessary political instrument* or a *political necessity* to hold together a multi-religious society like India and hence did not visualize the role of the state as an 'active agent' in the promotion of secular values in society as a whole. This national consensus has also been reflected in the very 'operational definition' of secularism[18] that implies the state upholding the principle of non- interference and equi-distance with regard to all religions. This is particularly true with regard to the Muslim communities. The Indian republic, since its inception, followed the British policy of non-interference in religious matters, particularly of the minorities.[19] Such a policy was justified with reference to the prevailing extraordinary situations such as the partition of the country and the growing majoritarian communalism during 1980s and 1990s; it was considered that any imposition of reform from above would only further alienate Muslims. On the other hand, the Muslim leadership not only never initiated reform, it successfully resisted any attempt to introduce even a modicum of liberal adjustment (particularly in matters related with the Muslim personal law), right from the introduction of an unofficial bill relating to ban the practice of polygamy among Muslim communities in the Maharashtra legislature in early 1960s until the Supreme Court Judgement on Shah Bano on the ground that this was a violation of the principle of secularism (for them, non-interference in matters of religion). Commenting on the Muslim position on secularism, Ziya-ul Hasan Faruqi rightly observed in the 1960s, 'In general, the Indian Muslims are prepared only to *tolerate* the idea of secularism; they are not ideologically equipped to support it actively or to strengthen its bases.'[20] It is hard to disagree with this observation and it holds even today as far as the attitude of Muslims towards secularism is concerned. Given (a) this reluctance of the state to introduce reform within the communities, (b) no prospect for the same from below and (c) the challenges of Hindutva, a great majority of Muslims are left with no alternative but to retreat into the ghetto. The cumulative effect has been that a great number of Muslims have failed to evolve a secular-modern outlook. They lack the skills and capacities to harness the benefits of 'general development' around them.

Muslim relationships with the political parties are characterized by the principle of 'votes in exchange for security'. The search for security is the dominant consideration and explains, in part, the shifting pattern of voting behaviour ranging from Congress party, to mainstream left like CPI(M), CPI, CPI(ML), to regional parties like BSP (Bahujan Samaj Party), SP (Samajwadi Party), RJD (Rashtriya Janata Dal), and others. No wonder a section of Muslims is willing to go with Hindutva forces provided they provide security. The late Rafiq Zakaria remarked, 'Muslims must learn to live in the Hindu state'. Of late there has been growing emphasis on the part of Muslim leadership to forge a coalition of Muslims, Dalits and OBC Hindus as a *political strategy* to counter the threat of Hindutva. The Jamaiat ul-Ulema-i-Hind has entered into a political alliance with the All India Confederation of SCs and STs of Udit Raj, forming the Bharat Bachao Morcha in order to unite against the Hindutva forces. However, such a political formulation suffers from a number of fallacies. It has been conceived in an electoral arithmetic and is not sustainable in the long term: social and political coalitions are always fluid depending on the political location and class character of the respective elites. Also, its tendency to identify the 'Hindu upper castes' as *the social base* of communal fascism, and Muslims, Dalits and OBCs as forming a *natural democratic and secular constituency* does not correspond with reality. It is not without reason that BJP has the largest number of SC and ST Members of Parliament. Intellectuals, liberals and left political activists expressed their surprise and were/are aghast to see the participation of Dalits, tribal people, and some OBCs in the pogrom against Muslims in Gujarat. The rapid growth of the BJP does indicate its capacity to transcend barriers of caste, class, tribe and region. This is not specific to the Hindu fundamentalists but a characteristic of all fundamentalist parties irrespective of religious affiliation. Hence any political mobilization on the criteria of caste and community cannot be antithetical to religion based political mobilization because both are premised on backward and inward looking ideology. As a result, the Mandalite plank of social justice in 1980s, though it halted the march of communal fascism temporarily, finally collapsed in 1990s and paved the way for Hindutva forces to capture state power. Erstwhile champions of social justice, whether the BSP, JD, or other DMK and TDP, were found enjoying power in alliance with the Hindutva brigade.

The question of the relationship of Muslims with the larger political forces involves the attitude of mainstream secular political forces towards the minority communalism, bearing in mind that the sustenance of a communal, collective, and monolithic image of Muslims has been one of the factors contributing to the rise of communal fascism. Historically speaking, the attitude of secular political forces ranging from the Nehruvian Congress to the radical left is one of 'toleration'. It appears that the tendency of tolerance within the liberal-secular-left spectrum has to do with its theorization of minority communalism as a by-product of majoritarian communalism. It is generally understood that minority communalism is a reflection of a 'perceived identity crisis' and sustained by mass illiteracy and poverty. Thus the issue of class is ignored. In fact there has hardly been any serious attempt to understand the persistence of minority communalism from *class perspective*. Hence the prescription is that with the demise of communal fascism and with the economic development and growth in literacy among Muslims, minority communalism will be automatically weakened, if not eliminated. However to deny autonomy to minority communalism is to ignore its historicity. The struggle against communal fascism has also an element of 'becoming champion of minority rights' and bringing minorities within the fold for electoral purposes, without making them realize the danger that communal fascism poses to the nation itself and criticism of communal tendencies amongst the minority. In fact this strategy even entails the active support of minority communalism in the fight against communal fascism. However the historical trajectory of the development of communal fascism in this country has proved the futility of such a political strategy. Significantly, while it has been demonstrated that both communalisms feed each other and grow together, no concrete initiative has been taken to unleash the democratic forces within the minority community.[21] Given the fact that almost 40-50 per cent of Muslim communities constitute the artisan class, their mobilization and participation is not only crucial to fight globalization and communal fascism but also to save them from playing into the hands of Muslim communalists. Hence the contention here is that struggle against communal fascism on national scale must combine with the struggle for democratization within minority communities.

IV

Today Indian Muslim communities are at the crossroads. They desire to live in a democratic and secular state without democratizing and secularizing themselves. Perhaps the votaries of multiculturalism will find no dilemma, as every community has the right to live with its collective religious and cultural rights within the secular nation-state. However in the absence of wider democratization of identity (that results in making the religious identity a personal matter) there is a real danger that the plank of multiculturalism might be hijacked by some communalist leadership to legitimize their politics, to maintain hegemony, and silence all democratic opposition. The dominant response of Muslim communities to Hindutva has occurred within such a framework and has taken the form of a legal battle demanding the implementation of constitutional articles pertaining to minorities, seeking larger support in the name of violation of human rights and reminding the state of its constitutional obligations. In a nutshell, the response is one of *bargain* within the existing situation and not to fight fascism on the principles of equality, democracy, freedom and citizenship. It does not see the danger of fascism. And hence in the process it isolates itself from the national political discourse. My submission here is that the Muslim communities must assert their national identity while fighting communal fascism; that Muslims and all other marginalized groups must assert that they, like all other groups, have a legitimate right to represent the nation. They will have to assert that democracy, secularism, equality and other ideals are needed for the construction of a healthy nation and that communal fascism is a danger to the nation itself. Only then will a viable political alternative to communal fascism become possible. Minorities must become an integral part of the larger democratic struggle in the society.

NOTES

1. These differences broadly range from theory advocating the linkage between globalization and rise of communal politics, to the theory that sees Hindutva as a form of cultural nationalism in terms of assertion of suppressed majoritarian identity against the imposition of alien, Western concept of secularism. For the former Stuart Corbridge and John Harris, *Reinventing India: Liberalization, Hindu Nationalism and Popular Democracy* (Cambridge, 2000), Baldev Raj Nayar, *Globalization and Nationalism: The Changing Balance in India's Economic Policy, 1500-2000* (New Delhi, 2001), Thomas Blom Hansen, 'The Ethics of Hindutva and The Spirit of Capitalism', in Thomas Blom Hansen, Christophe Jaffrelot (eds.), *The BJP and The Compulsions of Politics in India*, (New Delhi, 1998), pp. 291-314 and Achin Vanaik, 'The New Indian Right', *New Left Review*, 9, May-June 2001. For the latter explanation see T.N. Madan, 'Secularism in its Place', *The Journal of Asian Studies*, vol. 46, no. 4, 1987, pp. 747-59 and Ashis Nandy ' the Politics of Secularism and the Recovery of Religious Tolerance', in Veena Das (ed.), *Mirrors of Violence: Communities, Riots and Survivors in South Asia* (Delhi, 1990), pp. 69-93.
2. On the politics of the construction of a homogeneous Muslim identity, see Anwar Alam, 'Democratization of Indian Muslims: Some Reflections', *Economic and Political weekly*, vol. XXXVIII, no. 46, 15 November 2003, pp. 4881-5.
3. This observation is based on the author's personal conversation with a number of leading Muslim personalities in different fields.
4. See Asghar Ali Engineer, ed. *Communal Riots in Post-Independence India* (Hyderabad, 1984); Ashutosh Varshney, 'Ethnic Conflict and Civil Society', *World Politics*, 53, no. 3, 2001, pp. 362-89, and Mushirul Hasan, *Islam in the Subcontinent: Muslims in a Plural Society* (Delhi, 2002), pp. 373-83.
5. For details Jan-Peter Hartung, 'The Land, the Mosque, the Temple: More than 145 years of Dispute over Ayodhya', in Richard Bonney, ed. *Ayodhya 1992-2003: The Assertion of Cultural and Religious Hegemony* (Leicester, 2003), pp. 22-8.
6. Imtiaz Ahmad, ' Urdu and Madrasas', *Economic and Political Weekly*, 15 June 2002, pp. 285-92.
7. On the role of the government in the marginalization of Urdu, see Mushirul Hasan, 'In Search of Identity and Integration: Indian Muslims Since Independence', *Third World Quarterly*, vol. 10, no. 2, 1988, pp. 828-42, also his *Islam in the Subcontinent*, pp. 375-7.
8. Z.M. Qoreisi, 'Emergence of Muslim Majlis-e-Mushawarat', *Economic and Political Weekly*, 19 June 1971, pp. 1229-34.
9. Mushirul Hasan, *Legacy of a Dived Nation: Indian Muslims Since Independence* (Colorado, 1997), pp. 313-14.

10. A more recent example of such politics is the ordinance pertaining to a 5 per cent reservation of all governmental jobs and seats in the governmental educational institutions for Muslims in Andhra Pradesh, the benefits of which will mainly accrue to the already relatively privilege. Urdu-speaking Ashraf of Old Hyderabad at the cost of Telugu speaking lower caste Muslims, the bulk of whom have been included in the Mandal Commission for affirmative action.
11. See his 'Putting Gujarat in Perspective', *Economic and Political Weekly*, 27 April 2002.
12. For details Theodre P. Wright, 'Effectiveness of Muslim Representation in India', in Donald E. Smith, ed., *South Asian Politics and Religion* (Princeton, 1966), pp. 579-99.
13. Imtiaz Ahmad, 'Multicultural Discourse in India', paper presented in International Seminar on Multiculturalism in India and Europe, 6-7 November 2003, JNU, New Delhi, p. 18.
14. See an insightful article Zoya Hasan, 'Minority Identity, Muslim Women Bill Campaign and the Political Process', *Economic and Political Weekly*, 7 January 1989, pp. 44-50.
15. For literature on Dalit and OBC Muslim movements, Ali Anwar, *Maswat kee Jung: Pasemanjar: Bihar ka Pasmanda Musalman* (Delhi, 2001), A series of article in *Economic and Political Weekly*, 15 November 2003, Yogendra Sikand, 'Islamic Perspective on Liberation and Dialogue in Contemporary India: Muslim Writings in Dalit Voice', *Economic and Political weekly*, 14 September 2002.
16. Praful Bidwai, 'Age of Empowerment: Muslim OBCs Discover Mandal', *The Times of India*, 12 September 1996.
17. Asghar Ali Engineer, 'OBC Muslims and Their Problem', *The Hindu*, 12 September 1996.
18. The Constitution does not define the word 'secularism' except that the word has been incorporated into the Preamble by the 42nd Amendment and declared as one of the basic feature of Indian constitution by the Supreme Court. For the implications of lack of constitutional definition of secularism, Anwar Alam, 'Secularism in India: A Critique of the Current Discourse', in Paul R. Brass and Achin Vanaik, eds., *Competing Nationalism in South Asia* (Delhi, 2002), pp. 99-102.
19. With regard to the majority, the Indian state did enact the Hindu Bill despite the considerable opposition.
20. Z.H. Faruqi, 'Indian Muslims and the Ideology of the Secular State', in Donalad E. Smith, ed., *South Asian Politics and Religion*, Princeton, 1966, p. 140.
21. The CPI (ML) Liberation in Bihar has launched an Inqalabi Muslim Conference (IMC) to initiate mass contact with Muslims and to unleash democratic forces within the community. However the IMC is still in an embryonic stage.

7

The 'Cancer of Dowry' in Indian Muslim Marriages: Themes in Popular Rhetoric from the South Indian Muslim Press

SYLVIA VATUK

Today in India 'evil of dowry' has moved to centre stage as an object of social critique by the general Muslim public as well as by social reform-minded religious authorities and institutions. This development reflects the recent spread of a relatively new kind of transactional regime in connection with Muslim marriages. Whereas the specific object of the critique is new, the nature of some of the rhetoric is not. To be sure, the major themes in the popular Muslim discourse about 'dowry' closely echo those issuing from the Indian public at large and from women's NGOs and other feminist social reformers and activists. A careful reading of the Muslim press, however, also reveals the presence of other themes that represent a more specifically Muslim critique of the system. These recall some of the rhetoric of much earlier Muslim reformers in the subcontinent, who wished to purge Muslim lives of a wide range of customary rituals and ceremonial observances

* An earlier version of this paper was presented at a workshop sponsored by the Konrad Adenauer Foundation on the topic of 'Lived Islam: Liminality, Accommodation and Adaptation' held in Goa in December 2002. I thank the participants in that workshop and, in particular, its organizers, Helmut Reifeld, Imtiaz Ahmad, and Shail Mayaram, for giving me the opportunity to benefit from their knowledge of and ideas about the issues discussed here. I have also profited from conversations and e-mail exchanges with Frank Fanselow, Mary Hancock, Dennis McGilvray, Diane Mines, Mattison Mines, Filippo Osella, Martha Selby, Yogi Sikand, and Theodore Wright.

(Urdu *rasum*) regarded as objectionable because they had no religious sanction in the scripture and even involved activities contrary to the dictates of Islam. Furthermore, according to some, they were to be avoided because they represented cultural 'borrowings' or 'survivals' from pre-Islamic or Hindu modes of worship and life-cycle ceremonial.[1]

I use the term 'dowry' in its current popular Indian sense to mean cash and other valuables transferred at the time of a marriage by the bride's family to the groom and his family, often—though not necessarily—in response to explicit or implicit demands, rather than of their free will.[2] Over the past twenty-five to thirty years in southern India there has been considerable change in the pattern of marriage transactions associated with Muslim marriages.[3] Whereas previously parents endowed their daughters with a 'trousseau' of clothing, jewellery and household goods that were intended (in theory at least) to remain her personal property, now they are expected, in addition, to transfer significant wealth to her prospective groom and in-laws. I will first discuss the historical background of this change and then explore the community's response as reflected in discussions about the 'dowry' phenomenon that appeared in two south Indian Muslim newspapers in the late 1990s. I will analyse the various terms in which the critique of 'dowry' is framed in the press and assess their significance for understanding some of the social and political dilemmas in which ordinary Muslims find themselves today, as they pursue their daily lives as members of a minority community in an environment increasingly hostile to the kind of 'difference' they are perceived to represent.

HISTORICAL BACKGROUND

Already in the nineteenth century the British colonial state had become aware of the prevalence of the 'dowry' practice among certain segments of the Hindu population, especially in north-western India. Convinced that it led to widespread rural indebtedness and female infanticide, they made many attempts to suppress it, but to little avail.[4] After Independence those concerned with trying to rectify gender inequalities in the existing Hindu laws of marriage, property, and inheritance turned their attention to 'dowry'. Most acknowledged that the longstanding practice of endowing the daughter with valuables at the time of her marriage was a legitimate way of expressing parental affection and compensating her for the fact that, under Hindu law, she would normally inherit no share of her father's estate.[5] But reports of extortionate demands made during matchmaking negotiations by prospective grooms and their families were a cause for serious concern. In 1961 the Dowry Prohibition Act was enacted. It banned the transfer of 'any property or valuable security given . . . *as consideration for the marriage* [italics mine]' and made both giver and taker subject to prosecution.[6] Only a handful of cases ever came to trial under this Act, however, and in 1974 a government-appointed committee surveying all aspects of women's status in India had to report that 'dowry is on the increase, and has penetrated communities and regions which did not practise it earlier'.[7] Women's organizations all over India echoed the committee's call for strengthened legislation, and the original Act was twice amended, in 1984 and again in 1986.[8] The practice of giving 'dowries' continued to spread, however, and ever-rising amounts were reported.[9] Furthermore, 'dowry demands' were being made not only during the marriage negotiations but for years thereafter. Women who were unwilling or unable to comply with the demands often suffered psychological and physical abuse and, in extreme cases, death.[10]

There has been no perceptible decline in the prevalence of 'dowry' since the latest legislative enactments took effect. If anything, the custom has continued to spread. While one can find exceptions to this generalization, it is fair to say that most Indians today, of whatever social stratum or religion, take it for granted that, if they are to find a suitable husband for their daughter, the financial outlay will be substantial.

MARRIAGE TRANSACTIONS AMONG SOUTH INDIAN MUSLIMS: THE HISTORICAL EVIDENCE

Two fairly detailed descriptions of Dakkhani Muslim marriage 'customs' (*rasum*) are available. Both were written in Urdu by local Muslim men, one in the 1830s[11] and the other at the turn of the twentieth century.[12] Both works begin their discussion of marriage transactions by describing the *mahr*, a gift of money or other valuables that Islamic law requires the groom to offer his new bride.[13] The amount is always recorded in the marriage contract (*nikahnama*). It need not necessarily be handed over at the time of the wedding, but if not it remains an outstanding debt until either paid to, or 'forgiven' by, the wife.[14]

These early observers also prominently mention the *jahez*, the bride's trousseau.[15] Assembled and presented to their daughter by her parents, it included, according to Jaffur Shurreef, 'a quantity of the bride's clothes which have been worn, jewellery, cosmetics, bed and table linen, furniture (including a bed and a storage trunk), kitchen utensils, pots and pans, plates and cups, and one or two domestic slaves and some animals.'[16] The *jahez* goods, he says, remain in the bride's possession 'as long as she lives'. They then pass to her children or, if she is childless, to her closest [natal?] relatives.[17] On the night before the wedding ceremony (*nikah*) the entire *jahez* is taken in procession, often with musical accompaniment, to the groom's house and laid out there for his relatives and friends to inspect and admire. With it is delivered—in reciprocation of the wedding dress that the groom's party had earlier delivered to the bride's house—a set of clothes and an elaborate flower veil (*sehra*) for the groom to wear at the wedding ceremony.

Neither account mentions anything resembling the contemporary 'dowry'. Aziz Jang Wala, writing specifically about customs of the Nawwayat community (*qaum*), does mention a cash gift—called *pend* or *paind*—that is presented to the groom by his future in-laws at the conclusion of the engagement ceremony (*mangni*).[18] He indicates that poor families would offer sweets instead. He further explains that the word and the custom itself is of Telugu Hindu origin. Though it passed from the bride's parents to the groom, it does not appear to have been a gift on a par with the modern 'dowry', in terms either of size or function.

MARRIAGE TRANSACTIONS IN SOUTHERN INDIA IN THE MORE RECENT PAST

Several anthropologists carried out research among various south Indian Muslims communities between 1960 and the early 1990s. None of these reports addresses marriage transactions in great detail, but a careful reading suggests that, while it has long been customary to give the daughter as substantial a gift as possible of personal and household items at the time of her marriage, the practice of making payments of cash or valuable goods to the groom and his family was not followed in this region before the late 1970s or early 1980s. All mention the requirement that the groom make a commitment to give *mahr* to his bride. Otherwise, the principal marriage transfer described is the bride's 'trousseau'. Thus Mines says that among Muslim merchants in the town of Pallavaram, Tamil Nadu, in the late 1960s 'a woman is said to receive her share of [her natal family's] wealth in the form of dowry . . . such wealth belongs personally to her'.[19] The Tamil word used for this gift by both Hindus and Muslims in the area is derived from the Sanskrit *stri* + *dhan*, 'women's wealth'. Though Mines translates it as 'dowry', what he describes is not what is commonly meant by that term today but corresponds rather to Shurreef's description of *jahez* or 'trousseau'.

Fanselow, in an unpublished paper based on research among Muslim Ravuttars and Tarkanars in Tirunveli district, Tamil Nadu, in the early 1980s, likewise translates the Tamil *citanam* as 'dowry' in the context of a discussion of women's inheritance rights.[20] It consists of moveable property, mainly gold jewellery and silk saris, for the daughter's personal use. No mention is made in this account of any payments to the groom. However, in a later paper he documents from several decades of mosque records that by the 1980s a major portion of the *citanam* consisted of cash intended for the daughter's husband and in-laws. Whereas in the past the respective families' wedding expenses had been more or less equal, there was now a 'unilateral transfer of wealth' to the family of the bridegroom. Deploring this development, but unable to stop it, some local mosque committees (*jamaat*) had begun levying a tax on any groom who accepted a 'dowry'. But this experiment was later abandoned because worshipers objected to benefitting from an activity so clearly contrary to the dictates of Islam.[21]

A much more detailed account of Muslim marriage transactions is provided by C.G. Husain Khan, who conducted research in the early 1980s among Urdu-speaking Muslims in Karnataka.[22] There the principal marriage gift is the *jahez*, presented to the bride by her parents and consisting of 'many pairs of clothings [*sic*] and personal effects for the bride, normally including several pieces of gold and silver jewellery which will remain her personal property'. In addition, there are 'household furnishings like a bed with bedding . . . brass and copper cooking vessels . . . and other miscellaneous items'.[23] But Khan notes that well-to-do Muslims had recently begun giving substantial gifts of cash and gold to the families of their prospective sons-in-law.[24] He associates this new transaction, called *hunda*—which he identifies with the Hindu concept of *kanyadan*—with a growing preference among the wealthy for marriages outside the kin group, and notes the similarity between the Muslim practice and that of Hindus in the region.[25] Jackie Assayag, who did research in the early 1990s among villagers of both religions in the same general vicinity in Karnataka, makes a similar observation. He translates *hunda* into French as *dot* (the English dowry), 'a payment to the future husband', while translating *jahez* as trousseau.[26]

MUSLIM MARRIAGE TRANSACTIONS IN SOUTH INDIA TODAY

According to my own observations and interviews conducted between 1983 and 2001 in Hyderabad and Chennai, mainly among Urdu-speaking Muslims, the sequence of wedding rituals and gift exchanges followed are similar in most respects to those described in nineteenth-century and early twentieth-century sources.[27] Ritually the relationship between bride-givers and bride-takers tends to lack the element of asymmetry that typically characterizes this relationship among Hindus. Most material exchanges and feasting are reciprocal rather than one-sided, and the sequence of rites held at the groom's and bride's homes before and after the wedding are roughly mirror images of each other.[28] Likewise the sharp role distinction between the 'groom's side' and the 'bride's side', so crucial in Hindu marriage, is much less marked in a Muslim marriage, particularly, of course, when the union is endogamous to the *khandan* or local descent group.[29]

The major difference with the past is the expectation that the bride's parents will give substantial amounts of cash, goods, and other valuables to the groom and his family. With changing practices have come new linguistic usages. One expression that is frequently heard is *len-den* (literally 'taking-giving'). Traditionally a neutral term applied to the practice of exchanging gifts on a variety of ceremonial and festive occasions, it has acquired a more specific and negative connotation. The word *jahez* is still used, but its meaning has broadened as its content has changed. No longer consisting only of goods for the bride herself, a significant proportion of the goods are intended for use of the groom and his family. Furthermore, rather than being selected and freely given by the bride's family, what goes into the *jahez* is increasingly being dictated by the groom's family. The line between the bride's property and that of her conjugal family is consequently becoming blurred and her ability to retain or control the disposition of any part of her *jahez* is greatly reduced.[30]

While the word *jahez* is now often used in a broad sense for the entire set of transfers from the bride's family to their daughter *and* her new family, the cash portion of the gifts to the groom is often singled out from the material items as *jore ka paisa*, or *jore ki raqm*, 'money for the set (*jora*) [of clothes]'. As noted above, the groom's wedding outfit was formerly made to order by the bride's family and delivered to him shortly before the wedding. A tailor would be sent ahead of time to take his measurements and sew whatever the bride's family thought suitable. Over time, however, the parents of young men began to take responsibility themselves for ordering the wedding suit. The girl's parents would then be asked to reimburse them in cash. Eventually the amount demanded began to greatly exceed the actual cost of the clothes. Nowadays, under the guise of *jore ki raqm*, the girl's family may be asked to give anywhere from a few hundred to (in extreme cases) several lakhs of rupees. There is no longer even a pretense that it is directly related to the actual expense of clothing the groom.

In the extended family (*khandan*) with whose practices I am most familiar,[31] when cash began to replace the gift of a readymade outfit, a conventional amount of Rs. 50 was paid.[32] By the 1980s some families were paying amounts ranging from Rs. 500 and 5,000. When the groom was a close kinsmen the amount paid was usually nominal but larger amounts were transferred when the groom was a non-relative. This particular family is rather unusual in its collective reluctance to participate in the current practice of taking a large amount as *jore ki raqm* when they marry a son and paying out correspondingly when marrying off a daughter. One way that they are able to do this is by continuing to marry within their own *khandan*, insofar as this is possible, given changing criteria of 'suitability' or 'eligibility' of grooms in terms of educational qualifications and employment prospects.

If they aspire—or are forced by the lack of 'suitable' candidates within the *khandan*—to seek an 'outsider' for their daughter, parents are aware that they may be obliged to give a more substantial *jahez* and a larger amount as *jore ka paisa* than if the groom were a close relative. But when a young man of the *khandan* marries an 'outsider' girl, many prefer to adhere to their traditions and their religious principles and refuse to demand or even to accept 'free-will' offerings of cash or expensive goods from the girl's parents. Therefore, as one woman said to me, only partly in jest, young men of their *khandan*—particularly those who are educated in the professions or are working in the Middle East—are regarded as 'bargains' in the marriage market!

When urban residents of Hyderabad or Chennai talk about the way marriages are being celebrated today, the issue of 'dowry' is central. In the fall of 2001 I had such a conversation with a fairly well-to-do middle-aged Hyderabadi whose sons were just finishing high school. He explained that 'all middle class people' want their sons to become doctors. But admission to government medical schools is extremely competitive, so most must seek admission in one of the private medical colleges. These require, he said, a 'capitation fee' of up to Rs. 8 lakhs and annual fees of Rs. 80,000 to 86,000. Therefore, parents look for a bride whose family is in a position to reimburse them for their son's education. On top of this, they want a fridge, VCR, colour TV, and a motor scooter or even a car. They will say to each of the prospective brides' families, 'We have spent so much on our son's education. How much can you give?' Then they will send the proposal to the one that offers the most.

A young single woman bank employee in her early 20s, belonging to a lower middle class family and working as a computer operator in a bank, had a similar story to tell. The most desirable grooms, she said, are those working in the Gulf. They can command as *jore ki raqm* Rs. 3 or 4 lakhs. Those who have secure salaried jobs in India are worth closer to Rs. 2 lakhs. Even if the young man is unemployed, his parents may demand this much so as to set him up in business. Or the girl's family will be asked to make arrangements for a job overseas and a visa and also to fund his travel. They will also have to give their daughter a substantial amount of gold jewellery and numerous sets of clothes (11, 21, 51, 101 and so on) and at least one roomful of furniture as *jahez*. 'But it [the furniture] won't go into their own room. The husband's family will use it themselves!' As for the *jore ki raqm* (So much money for one suit of clothes!), the boy's family may use some of it to pay for the *valima* feast (on the day after the marriage is consummated). They may buy a few sets of clothes and perhaps some pieces of jewellery for the bride. The rest they will save for when their own daughter gets married.

Neither of these informants was describing the details of any particular marriage, and it is quite conceivable that they were exaggerating somewhat for maximum effect or at least presenting worst-case scenarios. Somewhat more specific—though not necessarily more reliable—are the data I obtained from interviews and case files of women whose failing marriages had brought them into the family courts of Chennai and Hyderabad. One young woman, a B.A. from a middle class family, told me that in 1985 her parents had paid her husband-to-be Rs. 15,000 as *jore ki raqm*. Her *jahez* included 5 *tolas* of gold and assorted furniture. After the marriage, her husband sold the gold and used the proceeds to finance his sister's marriage. He gave the furniture in his sister's *jahez* as well. The parents of several other women I interviewed, who had married between 1979 and 1989, had paid between Rs. 5,000 and 10,000 as *jore ki raqm*, in addition to the usual *jahez* items. Of course, to properly assess the significance of the cited amounts it would be necessary to have information about the income and assets of these women's families.

Detailed schedules of items presented in *jahez* are sometimes found in court files. For example, in connection with a marriage that took place in Chennai in 1986, 44 items of household use are listed, including furniture and kitchen utensils, with a total value of Rs. 36,000. The petitioner also claimed that her parents had given her 8 *tolas* of gold and 25 *tolas* of silver and her husband Rs. 10,000 in cash. Another bride, married in 1987, listed 19 silk saris, 65 *tolas* of gold, and extensive household furnishings and equipment as *jahez*. Her husband received Rs. 30,000 in cash. But soon after the wedding he and his parents further demanded a VCR, stereo, washing machine, cooking range, and Rs. 15,000 to invest in a 'side business'. When she refused to ask her parents to comply with these new demands, she was allegedly physically abused and eventually ejected from her marital home and forced to return to her natal family.

THE 'DOWRY EVIL' IN THE MUSLIM PRESS

That the custom of making payments to eligible grooms in connection with marriage is regarded within the Muslim community as a pressing social issue can be seen from the frequent discussions on the topic in Indian Muslim newspapers and magazines and, increasingly, on Islamic internet sites originating in the subcontinent. I have sampled two south Indian newspapers for relevant articles and letters to the editor on this topic. The first, the daily *Siasat*, published in Hyderabad, is distributed throughout south India and puts out a Web version that is read around the world. It is not a religious organ, though, as an Urdu-language paper, its readership is largely Muslim as are those who write for it. It covers local, national, and international news, sometimes written with a distinctly Muslim slant. It regularly prints articles about Muslim personalities and events in other countries and has a popular religious advice column. There is a once-a-week 'women's page' where most of the comments on 'dowry' that I discuss here have appeared. Women are well represented among the authors of articles on this page, as are most of those responding with letters to the editor. One can assume that its readership is also primarily female.

The other publication sampled is the *Islamic Voice*, published in Bangalore. It is India's most widely read English-language Muslim newspaper.[33] It appears to aim more explicitly than *Siasat* to speak for and to a self-consciously religious Muslim constituency. It devotes much space to religious, as well as to social and political, issues of particular relevance and concern to its largely middle class, Western educated, upwardly mobile Muslim readership. Articles dealing with social issues like that of 'dowry' appear irregularly. They tend to be written by locally or nationally prominent male religious and/or scholarly authorities and are typically highly didactic in tone. The paper does not provide a regular forum for readers' responses, so for this reason the voices of women are largely absent from its pages.

Both papers are very critical of the phenomenon that in the Urdu press is variously referred to as 'the dowry cancer' (*jahez ka nasur*) or 'the evil spirit of dowry' (*jahez ka bhut*). Writers address the topic from a variety of vantage points. Many write to document the current situation with respect to the practice of 'dowry', while others are more concerned about the social and personal consequences of excessive *len-den*. Some try to assign responsibility for the prevalence of the custom and its spread or to ask where and why the custom originally came from. Finally, there is the vexing issue of what to do about it. Most of the proposed solutions take the form of the usual exhortations to 'simply say no' when the time comes to arrange a marriage in one's own family, but these recommendations are frequently buttressed by appeals to Islamic ideals.

Letters to the editor of *Siasat* documenting current practice typically draw upon the writers' own experience or upon that of relatives and acquaintances. As one young woman explains,

> A very close friend of mine got married recently. Her parents had to pay 6 lakhs cash as *jore ki raqm*, in addition to all of the other expenses of the wedding. Altogether the marriage cost them 11 lakhs. When I asked her about it, my friend explained that the marriage was so expensive because he is a doctor. Otherwise, why should be marry an ordinary high school graduate like her?

A man reports the dilemma in which an acquaintance, the father of a young woman, currently finds himself:

> Five years ago, he negotiated the marriage of his daughter with a close relative. At that time there was no talk of dowry. Now, just before the day of *nikah*, the groom's father has demanded 5 lakhs rupees cash, a car, washing machine, fridge, colour TV and all the other household items! What can he do?

With respect to the issue of 'dowry demands', writers may refer to the time-saving device of presenting a 'list' at the onset of negotiations, in order to weed out unsuitable candidates and serve as a basis for serious discussion with the rest. Others outline the current 'market prices' for different kinds of grooms:

> A chauffeur, bus conductor, policeman, or office boy demands 2 *lakhs* rupees in cash, a motor scooter, 5 *tolas* of gold and plastic veneer furniture. A bakery worker wants 25,000 rupees cash, a motor scooter, 3 *tolas* of gold and metal furniture.

> The demand for grooms is shooting up like the market price of any other commodity. For example, for a doctor, five lakhs plus a Mercedes car. For a veterinarian, four lakhs plus a Suzuki car. For a civil engineer, five and a half lakhs and a Maruti. For a lawyer, three lakhs, etc, etc. These are the prices for professionals. Non-professionals have their own going rates.

Writers universally deplore the fact that the need to pay dowry is making it difficult for parents of moderate means to get their daughters married. Young women are remaining unmarried well beyond the desirable age for marriage and sometimes are unable to marry at all, because their parents cannot afford the dowries that are expected by 'suitable' grooms. One result of this is that girls are now seen as—and feel they are—burdens on their parents. This perception strikes at the very heart of the ideal parent-daughter relationship.

The question of who can and should exert control over the *jahez* is also raised by many writers. For example, one woman asks readers of *Siasat* to respond to the question of whether the bride ought to be required to share 'her' *jahez* articles with other family members. Some reply that she should be generous in allowing others to use her belongings but also note that family members should in turn acknowledge her rights and give the items back to her when they have finished with them. Other writers point out that, in practice, there isn't much a woman can do if in-laws take her belongings. In the words of one woman, 'There is nothing, other than her *jahez* clothes and jewellery, that the girl can keep for her own exclusive use'. In answer to this, several writers cite instances in which even the woman's jewellery has been taken by the husband or in-laws and sold to finance their own projects or to give away in the marriage of the husband's sister.

Many writers ask who is to blame for the 'aberration'. For some it is greedy grooms and their parents, for others it is the families of prospective brides who, in order to attract the most 'desirable' grooms, put ads in the paper offering large amounts of cash and promise an elaborate wedding. Such practices encourage dowry escalation and unfairly tempt young men who otherwise would be perfectly satisfied with modest gifts. The young women themselves are blamed by others for pressuring their parents to spend as much as possible, so as to heighten their own prestige and desirability. But most letter writers reserve their strongest ire for those bride-takers who make unreasonable 'demands', instead of looking at the qualities of the girl and accepting gladly whatever her parents choose to offer.

Writers also debate whether it is the younger or the older generation that is chiefly responsible for propagating the custom of dowry and whether men or women are more prone to insist on retaining it. So, for example, some claim that grooms are pressured by their mothers into going along with dowry demands, while others say that young people are at fault for indulging in the modern craze for fashionable clothes, expensive jewellery and consumer goods of all kinds. Their parents typically have no particular interest as such in these kinds of material things but are willing to do what they can to please their children.

Most of the anti-dowry rhetoric that I have cited so far conceptualizes the issue of *len-den* as a social problem adversely affecting the lives of individuals and their families. It is because of its deleterious social effects that the custom should be suppressed. But another approach to attacking dowry, repeatedly expressed in the *Islamic Voice* but rarely encountered on the 'women's page' of *Siasat*, makes use of the notion that dowry and other undesirable marriage customs should not be engaged in by religious Muslims because they were originally Hindu. While this discourse shares with others the assumption that the social consequences of participating in dowry transactions are deplorable, it differs in that its appeal for reform relies on an appeal to 'history' rather than to overall societal well-being or gender justice.

For example, one person writing in *Islamic Voice* introduces his essay by saying, 'Several traditions and customs which have been existing in the Indian subcontinent have nothing to do with the true Islamic spirit. They should be nipped in the bud at the earliest'. Another, after outlining how the demand for dowry places unbearable financial pressure on the parents of Muslim girls, elaborates upon this theme: 'The rich have copied this vulgar and criminal system from their counterparts in Hindu society and this practice has percolated to the poorest families too.' He goes on to criticize in particular the way that, before the *jahez* is delivered to the groom's house, the girls' parents

> display the vulgar luxurious goods in a mini-exhibition. . . . Where is the spirit of Islam here?. . . . If Islam is in danger right now in any sphere of human activities, it is here (dowry).

In another issue, the same author, in an article entitled 'Dowry Deaths and Mute Muslim Society,' reiterates that Hindu 'influence' is at the root of the problem:

Dowry is an alien feature and totally prohibited under Islamic principles. This is a social evil eating away the Hindu society. . . . Its influence on the Muslims disgraces the very Islamic notion of respect, affection and kindness expected to be showered on women. Muslims of India are victims of the social evil of the Hindus.

Finally, in both newspapers the all-important question of how to rid society of the 'dowry menace' is addressed. Suggestions include getting young people and their parents to refuse to participate in the practice of *len-den* themselves and to boycott weddings where they know that the dowry given is excessive. This is another area where appeals to Islam are often encountered. There are repeated calls for so-called 'simple' marriages, which are more pleasing to Allah than the lavish celebrations current in India today. For example, in an article published in 1998 in *Siasat* the writer points out that God has directed man 'to use all of his belongings in humility and moderation'. It is counter to His teachings to waste money and other material resources by spending excessively on unnecessary things just in order to impress others. It is especially so if one's means are limited. An essay in *Islamic Voice* entitled 'Simple Marriages are the Need of the Hour' echoes this theme: 'For those who are born with silver spoons in their mouths this waste is not felt at all, but for poor and middle class Muslims celebrating marriages has become a nightmare.' And a letter to the editor of *Siasat* advises readers: 'If all Muslims followed the sunnah of the Prophet (PBUH) and followed a simple life, then *insha'allah* this problem could definitely be solved.'

A male correspondent cites as an exemplary model his own son's recent wedding:

My son is employed abroad and earns 6400 *rials* per month. His marriage was very simple and according to Islamic law. There were no traditional rituals. *Nikah* was held in the mosque and the guests then came to the Function Hall [for a meal . . . *Mahr* was paid to the bride immediately. There was no band or videography. Those items of daily use that are usually given—such as copper and brass utensils, scooter, TV set, fridge, cooler, etc.—were absent. The bride brought only a bed, bed linen, a few clothes, a metal wardrobe, and fifty-five grams of gold. We did not make any demands.

And a woman reader writes in a similar vein about a cousin working in Saudi Arabia: 'He got many proposals offering *len-den*, but he chose a poor girl from a respectable family.'

Both letters reflect and doubtless reinforce the common perception that young men who live for a time in Saudi Arabia or the Gulf States tend to become more religious than they had been before leaving India. Upon their return they are believed to adhere to stricter standards of Islamic practice, based on what they have seen and heard preached there.

CONCLUSION

I have argued that the giving and taking of dowry is widespread among south Indian Muslims today. It is indulged in quite unselfconsciously, especially in urban areas, just as it is elsewhere in India among people of all religious communities. While recognized as a relatively new and decidedly negative addition to the repertoire of practices associated with Muslim marriages, it is reluctantly accepted as something that is perhaps an unavoidable accompaniment to the modern dilemma of growing economic insecurity and a lack of employment opportunities at a time of rising aspirations, among the young in particular, for the acquisition of ever more consumer goods and 'modern' lifestyles. But as the practice continues to flourish, so too does an ever more strident social critique that is reflected in the use of such phrases as *jahez ka nasur* and *jahez ka bhut*.

Most of the critique that emerges from the Muslim rank and file is identical in tone and content to the familiar pan-Indian anti-dowry discourse, whose history reaches far back into the early colonial period, though Muslims were not, until very recently, implicated among its perpetrators. It focuses on the deleterious effects of the practice on families and on marriageable and young married women and tries to find ways to explain and suppress its excesses.

Another theme, of more minor importance in the newspapers I sampled, reflects a more specifically Muslim critique. It stresses the 'alien' origins—from the perspective of world-wide Islam—of the 'dowry' custom. Underlying this critique of 'dowry' is an implied conceptual opposition between 'Indian culture' and 'the Muslim religion' that has been heard often over the centuries from Muslim religious reformers. In this discourse dowry is linked with a myriad of other undesirable Hindu customs that Indian Muslims have 'adopted' or 'retained' when their ancestors converted to Islam. I suspect that had I chosen to examine for this purpose one of the publications put out by any of the major Muslim religious bodies in India, this theme would have been even more prominent than it is in the newspapers I sampled. There is also an evident gender bias with respect to the terms in which the criticism is voiced. Women greatly predominate among the readers of *Siasat* who wrote to express their views about the 'cancer' of dowry. Women were also represented among writers of longer essays on the topic, though many were male. On the other hand, all of the authors of essays that I read in *Islamic Voice* were male. Many were clearly well-versed in the textual traditions of Islam, something that women are in general much less likely to be.[34]

For the vast majority of Indian Muslims, engaging in the practice of giving and taking dowry at the time of marriage presents no threat to their identity as both Muslims and Indians. Although they may resent its ubiquity for the entirely pragmatic reason that it so hampers their ability to arrange a secure and comfortable future for their daughters, they realize that it is a fact of life, something they must be prepared to deal with when the time comes. Some manage by resorting to such strategies as seeking a son-in-law within their immediate circle of close kin or—if they have a son of appropriate age—obtaining the necessary assets by first arranging *his* marriage to a girl whose parents are in a position to provide him a generous 'dowry'. Others turn to a like-minded community of devout Muslims pledged to stricter adherence to Islamic codes of conduct as a way of extricating themselves from dowry's stranglehold. For some of the latter, the familiar reformist discourse about fundamentally Hindu customs provides an especially strong and appealing rationale for going against the tide of lavish *len-den* that threatens a family's economic survival. To cease taking or giving dowry, then, becomes a compelling choice, not simply because of the harm it inflicts on them and their daughters, but because doing so threatens in a very fundamental way their identity as devout and observant Muslims.

I have noted here the presence of this latter discourse in some recent discussions in the contemporary Muslim press of the phenomenon of Muslim dowry. I am not in a position at present to say how prevalent it is in the Muslim press generally. It is not by any means the dominant theme of discussion in the two south Indian newspapers I was able to survey. However, it was encountered from time to time in the pages of a newspaper that attracts readers who are English speaking and therefore more highly Western educated and presumably better off than the average reader of the Urdu press. According to Sikand, who has analysed editorials in the *Islamic Voice* in considerable detail, it tries to deal seriously and constructively with issues facing the Muslim community today, promulgating a message that encourages readers to find a way to reconcile their dual identities as religious Muslims and Indian citizens by adapting themselves to the many challenges of the milieu in which they live. Among other things, the publication is said to be dedicated to a strategy of trying to establish more direct and more positive relations with fellow citizens of other faiths.[35] In the light of this overall assessment of the paper's orientation, it is therefore somewhat surprising to find that, at least with respect to the particular issue being discussed here, one finds in its pages numerous examples of utterances that might be interpreted as reinforcing negative stereotypes of Hindus and attempting to deliberately set Muslims culturally apart. To take this kind of position with reference to a social problem that afflicts Indians of all religions has its risks for Muslims living in a political environment where many in the majority community are eagerly looking for evidence that they are not only 'different' but that, in insisting on maintaining their difference, they represent a potential threat to the integrity of the Indian state. For this very reason there are many in the larger Indian Muslim community who are explicitly cautious about resorting to this kind of rhetoric when addressing issues like dowry.[36] My examination of the Muslim discourse leaves many open questions, not only about the political implications of some of the rhetorical choices that are being made by various individuals and segments of the community, but about the potential of any of them for bringing about real social change. Clearly, further research is needed before any of these questions can be satisfactorily answered.

NOTES

1. Barbara Metcalf outlines the major issues and reviews the central arguments of some of these reformers in 'Islam and Custom in Nineteenth-Century India: The Reformist Standard of Maulana Thawani's [*sic*] Bihisti Zewar,' *Contributions to Asian Studies* 17: 62-78 (1982). See also Book 6 of Muhammad Ashraf 'Ali Thanawi *Bihishti Zewar*, Delhi: New Taj Office, 1962 and Barbara Metcalf's translation of and comments on this chapter in her *Perfecting Women*: *Maulana Ashraf 'Ali Thanawi's Bihishti Zewar*, Berkeley and Los Angeles: University of California Press, 1991.
2. Some have suggested that the terms 'groomprice' or 'groom fee' are more appropriate than 'dowry' for the system as it operates today. However, since the latter is so widely used in India—often even when people speak in their mother tongue—I will use it here. On this question of terminology, see Lionel Caplan, 'Bridegroom Price in Urban India: Class, Caste and "Dowry Evil" among Christians in Madras', *Man* (n.s.) 19: 216-33 (1984) and Nicholas J. Bradford, 'From Bridewealth to Groom-Fee: Transformed Marriage Customs and Socio-Economic Polarisation amongst Lingayats', *Contributions to Indian Sociology* (n.s.) 19: 269-302 (1985).
3. I limit my discussion to southern India, although the phenomena that I discuss are widespread among Muslims elsewhere in India as well as in Pakistan and Bangladesh. My remarks are based largely upon my own research among Urdu-speaking Muslims in Chennai and Hyderabad, conducted since 1984 during several visits for periods ranging from 2 to 10 months in length. I also refer to the ethnographic literature on Muslims elsewhere in the south, excluding Kerala.
4. Veena Oldenburg subjects British analyses of the connection between dowry and female infanticide to critical examination in *Dowry Murder: The Imperial Origins of a Cultural Crime*, New York: Oxford University Press, 2002.
5. On the question of the relationship between dowry and female property rights in India see Jack Goody and Stanley J. Tambiah, *Bridewealth and Dowry*, Cambridge: Cambridge University Press 1973; Stanley J. Tambiah, 'Bridewealth and Dowry Revisited: The Position of Women in Sub-Saharan Africa and North India', *Current Anthropology* 30, 413-35 (1989); Bina Agarwal, *A Field of One's Own: Gender and Land Rights in South Asia*, Cambridge: Cambridge University Press, 1994, pp.198-248; Srimati Basu, *She Comes to Take her Rights: Indian Women. Property, and Propriety*, Albany, NY: State University of New York Press, 1999.
6. The law applied to people of any religion, although at that time the practice of giving 'dowries' had not yet become widespread among Christians or Muslims.
7. Committee on the Status of Women in India, *Towards Equality*, New Delhi: Government of India, Ministry of Education and Social Welfare, Department of Social Welfare, 1974, pp. 73-4.

8. For more details see Werner Menski, 'Legal Strategies for Curbing the Dowry Problem', in W. Menski (ed.), *South Asians and the Dowry Problem*, London: Trentham Books, 1998, pp. 97-149.
9. It is not entirely clear to what extent this increase simply reflects an overall inflationary trend over the period.
10. M.N. Srinivas analyses these and other post-Independence developments in his *Some Reflections on Dowry*, New Delhi: Oxford University Press, 1984.
11. Jaffur Shurreef [Jafar Sharif], *Qanoon-e-Islam, or the Customs of the Moosulmans of India; Comprising a Full and Exact Account of Their Various Rites and Ceremonies from the Moment of Birth till the Hour of Death*, G.A. Herklots, trans, London: Parbury, Allen, and Co., 1832, pp. 83-144. The author was a Dakkhani Muslim employed as a *munshi* by the East India Company. His original Urdu manuscript was never published and was apparently lost shortly after it was edited and translated into English by the British Army surgeon who had commissioned it. For further details about this book and its history see my 'Shurreef, Herklots, Crooke, and *Qanoon-e-Islam*: Constructing an Ethnography of "the Moosulmans of India"', *South Asia Research* 19: 5-28 (1999).
12. Aziz Jang Wala, *Tarikh-un Nawwayat*, Hyderabad: Wala Akadami, 1976 [orig. 1904], pp. 84-132. The Nawwayats are a relatively small community whose members are found widely dispersed throughout southern India. They trace their ancestry to Arab traders and preachers who came by sea to the western coast of India in the eighth century. Some of their descendants moved gradually to the east and south, serving in various religious and civil capacities in the administrations of successive Muslim rulers of the Deccan. See Victor S. D'Souza, *The Navayats of Kanara: A Study in Culture Contact*, Dharwar: Kannada Research Institute, 1955; Sylvia Vatuk, 'Identity and Difference or Equality and Inequality in South Asian Muslim Society', in C. Fuller (ed.), *Caste Today*, Delhi: Oxford University Press, 1996, pp. 227-62 and 'The Cultural Construction of Shared Identity: A South Indian Muslim Family History', in P. Werbner (ed.), *Person, Myth and Society in South Asian Islam*, Special Issue, *Social Analysis* 28: 114-31 (1990).
13. When Muslims speak or write in English they often use the word 'dowry' for *mahr*. This leads to considerable confusion, even in some of the scholarly literature. A more appropriate translation, long used by scholars writing about marriage transactions generally, is 'dower'.
14. Sunni Hanafi law—followed by most Indian Muslims—recognizes two categories of *mahr*, the 'prompt' and the 'deferred'. In some parts of the Islamic world the groom normally hands over all or a substantial portion of the *mahr* at the time of the wedding (see, for example, Annelies Moors, *Women, Property and Islam: Palestinian Experiences 1920-1990*, Cambridge: Cambridge University Press, 1995, pp. 77-150; Judith Tucker, *In the House of the Law: Gender and Islamic Law in Ottoman Syria and Palestine*,

Berkeley: University of California Press, 1998, pp. 52-7). The rest comes due when her husband dies or divorces her by *talaq*. But in India the entire *mahr* is almost always 'deferred' and in practice few women ever receive it, even if divorced or widowed.

15. The Urdu word *jahez* comes from the Arabic *jahaz* or *jihaz*, the trousseau that is customarily given to the daughter in Arabia and other Middle Eastern countries. See, for example, Tucker, *In the House*, pp. 55-7.
16. Shureef, *Qanoon*, p. 117. The apparent reference to clothes that have been *previously worn* is somewhat puzzling and certainly inconsistent with the contemporary practice of sending the bride to her new home with a generous set of brand-new clothes, ideally enough to last her for several years.
17. Ibid., p. 121.
18. *Pend* is also included in a list of 'harmful' wedding rites in a manifesto against 'wasteful' and non-Islamic ceremonials issued in 1863 by a group of reformist Nawwayat *ulama* in Madras (Muhammad Sibghatullah et al., *Zabitah-i Rasum-i Nikah*, unpublished manuscript). See also the same author's *Gulzar-i-Hidayat*, Madras: Nizam-ul-Mutaba, 1873-4 (orig. 1847).
19. Mattison Mines, 'Urbanization, Family Structure and the Muslim Merchants of Tamilnadu', in Imtiaz Ahmad (ed.), *Family, Kinship and Marriage Among Muslims in India*, Delhi: South Asia Books, 1976, p. 303.
20. Frank S. Fanselow, 'Law and Custom Reconsidered: A Comparative Study of Hindu and Muslim Inheritance Laws and Practices in Southern Tamil Nadu', unpublished paper (n.d.), p. 28.
21. Ibid., 'Dan, Dakshina and Dowry: An Analysis of the Muslim Marriage Market in Tamil Nadu', unpublished paper (n.d.), pp. 11-14.
22. C.G. Hussain Khan, *Marriage and Kinship among Muslims in South India*, Jaipur and Delhi: Rawat Publications, 1994.
23. Ibid., pp. 133-4.
24. This term is doubtless the same as the Marathi *hunda*, 'money given at marriages by the father of the bride to the bridegroom and his party, instead of ornaments and clothes usually presented' (J. Molesworth, *Marathi-English Dictionary* [Pune: Shabhada Saraswat, 1986 (orig. 1857), p. 905], cited in Veronique Benei, 'Changing House and Social Representations: The Case of Dowry in Pune District', in *Home, Family and Kinship in Maharasthra*, Irina Glushkov and Rajendra Vora (eds.), Delhi: Oxford University Press, 1999, p. 130.
25. Khan, *Marriage*, pp. 110-19. Poor Muslims, who were continuing to marry close kin, had not begun giving *hunda*.
26. Jackie Assayag, *Au Confluent de Deux Rivieres: Musulmans et Hindous dans le Sud de l'Inde*, Paris: École Française d'Extrême-Orient, 1995, p. 51.
27. In 1998-99, in the course of research on women and Muslim family law in the Chennai Family Court, I also obtained some data on marriage transactions among Tamil-speaking Muslims in that city.

28. This is consistent with a general Muslim tendency to endogamous and isogamous patterns of marriage alliance.
29. In such cases the bride and groom and their other kinsmen are typically related to one another in multiple ways, making it difficult to definitively assign everyone to one or the other 'side' for ritual purposes.
30. Of course, even in the past a husband or mother-in-law could (and did) forcefully or otherwise take possession of some or all of a woman's *jahez*. But the fact that it was well understood that this meant appropriating wealth that properly belonged to her doubtless served to constrain people from taking such actions. Such constraints have now largely disappeared.
31. This family, whose forebears were well-known Sunni *ulama* in Madras and Hyderabad, belongs to the Nawwayat community. See my 'Identity and Difference' and 'The Cultural Construction'.
32. It is not clear when this change began to take place.
33. See Yogendra Sikand's chapter on *Islamic Voice* in his *Muslims in India Since 1947*, London: Routledge Curzon, 2004.
34. It is conceivable, though I have no evidence of it, that *Siasat* may have a policy of not publishing comments that could be seen as reinforcing religious stereotypes.
35. Sikand, *Muslims in India.*
36. I am indebted to a recent conversation with Filippo Osella for his insights on this question.

8

From Custom to Scripture: Observations on the Direction of Indian Islam

ARSHAD ALAM

Muslims in India are as varied in their religious and social practices as any other group. Despite attempts to paint a stereotypical image of 'Muslim community', religion has only been one among the many social facts of caste, gender, and locality constituting the operational reality of everyday Muslim praxis. Moreover, religion is in itself a highly contested terrain as its actual experience may depend on the differential access of particular groups to cultural, economic, and social capital. That is to say, the experience of religion is bound up with other social facts such economy, polity, and technology. Changes within the ambit of religion are thus closely related with changes in other spheres of society. Scholarship on change in Muslim societies has recognized this need to treat Islam as a dependent variable, rather than explaining changes through recourse to texts (Malik 1998, Geertz 1971, Ahmad 1983). The present paper, locating itself within such a

*This paper is the result of few weeks of observation in both the relevant *madrasas* (mentioned in the text), in Gaya, Bihar. I take this opportunity to thank Hafiz Janab Md. Shahiruddin Saheb, Janab Abdullah Saheb and Janab Maulana Md. Naimuddin Saheb for letting me stay within the precincts of the *madrasa*. Without their permission and the co-operation of the teachers, this paper would not have been possible. I would also like to thank the students who were generous enough to share their time and accommodation with me. Part of this paper was presented in the ECMSAS Conference, University of Lund, Sweden, and I thank all those who commented on my paper.

tradition of scholarship, seeks to understand the direction of change within Indian Muslim society. However, far from being an attempt to 'generalize from above', the paper seeks to describe the 'fragment', the micro-processes of change, the changing conceptions of Islam at the local level and the role of religious schools (*madrasas*) in this process. The paper starts with a general observation of the denominational plurality of Indian Muslims, locating it within the increasing differentiation of colonial society. By looking closely at the workings of two different denominational *madrasas*, one Barelwi and the other Deobandi, it goes on to understand the appeal of these two sets of ideologies within different sectors of the Muslim population and how one ideology is gaining over the other. The paper concludes with some comments regarding the reasons and meaning of increasing dominance of Deobandi ideology and what it portends for the future of Indian Muslims.

ISLAM IN INDIA

Muslims in India have been denominationally plural. Apart from global schism between Shia and Sunni Islam, they both are internally divided into numerous denominations. Within Sunni Islam, a majority of Indian Muslims owe their allegiance, or are considered to be the followers of either the Barelwi or Deobandi denomination (*maslak*).[1] This denominational plurality has much to do with Islam's encounter with colonialism. Faced with the loss of power and privilege, the elite Muslim self introspection sought the reasons for the decline of its power within the realm of religion. This led to the reformulation of religious thought, often producing varied results. Thus both Aligarh and Deoband, differing radically in terms of tactics but united in the ultimate aim of reformulating Islam in India, were the product of this same introspection. Aided by the technology of print, these *maslaks* sought to create a 'public' of their own so as to educate them in the finer points of their version of Islam (Robinson 1993, Freitag 1989, Sanyal 1999). Slowly but surely this led to a certain crystallization of denominational identities.[2] These identities were not merely the result of philosophical exercise by the learned ulama but were embedded in the material location of its followers. Thus very often different denominations appealed to different 'sectors' of Indian Muslims (Malik

1998). Within the specific scope of this paper it suffices to note that Deoband appealed more to the semi-urban, petty bourgeoisie while the Barelwis were represented mostly by the rural Muslims; a division which more or less continues to the present. This differential socio-economic location may be at the root of differing interpretations of Islam and a passionate mutual dislike.[3]

Understanding society as a network of diffused power relationship (Foucault 1980) the establishment of an educational institution becomes a profoundly political act. The establishment of various religious seminaries thus was not just an act of 'saving the traditional sciences' from the ravages of English education, its politics went much further and indeed was based on an understanding of the new, alternative, emerging bases of power, legitimacy, and authority. The failure of the uprising of 1857 still fresh in memory, a section of *ulama* sought institutional bases which would not only act as a shield for the *batini* (inner) realm of religiosity but would at the same time be engaged in the creation of a 'religious field'.[4] The successful reproduction of this field would then depend upon the strategies of producing certain specific forms of 'capital' so that the workings of these capitals in turn create the conditions for such fields to reproduce.[5]

The establishment of a Dar ul-Ulum at Deoband in 1866, later to become the most popular *madrasa* in South Asia, was indeed a 'moment', since it changed the way in which *madrasas* were organized. Deoband altered the aims, methods, and content of *madrasa* education in India. Today Deoband is not just a *madrasa*; it is fountainhead and perhaps the most important institution of 'renewal' in Islam, so much so that it crystallized into a distinct denomination within South Asian Islam. Pre-Deoband *madrasas* were mostly organized around a few families or students studied at the feet of revered scholars (Metcalf 1982, Nizami 1996). Often students would travel great distances to learn a certain text from the master after which he would proceed to learn some other texts from some other scholar of repute. Education was not restricted within the confines of a particular institution. Status, cultural capital, and prestige were derived from students' association with particular religious personae rather than as students of a particular *madrasa* (Eickelman 1992, Chamberlain 1997; Berkey 1992). In sharp contrast, the prestige of Deoband was from the beginning institutional. Much like the modern education system, Deoband had various classes for different courses of study, a system of annual examinations and time tables, all innovations in the field of religious education in India (Metcalf 1982). But perhaps the most important differences emanated from the curriculum and the system of finances which Deoband adopted.

Deoband taught the *dars-e-nizami*, the curriculum developed by Mulla Nizamuddin of the Firangi Mahall of Lucknow during the early eighteenth century. However, they significantly reduced the content of 'rational sciences', supplanting them with books on *hadith*, which earlier used to be peripheral to *madrasa* curriculum (Sufi 1941).[6] In fact in earlier *madrasas*, both the rational sciences (*manqulat*) as well as the transmitted sciences (*maqulat*) were taught; the choice depending on the proclivities of particular students and teachers. The 'secular' *dars-e-nizami* catered to the interests of the contemporary service elite and was at the same time a tool in the service of the state. By reducing the content of rational sciences, Deoband subtly altered the very definition of what constituted a *madrasa*. From being an educational institution where one could study books ranging from arithmetic to Koranic exegesis, it was now being defined solely as a place for acquiring religious knowledge. Deoband thus defined itself as a specialized institution for the study of Islamic religion, a definition that fitted quite well with the growing differentiation of colonial society.

Such 'modern' internalization of religion as occupying a separate and distinct sphere of society (Zaman 2002) was combined with a novel system of financing. Earlier *madrasas* such as the Firangi Mahall depended on the largesse of the nawabs and later on the Crown. The dwindling resources and the uncertain socio-political climate of the times made the financing of these *madrasas* extremely difficult. The novelty of Deoband was its system of popular financing, legitimized by one of its cardinal principles, namely that the participation by the state or the wealthy would be harmful for the *madrasa* (Metcalf 1982; Quraishi 1980). Popular finance made the institution dependent on those Muslims whom they sought to educate about 'true Islam'. A 'latent function' of this dependence was to bring them closer to ordinary lay Muslims who were ultimately both the subjects as well as the objects of their hegemonic exercise.[7]

In sharp contrast to Deoband, Barelwi Islam has no founder but considers itself as the traditionally true Islam. Calling themselves the Ahl-e-Sunnat-wa-Jamaat, they represent the whole repertoire of traditional Muslim practices around shrines, saints, and Sufis, often giving local traditions and customs an Islamic hue. Islamic revivalism in India, as elsewhere, made these very practices the subject of virulent attacks and indeed blamed it for the downfall of Islamic power worldwide. In India these attacks were best articulated by Shah Ismail Shaheed in his book *Taqwiyat-ul-Iman* (Strengthening of the Faith), published in 1826-7. An ardent follower of Sayyid Ahmad of Rae Bareilly, Shah Ismail sought to purify Islam from what he considered the customary corrupt practices of the Muslims of the subcontinent. His denounced the concept of intercession as antithetical to the core Islamic belief in *tauheed* (oneness of God) and thus struck at the very heart of Islamic understanding of the Ahl-e-Sunnat-wa-Jamaat. It was left to Ahmad Riza Khan (1870-1920), to respond to the charges of *shirk* (associating partners to God). The cardinal importance attributed to Ahmad Riza Khan in the Barelwi discourse has therefore much to do with his resolute defence of traditional Islam practised by the vast majority of Muslims, which had come under attack from the likes of Deoband and the Ahl-e-Hadith (Sanyal 1999). Indeed the Deobandis considered the Barelwis innovators (*bidati*) while Ahmad Riza Khan termed the *ulama* associated with the Deoband 'leaders of heresy', Satan-inspired Wahhabis.

Central to their different yet competing interpretation of Islam was the understanding of Prophet Muhammad. Islam all over the world has revered its Prophet often making him an object of worship. The path to God was illuminated through the *Dhikr* of Muhammad. This episteme made the Prophet an intercessor between God and his people and Islam a much more personally felt experience. The way to the Prophet, however, was through those who were close to him. The *ashiq-e-rasul* (lover of the Prophet) used to be a saint or *pir* whose blessings formed the chain of intercessors (*silsila*) reaching ultimately to the *rasul* (messenger). Clearly, then, such a practice spawned a large number of *dargahs* and *mazars* (mausoleums) whose rituals were connected closely with the economic and social rhythm of mostly peasant rural societies.

Offerings and pleadings on the *mazars* and graves was vehemently opposed by the puritan Wahhabis in Arabia and eventually by a large number of Islamic movements in India, ranging from the Faraizis of Bengal to the more recent Deobandis. Central to the latter argument was that only God should be the object of worship. For them Prophet Muhammad was important as a model Muslim but no extraordinary powers be attached to him. They accused the Barelwis of elevating the status of Muhammad and some of the saints as being equal to God. Moreover, worship at the graves and asking for intercession were considered akin to idolatry and, in the specific context of India, direct influence of Hinduism. It was this *shirk* that had led to the downfall of Muslims in the subcontinent. Therefore movements like Deoband took it as their duty to educate the Muslims in true practices of the *din*. On the other hand, for Barelwis this was nothing new, they were just following the Islam of the *sahabas* (companions of the Prophet) and their descendants and it was the likes of the Deobandis who were innovators under the influence of the Satan-inspired Abd Ibn Wahhab.

The resolute defence of traditionalist Islam by Ahmad Riza Khan spawned a number of tracts that now almost have a canonical status for the movement. However, this defensive movement was not organized around educational institutions like the other Islamic movement of Deoband (Sanyal 1999). It was not until 1904 that the first *madrasa* was started by Ahmad Riza in Bareilly. By all accounts this *madrasa* was nothing as compared to Deoband in terms of the meticulous attention given to organization and fiscal arrangements. Moreover, it seems that the charisma of Ahmad Riza outweighed any effort to organize a movement around an educational fulcrum. Nevertheless a number of *madrasas* professing faith in Barelwi educational thought (*maktab-e-fikr*) did open with varying degrees of success in the early twentieth century. Often small and ephemeral, they were nevertheless instrumental in creating personal links between *ulama* and new leaders. The Barelwi *madrasas* too used novel methods such as a fixed syllabus, annual examinations, and specialized departments for preaching, publication, and debate (Sanyal 1999; Metcalf 1982). Moreover, they also appealed to the local public for financial donations, a method pioneered by Deoband.

MADRASAS AND THEIR PEDAGOGY

Located in the same district of Gaya and separated by a distance of almost 17 kilometres, *madrasas* Zeya ul-ulum and Ain ul-ulum appeal to very different sets of students, in the process creating two very distinct fields which they help maintain and reproduce. While the former belongs to Deobandi *maktab-e-fikr*, the latter is a Barelwi *madrasa* and considerably older. The former was founded by Maulana Muhammad Shahiruddin in 1964, while the latter has a much older pedigree, being a *khanqah* of Pir Miyan in early twentieth century to which a formal *madrasa* was added only in 1951. In both cases, the call to spread the *din* came in the form of a dream. And in both the cases, there was *hijrat* (migration) that made their callings even more pious, retracing the original *hijrat* of Prophet Muhammad from Mecca to Medina. Both dreams and migration have been used as powerful signs of legitimation throughout Islamic history.[8] While the former came from a family of religious scholars in the district of Arwal, the latter migrated from Calcutta on orders from his *pir*. Presently the Deobandi *madrasa* has 154 students and the Barelwi *madrasa* around 90, studying different courses. In both, the majority of students belong to *hifz*, the post *hifz* courses having relatively few students.[9] Most of the students of these *madrasas* are boarders. Both *madrasas* draw students from the different areas that belong to their sphere of influence. While the Deobandi *madrasa* recruits its students from villages adjacent to Gaya and neighbouring districts, the students in the Barelwi *madrasa* come from interior villages of Palamau and Garwah district of the new state of Jharkhand.[10] It was observed that the villages from where the students came to the Zeya ul-ulum were Deobandi and had a strong tradition of *tabligh*.[11] The students of Ain ul-ulum however, came from areas where Pir Miyan had had its largest number of *murids* (followers) who came for his annual *urs*,[12] thereby renewing ties with their *pir*. In both the *madrasas*, teachers mostly came from these very areas, leading one to believe that often they also acted as recruiters of students in their respective areas.[13] It was intriguing to note the presence of very few students from the neighbourhood or the immediate vicinity of the institutions themselves. On further inquiry it was revealed that within the local setting these *madrasas* command very little social and cultural respect, local Muslims accusing them of being denominational rather than religious *madrasas*. The local Muslims therefore prefer to send their wards to government schools. One informant had a whole list of complaints against one of these *madrasas*, accusing it of financial irregularities. Such close oversight being not available to far flung villages, the respect there for both these *madrasas* was much greater. Moreover, since government schools somehow still manage to function in Gaya district, parents are inclined to send their wards there, an option which in some of the villages that I visited was simply non-existent. However, mostly the reasons ascribed for sending their children to *madrasas* were couched in terms of *Islami tarbiyat* (character and discipline), accusing the government schools of teaching Hindu precepts and ideas.[14]

The pedagogy within both these *madrasas* was very similar. A normal day starts with the early morning prayer which all the students were required to attend. Some start with lessons right away: students must memorize and recite in front of their teachers. Formal classes start at eight in the morning go on until five in the evening, breaking in between for breakfast, lunch, and prayers. The students then get two free hours, after which dinner is served. Some students continue to study in the mosque while most retire for the day. Since the teachers also live within the same precincts, they are constantly available for any clarification which students want after class hours; an option not available in government schools. However, the presence of teachers within the same quarters also leads to the surveillance and control of students all the time. Control is inbuilt within *madrasa* pedagogy, often going to the extent of control over students' bodies. In both the *madrasas*, teachers were considered fathers responsible for the discipline and character of every student. The authority pattern within the household in which the father is at the centre of the authority structure is replicated within the *madrasa* setting, thus embedding such a patriarchal authority pattern deep in the minds of students.

Among the various techniques of control are corporeal punishments. The hierarchy, respect for authority and consequently an inegalitarian worldview is further reinforced by indexing of class timings with that of breakfast, lunch and dinner.[15] Often denial of food is an effective form of punishment. For children who come from families who can only afford two meals a day, this form of punishment was enough for them to comply with the 'regime' within both these *madrasas*. Controlling students was also reflected in the students' 'proper' way of talking, sitting, and even reading in front of teachers. These constituted the 'adab' within the settings of both the *madrasas* which teachers were mandated to teach the students along with knowledge. *Talim* (education), therefore, incorporated both the mind as well as the body. In both *madrasas* there is there very little writing. Mostly students read aloud a particular portion of a text in front of a teacher who then commends the student or makes corrections. Writing about medieval Cairo, Chamberlain (1992) argues that the practice of reading aloud a text reinforced the authority of the teacher, as the reading of the student had to constantly be checked against the Shaykh. As in Jewish tradition, reading aloud is considered an important aid to memorization. Such control and surveillance starts early in life of these students. As mentioned earlier, children doing *hifz* belonged to the age group of 8 to 10 years. And for three years they are supposed to do nothing but memorize the Koran, since most of the teachers were of the opinion that everything else, like learning to write, in this period constitutes a distraction. After three years the impact of such pedagogy can only be fathomed. These pedagogic techniques constitute an important part in the formation of what Bourdieu has called habitus. Habitus refers to the total ideational environment of a person. It includes beliefs and dispositions, and prefigures everything that a person may choose to do. The concept of habitus challenges the concept of free will, in that within a certain habitus at any one time, choices are not limitless. There are limited dispositions or readiness for action. A large part of the concept of habitus is that it brings attention to the fact that there are limitless options for action that a person would never think of, and therefore those options don't really count. In normal social situations, a person relies upon a large store of scripts and a large store of knowledge, which present that person with a certain picture of the world and how she or he thinks to behave within it. A person's habitus cannot be fully known to the person, as it exists largely within the realm of the unconscious and includes things as visceral as body movements and postures, and it also includes the most basic aspects of thought and knowledge about the world, including about the habitus itself (Robbins 2000). Pedagogic techniques within these *madrasas* are therefore crucial in understanding the habitus of the average student. However, the habitus as embodied personal capital can only be actualized or operationalized within the context of a given field.[16]

THE DIRECTION OF INDIAN ISLAM

Despite the doctrinal differences within these two denominations, one finds that within the setting of the *madrasa*, there is little difference in techniques of transmission. Curricular differences too are not major, with only a few books on their respective *maktab-e-fikr* being prescribed differently to students. And yet the production of denominational differences is institutionalized in both these *madrasas*. This institution is called 'debate' in the Zeya ul-ulum and 'munazra' in the Barelwi Ain ul-ulum. It is here that the students, with kits and other methods, learn the finer points of differences of their respective *maslaks*. Held once a week, this institution is also the space where the students learn oratory and the ways to counter the opponents' arguments about the correct *din*. It is here that students of Zeya ul-ulum learn that the Barelwis are *bidati* while the students of Ain ul-ulum learn that Deobandis are the masters of *fitna*, masquerading as Muslims. These students after graduation circulate their point of view in their own villages and towns. More often, they do so by founding their own *madrasa*, an option which offers them the full potential of utilizing the capital of their habitus, making the circle of reproduction complete.

However, in one sense the Deobandis have over the years, been more successful than the Barelwis. Thus the Barelwi Ain ul-ulum which was once the only *madrasa* in the locality concerned, has seen student enrolment dwindle over the years, especially those of the non-boarders. On the other hand Zeya ul-ulum, which was the first Deobandi *madrasa* founded in this locality, now boasts of three new Deobandi *madrasas* in the area, all with substantial numbers of students, Moreover, Muslims who were previously close to the Barelwi *madrasa* and *khanqah* are now very much within the Deobandi influence. Indeed, within the previously Barelwi locality, one notices marked changes in religious practice. Thus, fewer Muslims today engaged in—*maulud*, which was a prevalent and accepted ritual not very long ago. Participation in the annual *urs* has similarly declined. Moreover, customary practices among Muslims coexisted with religious practices and were accepted as inevitable part of Muslim social life.[17] The salience of customary practices sustained a liminal space shared with Hindus on certain occasions. Thus in another timeframe, but very relevant to our discussion here, the *dargahs* or shrines of holy men were visited by Hindus and Muslims and *diyas*/lamps were lit at night (Crooke 1972), a practice still observed at some shrines. Not only the Muslims but also the Hindus participated in Muharram festivals in great numbers (Crooke 1972). Similarly Holi was celebrated with equal reverence and gaiety by both Hindus and Muslims. One has only to listen to Khusrau's verses to understand the importance of Holi and Basant in both Hindu and Muslim popular culture. Moreover, 'cultural mediators' used Hindu symbols to communicate and attune Islam to the local ecological setting, as in the case of Bengal (Roy 1983). Religiously labeled as syncretic, considered to be Hindu influences on Islam, anthropologically conceptualized as folk and little traditions, these were the shared spaces that came under vehement attack from the Deoband and later were internalized by those who had hitherto considered nothing wrong with them. Indeed as one tablighi remarked, 'We were in the phase of *jahiliyya* before'.[18]

Such reasons alone cannot however explain why such large numbers of Indian Muslims have chosen one form of Islam over the other. Perhaps another important reason lies in the observation of a practising Barelwi. During informal discussion he remarked that most educated Muslims are Deobandis and this fact had already started making him uneasy about his own convictions. We have already noted that Barelwis are mostly concentrated in rural areas, are less educated and predominantly of lower castes. Thus the Deoband school has a starting social and cultural advantage over the Barelwis. Being well educated and urban they are able to wield influence over semi-literate rural Muslims. More often than not, this influence is in the secular domain, but this influence gets translated into the domain of religious beliefs also.

Migration to urban areas is a common phenomenon in India. Many Muslims do so in search of better avenues. In the urban areas they come in contact with the Deobandi Islam. They see for themselves that richer and better educated Muslims follow this variety of Islam and they start questioning their own understanding of religion. Moreover, the urban setting itself necessitates certain changes in life-style due to routine and constraints of time. The urban lifestyle demands a less ritualistic routine, which Deoband offers them. Being personally responsible to Islam is what Deoband teaches them. In contrast, in Barelwi Islam, merit is earned through the organization of *milads* and other highly ritualistic ceremonies held regularly at local shrines. This is not only time consuming but it also constitutes a financial burden. It comes as no surprise in my survey that most of the villages which had Deobandi influence were also the villages with a considerable number of male members working in big cities like Calcutta. Thus it seems that there is some kind of an affinity between the urban way of life and Deobandi Islam.

One also notices that over the years there has been a greater proliferation of Deobandi *madrasas* than Barelwi ones. Perhaps the initial lack of Barelwi enthusiasm for establishing *madrasas*, as noted above, has something to do with it. But perhaps a more credible reason seems to be the availability of funds from countries like Saudi Arabia to the Deobandi *maslak*. The Barelwis have always to depend on local support. This in turn has the effect of granting much greater visibility to the Deobandi Islam even though in real terms it would be a numerical minority as compared to the Barelwis. This visibility consequently attracts more Muslims to the Deoband way.

What then does the spread of Deobandi Islam mean for the religious future of Indian Muslims? For one, Muslims will become increasingly conscious not only of their Muslim identity, but as to what kind of Muslims they are. Deobandi Islam will be the Islam against which all other Muslim denominations will be judged; non-Deobandi groups will essentially be oppositional categories. The increasing hegemony of Deoband ideology will also mean that boundaries will be ever more sharply drawn between Hindus and Muslims, thus further limiting whatever shared space that survive. This however, is not to suggest that the Barelwi Islam is the upholder of shared practices between Hindus and Muslims, in India Indeed the *fatwa* of Ahmad Riza Khan make it plainly clear that he did not want any cooperation between Hindus and Muslims (Sanyal 1999). However, the very practice of an intercessory interpretation of Islam creates spaces in which identities become blurred. Indeed, necessitated by the dictates of the political economy, Barelwi Islam can only prosper when identities and boundaries between communities are not clear cut. This is the reason why, until some years ago, non-Muslims were allowed to pay respect and offerings at the *mazar* within the precincts of the Ain ul-ulum *madrasa*. However, now this practice has stopped altogether. Indeed under the Deobandi accusation of being influenced by Hinduism , the Barelwis are trying to portray themselves as more Muslim than the others; in the process having clearly defined boundaries of who is a Muslim and who is not; what constitutes true Islamic practice and what is *bidah*. During my interviews with the teachers of this *madrasa*, it became clear that they were no longer ready to tolerate certain practices within the precincts of the *mazar* which could give leverage to any Deobandi to call them deviants. Thus, practices which were earlier tolerated as customary were being increasingly scrutinized with in the Barelwi space of Ain ul-ulum, which has led to a marked decline in the number of people who used to visit the *rauza* of Pir Miyan earlier. Inherent within this process is its own nemesis, the Deobandization of Barelwi Islam, which not only threatens the very denominational plurality of Indian Islam but also would sharpen the boundaries between Muslims and other communities.

Among other things, the spread of Deobandi ideology could also mean the segregation of lower-class Muslim women within the household. *Mazars* and *khanqahs* offered many of these women an escape from daily drudgery. On occasions these were the places where women could pour their heart out in front of the Shaykhs or other women in similar situations. It was not without reason that women more than men populated the mausolea and indeed they continue to do so, giving Islam a feminine character. The spread of the text-based Deoband threatens this face of Islam, veiling it behind the thick walls of the household. Paradoxically though, Deoband Islam, through its reliance more on the text than on tradition, opens up spaces for educated Muslim women who want to challenge the patriarchal set up of Muslim societies. In the educated Muslim societies everywhere, women are increasingly appropriating rights given to them by Islam but denied by traditional patriarchal structures. They are increasingly seeking recourse to the scripture to legitimize their increasing social visibility in terms of opting to be working women or even challenging their inferior status within the family. This should not, however, make us oblivious to the fact that such tendencies often lead to exclusionary religious and cultural boundaries by making them more 'Islamically conscious'.

Thus we see the future that Muslim women share with Muslim society in general. The general march is definitely towards what I have termed as 'Deobandization' of Indian Islam. Linked to rural urban migration as well as to migration to Saudi Arabia, this scriptural Islam definitely has the potential of questioning the traditional Muslim social structure in India. Theoretically, by enabling every Muslim to access the sources personally, Deobandi Islam carries within itself the subversive potential of altering traditional structures based on caste, class, age, and gender. Increasing Deobandization can indeed be a liberating experience for many sections of Indian Muslims. Yet the question remains as to whether, despite this theoretical possibility, Deoband would be able to actualize its own potential. Already the popularity of the post-Deoband denomination, the Ahl-e-Hadith, points in the other direction. More scriptural than even Deoband, the Ahl-e-Hadith, with its own network of *madrasas*, is emerging as one of the most important claimants of modern Islam. Moreover, as was noted earlier in the paper, pedagogic techniques within the *madrasas* make it increasingly difficult to question entrenched authority structures. Indeed the habitus created within the *madrasas* can only become 'capital' if the existing field of power relationship is left undisturbed . As we have noted above in the case of women (but which is equally true for men) those scriptural Muslims who are challenging the existing authority structures are already endowed with other forms of social and cultural capital which their modern schooling has provided them. From an average *madrasa* student, whose capital remains tied to the existing social order, it is too much to expect change.

To conclude therefore, there is nothing inherent about the Deobandi version of Islam that is making it the dominant Islam in India. Rather it is its social location that gives it more visibility and dominance. The hegemony of scriptural Islam is, therefore, at the same time the hegemony of urban educated and religiously conscious Muslims. We have seen that Barelwi Islam, through its espousal of the intercessory role of saints, reproduces certain praxis congenial to the rural, semi-literate population. Rituals associated with this Islam are attuned to the seasonal rhythms of a peasant rural life-world. Barelwi Islam is therefore more suited to spaces where capital (in the form of *baraka*) is embodied within the personae. It is thus an Islam of a predominantly ascriptive society. On the other hand, Deoband strikes at the very roots of this form of Islam by pronouncing these practices as *bidah*. Indeed Deoband is much more about creating a different kind of capital, a form of capital which is achieved and earned through personal merit rather than through associations with holy saints. As noted above, this form of Islam is most congruent with modern city life where achievement is highly valued. Going with the trend of urbanization in India, Deoband, in seeking to make personally responsible, scriptural Muslims, would promote a very sanitary, clear-cut and in a sense positivist interpretation of Islam. The religious future of Indian Muslims is moving towards a non-ritualistic, simple, purified and homogenizing Islam which like all other social formations is partaking of an increasingly rationalizing social world. However, being intrinsically antithetical to shared traditions of living, such a rationalist, positivist Islam in bound to make boundaries between different communities still more clear cut and knowable; a possible future which should make those of us living in the present very uneasy.

NOTES

1. It must be noted that the appellations of Barelwi and Deobandi began as pejoratives. The former call themselves as the followers of Ahl-e Sunnat wa Jamaat and the latter refer to themselves as Sunnis, both contesting that they are the true followers of the Sunna of the prophet, while referring to the other as a Barelwi or a Deobandi. However, the terms have become so popular that it has been adopted as an unproblematic term for self-description, except by higher *ulama*. Thus the students and teachers whom I interviewed had no problem in referring themselves as Deobandis or Barelwis. It is with this understanding that I am using the terms here. It must be noted, however, that naming in itself is a political act; the object being to undermine the legitimacy of other denomination. Thus, the purpose of terms like Barelwi, Deobandi, and Wahhabi is to deny the 'truthfulness' of their message by pinning it down as the ideology emanating from a place (Bareilly) or an institution (Deoband)

or a person (Abd-al-Wahab) which cannot be 'true Islam' since Islam is beyond the matrix of time and space.

2. Such crystallization, however, was not divorced from the overall encounter of Indian society with colonial modernity. Indeed the eighteenth and nineteenth centuries in India are the most important for any discussion of the identity question. The categorizing and classifying zeal of the colonial state, often based on a faulty understanding of the complexity of Indian society, in many ways led to the reification of identities, aided of course by certain immanent processes.
3. While scholars have often highlighted their ideational differences, there has been a neglect of locating these differences within different kinds of social, economic or cultural capital. See for example the works of Metcalf and Ṣanyal.
4. Initially synonymous with structures, the concept of field was enhanced by Bourdieu's conception of 'cultural', 'symbolic' and 'social', as well as economic forms of capital. A field consists of relationships between different 'positions', with various types of 'resources', economic, symbolic, etc., flowing between them. There is, therefore, the economic field, the intellectual or academic field, the political field, the religious field, and so forth.
5. Reproduction entails the production of conditions of reproduction as well.
6. The study of Hadith relates to the everyday practices of Muslims. Its importance is thus most felt in times of political uncertainty and upheaval. Post 1857 Indian history was indeed one of those times. Earlier during the unstable times of the Delhi Sultanate, Hadith studies were similarly valued. However, the nineteenth-century emphasis on Hadith had much to do with the location of non-Islamic practices within the everyday life of ordinary lower caste Muslims. Sincere attempts to 'cleanse' them of all so called Hindu influences began in earnest with the popularization of Hadith studies.
7. Taking financial aid from the state would definitely have meant it being tainted by a non-Islamic source, as suggested by Metcalf. However, the alternative of popular donations was not just the search for an alternative patron; it went much farther than that. It needs to be understood that this arrangement was one of the important tools through which hegemony was asserted over the common Muslims. Moreover, having the interest of lower class Muslims tied to religious education meant that the upper class Muslims were free from internal competition. Indeed much of the scholarship on Muslims belies any understanding of the role of class and caste—as if these do not exist in Muslims societies!
8. For the uses of dreams see Nile Greens 'The religious and Cultural Roles of Dreams and Visions in Islam', *Journal of the Royal Asiatic Society*, Series 3, 13, 2003.
9. *Hifz* is the first stage of learning in a *madrasa*, which is the recitation and memorization of whole of Koran. Generally the students are very young (8-10 years) taking up to three years to finish the course and become *hafiz*. It is only after this that they do higher courses like *maulvi* or *fazilat*.

10. The districts of Palamau and Garhwa in the now new state of Jharkhand are solidly Barelwi in orientation. The villages are in the interior with considerably difficult access by road. During my interaction with the families who sent their children to the Ain ul-ulum Madrasa in Gaya, it became clear that they relied heavily on the local *ulama* who belonged to the same denomination, to tell them about the evil influences of Deobandi Islam. They believed that the Deoband school was nothing more than a *munafiq* (heretical) conspiracy to weaken Islam. It also came to notice that the majority of Muslims in this area were the followers of the Pir Miyan and thus had no hesitation in sending their wards to the *madrasa* associated with his name. On the other hand the villages from which the Zeya ul-ulum recruited its students were not so remote, being much more easily accessible and having much more communication with the urban centres. This observation, however, should not make us oblivious to the fact that the government school system was almost non-existent in both the areas of study. Families who could afford to mostly sent their children to privately run 'English medium' schools and these included some *madrasa* trustees.
11. The faith movement started by Maulana Muhammad Ilyas was meant to strengthen the inner boundaries of the community. An offshoot of the Deobandi school, tabligh means spreading *dawa* through persuasion and perseverance.

    The Tablighis move within the Muslims telling them about *namaz* and other *akayad* as well as the correct way to do it. Closely related to the Deobandis, the latters' *madrasas* serve as effective networks through which they operate.
12. *Urs* literally means marriage of the *pir* with the Almighty; the celebrations and *jiyarat* taking place on the day this great union happened, i.e. on the day of his death.
13. In one of my informal conversations, I was told that a teacher who brought more students to *madrasas* had a much higher status than the others, since he was 'preparing the army of deen'.
14. I recall that in one these *madrasas*, once a father came with his son to get him admitted in the *madrasa*. On being asked what his son did before coming here, he answered that he was going to a government school. Later on I inquired what made him decide in favour of a *madrasa* rather than the school. His simple answer was that the school used to teach him 'vande mataram' every morning. However, upon further inquiries, I came to know that he did not know the meaning of 'vande mataram' except for the fact that it was anti-Islamic.
15. Theoretically Islam is considered as a religion which gives thrust to egalitarianism. Thus the institution of *namaz* is a great leveling space wherein ascriptive distinctions of caste and status gives way to achieved marks of distinction based on piety. However, the point cannot be stressed too much. Often at local levels, worldly distinctions do find their way within the space of mosques also. Moreover, within the setting of *madrasas*, wherein majority

of the students are from the same class location and more or less comparable caste statuses, *namaz* cannot have such an egalitarian potential as often thought. Other disciplinary techniques discussed in the text have much more of influence since they constitute the 'operative regime' within the *madrasa* of which *namaz* is just one part.

16. For an explanation of the concept of field see note 4, above. Here I do not suggest that there are no objective conditions of reproduction of *madrasa* education in India. What is being highlighted here is the role of *madrasas* themselves in sustaining and creating its own conditions of reproduction.
17. For legal legitimacy of Muslim customary practices even within Islamic law, see Micahel Anderson, *Islamic Law and Colonial Encounter*, 1993.
18. *Jahiliyya*/ignorance denotes the pre-Islamic practices of Arabia which included such acts as idolatory, etc.

REFERENCES

Ahmad, Imtiaz, 1983, *Modernization and Social Change Among Muslims in India*, Delhi: Manohar.

Bourdieu, Pierre, 1985, 'The Genesis of the Concepts of "Habitus" and "Field", *Sociocriticism* 1(2), 11-24.

———, 1986, 'From Rules to Strategies: an Interview with Pierre Bourdieu', *Cultural Anthropology* 1(1), 110-20.

———, 1967, 'Systems of Education and Systems of Thought', *International Social Science Journal* 19(3), 338-58.

Berkey, Jonathan, 1992, *The Transmission of Knowledge in Medieval Cairo: A Social History of Islamic Education*, Princeton: Princeton, University Press.

Chamberlain, Michael, 1997, 'The Production of Knowledge and the Reproduction of the Ayan in Medieval Damascus', in Marc Gaborieau and Nicole Grandin (eds), *Madrasa: La Transmission du Savoir Dans le Monde Musulman*, Paris.

Crooke, William, 1972, *Islam in India: The Customs of the Muslmans of India*, Delhi: Oxford University Press.

Eickelman, Dale F., 1992, *Knowledge and Power in Morocco: The Education of a Twentieth-Century Notable*, Princeton: Princeton University Press.

Freitag, Sandra, 1989, *Collective Action and Community: Public Arenas and the Emergence of Communalism in North India*, Berkeley: University of California Press.

Foucault, 1980, *Power/Knowledge: Selected Interviews and Other Writings, 1972-77*, edited and translated by Colin Gordon, Harvester, Sussex.

Geertz, Clifford, 1971, *Islam Observed: Religious Developments in Morocco and Indonesia*, Chicago: University of Chicago Press.

Green, Nile, 2003, 'The Religious and Cultural Roles of Dreams and Visions in Islam', *Journal of the Royal Asiatic Society*, Series 3, 13, 3.

Malik, Jamal, 1998, *Colonization of Islam: Dissolution of Traditional Institutions in Pakistan*, Delhi: Manohar.

Metcalf, Barbra Daly, 1982, *Islamic Revival in British India:Deoband; 1860-1900*, Princeton: Princeton University Press.

Nizami, K.A., 1996, 'Development of Muslim Educational System in Medieval India, *Islamic Culture*, October.

Robinson, Francis, 1993, 'Technology and Religious Change: Islam and the Impact of Print', *Modern Asian Studies*, 14: 3.

Robbins, Derek, 2000, *Bourdieu and Culture*, Delhi: Sage.

Roy, Asim, 1983, *Islamic Syncrestic Tradition in Bengal*, Princeton: Princeton University Press.

Sanyal, Usha, 1999, *Devotional Islam and Politics in British India: Ahmad Riza Khan and his Movement, 1870-1920*, Delhi: Oxford University Press.

Sufi, G.M.D., 1941, *Al-Minhaj: Being the Evolution of Curriculum in the Muslim Educational Institutions of India*, Idarah-i-Adabiyat-i-Delhi, Delhi.

Quraishi, M.F., 1980, *History of Darul al Ulum Deoband*, vol. 1, Ahmedabad: Sahitya Mudranalaya.

Zaman, Muhammad Qasim, 2002, *The Ulama in Contemporary Islam: Custodians of Change*, Princeton: Princeton University Press.

9

The Bajrang Dal: The New Hindu Nationalist Brigade

SMITA GUPTA AND CHRISTOPHE JAFFRELOT

Since the nineteenth century Islam and Christianity have been the targets of Hindu militant ideologues. In Punjab, as early as the 1870s the Arya Samaj confronted these two religions through the Shuddhi movement which was intended to counter the proselytizing activities of Christian and Muslim missionaries. Soon after, waves of communal tension and riots prepared the ground for the development of Hindu nationalist organizations. The anti-cow slaughter movement set the stage for the creation of the Hindu Mahasabha in 1915, and reactions to the Khilafat movement did the same ten years later for the RSS, an organization that has become the matrix of a larger network of Hindutva oriented groups, the 'Sangh Parivar'.

Shortly after its creation in 1925, the Rashtriya Swayamsevak Sangh (RSS) or the National Volunteer Corps acquired attributes characteristic of contemporary fascist-leaning groups in Europe. From these it partly drew its inspiration, in terms of uniforms, techniques of group discipline ranging from daily calisthenics in small groups to parades to the beat of drums, and lessons in the use of weapons. The RSS founder, K.B. Hedgewar, had assigned the organization the primary mission of defending the Hindu community against Muslim aggression, real or imagined. To some extent, the RSS was founded as a self-defence militia,[1] hence the paramilitary overtone.

However, this paramilitary style went together with the promotion of a system of quietist values, especially after the British compelled the movement to give up the use of firearms in the 1940s.[2] But RSS leaders had right from the beginning resorted to alternate techniques that they presented as a training in Karma Yoga – or the Yoga of action. The cadres of the organization, indeed, had to develop an ascetic way of life which obliged them to renounce both family and career and devote themselves entirely to the cause.[3] The prestige of this cause and renunciation for it—especially by the elite pracharaks or preachers—were expected to attract new members to the movement. Leaders brought their followers together everyday at sunrise and/or sunset to their local *shakhas* (branches) for ideological training sessions and physical exercise that often took the form of games calculated to create a sense of unity across caste and class differences. The pracharaks were supposed to instil in the novices Hindu *samskars* or noble values, and the key elements of the personal discipline that they must strive for.

This emphasis on discipline and austerity, however, in no way ruled out the use of violence. RSS members were as active in anti-Muslim violence in the riots of the 1920s, as they were in the Partition massacres. But they were not specially trained to use firearms and, interestingly, were reluctant to use their strike force against Hindus, unless they were Communists. The RSS hoped to spread its message through example, not force; it wished to attract Hindus to the *shakhas* to reshape their minds, not bludgeon them into adopting its worldview.

Things changed in the 1990s with the rise of the Bajrang Dal, the new armed wing of Hindu nationalism. Not only was this militia trained for far more systematic violence than that practised by the RSS, its self-appointed role as the new cultural police saw it using violence against Hindus as well.

THE BAJRANG DAL, BY-PRODUCT OF THE AYODHYA MOVEMENT AND THE PLEBEIANIZATION OF THE SANGH PARIVAR

The Bajrang Dal is not a direct creation of the RSS but the offshoot of a third party, the Vishva Hindu Parishad (VHP) or Universal Hindu Association. Founded in 1964 by RSS leaders, this organization was assigned the task of federating the various Hindu sects and mobilizing the Hindu masses by exploiting emotive religious issues and symbols. Movements to enforce a ban on the slaughter of cows and for the construction of a Ram Temple in Ayodhya[4] were ideal vehicles for mass mobilization and, in the process, the VHP developed a plebeian and populist style.

Subsidiary of the VHP

In the spring of 1984 the VHP passed an official resolution demanding restoration of the site in Ayodhya, where the 400 year-old Babri Masjid stood, to the Hindus so that they could build a temple devoted to the Hindu god, Ram. Soon thereafter it founded the Bajrang Dal. The new organization's name indicated that the VHP had created an armed wing for itself: *bajrang*, meaning 'strong', is associated with, Hanuman—sometimes also referred to as Bajrang Bali—who is generally depicted brandishing a club.[5] In mythology Hanuman is dedicated to Ram, and it is before an image of Hanuman that RSS members, traditionally, pledge themselves—'body, heart and money'—to their organization.

The Bajrang Dal was created 'with the temporary and localized objective of awakening youth of Uttar Pradesh and get their involvement in the Ramjanmabhoomi movement'—according to the VHP's official website—to protect the Ram-Janaki *Rath Yatras*, the campaign to create public opinion for the construction of the Ram Temple.[6] If that was the primary objective behind the creation of the Bajrang Dal, VHP functionary Rukun Singh Payal provides a subsidiary reason: after 1984 Pakistan's Inter Services Intelligence became more active in India and trained terrorists to operate in Punjab and Kashmir.[7] 'It was important', said Payal, 'to have an organization that could protect Indian culture from these Muslims.'

The Bajrang Dal cut its teeth protecting the Ram-Janaki *Yatras* in 1984, and the *shilanyas* or foundation ceremony for the Ram Temple in 1989 took place in Ayodhya amidst a belligerent show of strength by its members. They re-surfaced in 1990, in saffron bandanas and shirts, carrying banners, as the motorcycle-borne outriders for the *Rath Yatra* of the then BJP President, L.K. Advani. This journey went from Somnath in the western province of Gujarat to Ayodhya. Advani was arrested in Bihar, but the journey catapulted the BJP to political centrestage. Then, on 6 December 1992, the organization saw 'action' at the Babri Masjid—its members spearheaded the destruction of the mosque. Finally, the Bajrang Dal has also been involved in riots, instigating Hindus against Muslims, all over India, from Madhya Pradesh to Gujarat. In the wake of the demolition of the Babri Masjid, Bajrang Dal members played, for instance, a key role in the riots in Bhopal which left 161 dead—most of them Muslims. One of the protagonists in the riot recalls, 'We received the order from the Sangh Parivar not to go to Ayodhya [6 December 1992] because there was the premonition [*purvabhas*] that a fight might happen here [in Bhopal]. Therefore, a few people stayed here on alert. . . . We took part in the riot. Muslim people killed policemen and looted the people. Therefore we took part and then scared the Muslims away.'

The Bajrang Dal was declared illegal by the Congress government headed by P.V. Narasimha Rao, as was the RSS and the VHP, soon after the demolition of the Babri Masjid. However, the ban was lifted in 1993. But it could not revert to its earlier activities immediately as the RSS and the rest of the Sangh Parivar—starting with the BJP—wanted to have a better grip over the organization that had resisted any form of discipline during the Ayodhya movement.

On 11 July 1993, the Bajrang Dal which, at that time, existed legally only in Uttar Pradesh, became the nationwide organization officially designated as the youth wing of the VHP. It acquired a uniform—blue shorts, a white shirt and a rust-coloured scarf—and a handbook for trainers at its 350-odd camps run all over India. In the preface to this little book written in Sanskritized Hindi, Acharya Giriraj Kishore, second in command of the VHP, paid tribute to the heroes of 6 December 1992:

> On that day the force of youth, escaping its leaders, and despite their repeated injunctions, went forward to accomplish its mission—mission aimed to erase the shameful scar [that was, for him, the Babri Masjid]. . . . Whether it is an individual or a nation, the entire society or an organization, only one who knows discipline can achieve success, awareness and excellence. Without discipline, there can be no success. Discipline comes from training and exercise. And if a disciplined man is also brave, what more can you ask for?

Kishore's emphasis on discipline was translated in the 1990s into Bajrang Dal training camps. Though they did not number 350, the figure claimed in 1994, they were many, and, more importantly, different from those run by the RSS.

The first Bajrang Dal chief in 1984, Vinay Katiyar, was a former RSS pracharak: the fact that he belonged to the backward Kurmi caste from Uttar Pradesh—rather than an upper caste—hinted at the more plebeian nature of the Bajrang Dal, as well as the desire of the Sangh Parivar, with its upper-caste base and mindset, to now enlarge its constituency. But the three Bajrang Dal chiefs who followed Katiyar were all upper caste—Jaibhan Pawaiya was a Rajput, Surendra Jain a Bania, and now Prakash Sharma, a Brahmin. All three are university-educated and, on the surface, polished and articulate, a contrast to Katiyar, who though educated has a rough exterior and a criminal record to boot. But the rank and file of the organization remains mixed. Bajrang Dal members we met on fieldwork were for the most part unemployed or involved in part time (and half legal activities like lotteries). They were ready to be mobilized at any time to do the dirty work, for they were lawless and fearless. Katiyar, in fact, declared in an interview, 'Might is the only law I understand. Nothing else matters to me. In India it is a war-like situation as between Rama and Ravana'.[8]

The Bajrang Dal and Violence and the Other

For the RSS and its affiliates, violence is not new. As far back as in 1927, RSS volunteers were involved in a riot during the procession of Mahalakshmi, the goddess of prosperity. But over the years, as its family expanded, ambitions grew, and the party moved closer to political power, the RSS realized the importance of insulating itself and some of its affiliates, such as the BJP, from accusations of breaking the law. After all, the RSS has been banned three times since Independence—in 1948 after Mahatma Gandhi's assassination; in 1975, after the then Prime Minister Indira Gandhi imposed Emergency and, in 1993, after the destruction of the Babri Masjid.

After facing a third ban, the RSS decided it needed an organization to take care of the rough action so that its other affiliates could remain law-abiding. For the BJP, which was then hoping to come to power, this was particularly useful: it could dissociate itself, if needed, from the more heinous of the Bajrang Dal's crimes while deriving political advantage from the communal polarization that would result from its activities.

So, in 1993, the Bajrang Dal became the youth wing of the VHP officially and was brought under the latter's control, even though it did not claim to have the same ethos as the RSS nor the same degree of discipline. Its members did not meet daily like the swayamsevaks in the RSS *shakhas*; they simply took part in training camps where they were taught 'how to be bold'.[9] Till 1993, the Bajrang Dal, an army of 'lumpen elements', did not even sport a uniform. Even today, the uniform has not particularly caught on: Bajrang Dal members prefer to recognize each another by saffron-coloured headbands emblazoned with 'Ram'.

If the Bajrang Dal being a subsidiary of the VHP distances it from the RSS, this is just a thin cover. Not only do members of the RSS family move from one organization to another, they also work on projects together. For instance, Katiyar became an RSS pracharak in 1972, then a functionary of the Akhil Bharatiya Vidyarthi Parishad, the student union of the Sangh Parivar, before he became the founder president of the Bajrang Dal in 1984. Later, he graduated to the BJP and was the MP from Faizabad, the constituency where Ayodhya is located.

Structurally, the Bajrang Dal works in close conjunction with the VHP. Surendra Jain, a former Bajrang Dal president and currently the VHP all-India secretary in charge of the Bajrang Dal, explained: 'It is a father-son relationship and the VHP is the chief patron of the Bajrang Dal—there is total co-ordination and consultation between the two.'[10] Or as Katiyar put it, 'In 1993, when it officially became the VHP's youth wing, it was placed under the latter's sanrakshan and marg darshan' (or protection and guidance).[11] Functionally, this means that at the village, district, state, and central level, the two key functionaries, the president and convenor, are from the VHP and Bajrang Dal respectively. Payal, the VHP president of Uttar Pradesh's Bulandshahr district, put it succinctly, 'The VHP decides, the Bajrang Dal implements'.[12]

The Bajrang Dal and the VHP are officially and emotionally linked, but the former's activities are also often undertaken in conjunction with other fraternal RSS outfits. For instance, it provides the muscle for the Vanvasi Kalyan Ashram which works in tribal areas to prevent religious conversions to Christianity, and for the ABVP and BJP during elections, literally providing the cutting edge of their joint ventures.

While Bajrang Dal leaders uniformly deny any connection with violence, an explanation provided by its current president, Prakash Sharma, of the symbolism of Hanuman as the organization's presiding deity is revealing:

> Hanuman, as you know, could change his shape. He could assume the form of a fly to elude Surasa the giant. He could make himself strong enough to carry on his shoulders a mountain on which the lifesaving (chiranjivi) plant grew. He could jump across the Palk Straits to Lanka, and help Ram build a bridge to Lanka in five days, and when Ravan had his tail set on fire, he just lengthened it and set Lanka ablaze. Similarly, depending on the circumstances, and the VHP's Programmes and evolving worldviews to protect our religion, culture and nation, the Bajrang Dal can play different roles. Just as Hanuman was always ready to help Ram in times of emergency, so the Bajrang Dal is in constant readiness to assist the VHP and the sadhus. The youth power of the Bajrang Dal can be mobilised at any time for conflict situations.[13]

In the same spirit, the VHP's official website says, 'The Bajrang Dal has proved as a security ring of Hindu society. Whenever there is an attack on Hindu Society, Faith and Religion, the workers of Bajrang Dal come forward to their rescue.'[14]

Over the years, the Bajrang Dal has shifted focus from mobilizing support for the Ram temple to what Sharma describes as 'problem solving'.[15] The problems have been identified as terrorism in Jammu and Kashmir, the influx of refugees from Bangladesh referred to as 'infiltration', and conversions to Christianity. It also helps government agencies to enforce laws banning cow slaughter. If government agencies don't act against those whom the Bajrang Dal has identified as an ISI agent or involved in the slaughter of cows, then 'we just uproot them from society ourselves', says Payal.[16]

In some areas, the Bajrang Dal operates secretly: Jain admits that the organization has members in Hindu-dominated villages in Jammu, Poonch, Doda and Rajouri who 'work undercover'. He refuses to name the villages or persons as that would 'endanger their safety' but says these Bajrang Dal activists have penetrated the government-sponsored village safety committees set up to protect villagers from terrorism without fellow committee members knowing anything about their allegiance to the Bajrang Dal.[17] VHP international general secretary Praveen Togadia told a press conference in Lucknow on 26 March

2000 that the VHP and Bajrang Dal had decided to set up private armies by deploying their activists in villages along the borders in Kashmir, the north-east, Punjab, Rajasthan, and Gujarat. These volunteers of the People's Defence Committee, he said, were being trained in Vrindavan in Uttar Pradesh to help people fight ISI-spawned terrorism.

Over the years, the Bajrang Dal has grown: in 2001, its official strength stood at 1.25 million, according to Sharma, who adds that a massive membership drive planned between September and November 2004 should double that figure.[18] It may not be that hard: Payal, VHP president of Bulandshahr district in Uttar Pradesh, for instance, says there are 15,000 Bajrang Dal activists in his district alone—which would mean that UP could currently have about 500,000 members. The problem with assessing the Bajrang Dal's numerical strength is that the cadres of the various RSS organizations move from time to time from one to the other.

The Making of a Bajrang Dal Volunteer

According to Jain, the training camps started in 1984 were held in every state by 1993. For the 250-odd camps each year, there is a set syllabus, Jain says, 'to cater to intellectual and physical growth'.[19] For intellectual growth, there is the *baudhik*, the discourse, in which new recruits are taught the 'dangers of globalization, the cultural attacks on Hinduism, the various religions in the world, the problems confronting Hindu society, and the real history of India'. The recruits are also taught yoga, meditation, and martial arts—a mixture of judo, karate and ju-jitsu 'specially created by the Bajrang Dal'. Sharma insists that all this is for self-defence and to 'defend society and the social fabric against abductors and molesters of women, thieves, Pakistan's Inter Services Intelligence agents, and Bangladeshi infiltrators'—all euphemisms for Muslims. Then he adds, 'I don't know why this question is repeatedly asked of us—after all, Boy Scouts are given arms training. It helps improve self-esteem and confidence.'[20]

Each year, roughly 250 to 300 activists are prepared for the role of Bajrang Dal 'missionaries'. As simultaneously educationists and ambassadors for the VHP and Bajrang Dal, Jain says, they are expected to strengthen the organization, recruit new members, and ensure that the programmes are implemented effectively.[21] At least once a week, in every block of the country where the Bajrang Dal exists, members meet either for group worship, to read the Hanuman chalisa, or to discuss the social and political situation in the country. Organizational meetings are held regularly—once a week in every block, once a fortnight in every district, once in three months in each province and twice- and sometimes three times a year at the all-India level.

Five times a year, the Bajrang Dal observes special festivals. In April Hanuman Jayanti is celebrated as Balupasana Diwas or Worship of Strength Day; next comes Valmiki Diwas[22] when a fresh resolve is taken to establish *samajik samrasta*. In the RSS lexicon, *samajik samrasta* or social harmony is a euphemism for the acceptance of the caste hierarchy by those on its lower rungs, and is essentially aimed against any sort of positive discrimination. Then on 14 August, All-India Memorial Day, members pledge to strengthen the Bajrang Dal, with the goal of establishing an Akhand Bharat or an Undivided India. 14 August or Pakistan's Independence Day, rather than 15 August, India's Independence Day, has been chosen for this annual pledge to emphasize the view that Muslims, not Hindus, divided India. This is followed by Martyrs' Day, on 2 November the day in 1991 when Bajrang Dal workers clashed with the then UP administration as they made their first assault on the Babri Masjid, climaxing on National Glory Day, commemorating 6 December 1992 when the mosque was razed to the ground.

The training at the Bajrang Dal camps is geared to help new recruits internalize the three key elements of the organization's mandate, says Sharma.

> *Suraksha* or security lays emphasis on making Hindu society strong, learning to protect ourselves, our mothers and sisters, our temples and the nation, with the area of operation ranging from our immediate neighbourhood to the border. Then comes *sewa* or service—by providing health, educational, developmental and relief facilities, we help in the task of social harmony to counter the vote bank politics of the pseudo-secular parties. Finally there is *samskar* or culture—the recruits must absorb the ideology of the organization, and follow its rules and be bound by its discipline.[23]

Arming Bajrang Dal volunteers and readying them for battle is the next step: the organization has, appropriately, chosen the *trishul* or trident as its main weapon, which it distributes among its members at special convocation ceremonies: Jain claims that 500,000 have been distributed since 1986.[24] The pledge taken by the chosen ones is: 'With God as my witness, I pledge I will always be ready to rise to the defence of my country, religion and society while promising that I will not misuse this trishul.' The Bajrang Dal likes to describe the trident as a harmless religious symbol of Shiva, whose incarnation is Hanuman. But these are 10.16 cm-long, sharp-edged, instruments capable of maiming and killing, cleverly camouflaged Rampuri knives, which, like Sikh daggers are exempt from the provisions of the Indian Arms Act.

The *trishuls* are lethal enough, and *trishul* distribution ceremonies have hit the headlines often. But from 1996, Bajrang Dal workers have also been given training in firearms, a fact that has been widely reported. Though the training has been given with airguns, Bajrang Dal functionaries say that those who excel will graduate to more sophisticated guns. As part of extremely rigorous physical conditioning, Bajrang Dal militants also practise judo and karate, learn to climb ropes, go through circles of fire, and are trained in the use of rifles and pistols. This echoes the training Islamists in Osama bin Laden's organization undergo as shown in TV reports of the Al Qaeda camps in Afghanistan before the fall of the Taliban. A camp head in Ahmedabad explained in one of the rare interviews published on the subject: 'The jehadis have no fear of death. They learn this at an early age in the madarsas. We must also end our fear of death.'[25] All available interviews on the subject show that the physical training that activists undergo aims to counter a perceived rise in Muslim threats due to the appearance of suicide attacks in the region—in Jammu and Kashmir to begin with—something that led Shiv Sena leader Bal Thackeray to talk of setting up Hindu 'suicide squads'.

Similarly, the Bajrang Dal's 'Hindu proselytization' seeks to duplicate the tactics used by Christian and Muslim missionaries in India.[26] Here too Hindu nationalists try to imitate the methods of those they perceive as threats to their identity and survival. Occasionally, the process results in a highly revealing mental transposition, observed among some Bajrang Dal leaders, of the situation prevailing in Israel.

At a camp in Ayodhya in 2000, one of them explained that Hindu nationalists draw their inspiration from Israel, as that country tries to train all its citizens to defend themselves in a hostile environment. One of the activists declares: 'India's [situation is] even worse. Israel has threat only from outsiders while India faces threat from even those inhabiting it'.[27] Another Bajrang Dal member at this camp added, 'I am of the secret service of Bajrang Dal. Israel's Mossad is my inspiration'.

Simultaneously, the Durga Vahini or Durga brigade appeared in the 1990s to band together Hindu nationalism's female 'youth'. This organization too stresses defence—especially self-defence—of young Hindu women, including training in the use of firearms.[28] It also continues the tradition started by the Rashtra Sevika Samiti, a women's organization founded in 1936 alongside the RSS, whose primary objective was to train Hindu women in self-defence techniques to enable them to resist Muslim aggressors.[29]

THE BAJRANG DAL AND VIOLENCE AGAINST CHRISTIANS, MUSLIMS . . . AND HINDUS

Targeting the Minorities

The VHP was created in 1964 directly to counter a perceived threat from Christianity that the Hindu nationalists took to be the most proselytizing religion in India. The imagined 'enemy's' strength was seen to come from the organizational solidity and transnational character of this creed. To counter such an adversary, therefore, it was necessary to equip Hindus with a centralized international ecclesiastical body of their own.

'The declared object of Christianity is to turn the whole world into Christendom—as that of Islam is to make it "Pak",' warned Shiv Shankar Apte, who had joined the RSS in 1939 and was to become the first VHP chief. 'It is therefore necessary in this age of competition and conflict to think of, and organize, the Hindu world, to save itself from (their) evil eyes.' Fifty nine years after Apte made this declaration, the objective and ideology remains unchanged, even if there have been innovations in methods of mobilization.

Through the 1980s and 1990s, the RSS family carried on its hate campaign against the religious minorities, demonizing in particular the Muslims and portraying them as either drug mafiosi, terrorists, or agents of Pakistan. But after Congress party president—now India's ruling Congress-led United Progressive Alliance chairperson—Sonia Gandhi joined active politics in 1998, an event that coincided with the BJP-led coalition coming to power at the Centre, the attacks on Christians escalated. Christian missionaries in tribal areas were targeted and the twin weapons of persuasion and coercion were used to compel newly converted Christian tribals to 'return' to the Hindu fold where, incidentally, they were never accepted.

In an interview in 1998, Katiyar, asked whether Christians were being targeted because of Sonia Gandhi's entry into politics, gave it his own spin: 'It is . . . the other way around. Christians have become aggressive ever since Sonia Gandhi took over as Congress president. Christians feel they have the perfect protector . . . to convert Hindus.' If Sonia Gandhi's appearance was a fresh impetus for the interest in Christians, another reason was that though the reorganization of the Bajrang Dal begun in 1993 had not diverted it from its original mission, Ayodhya, the fact that the issue had been put on the backburner by the BJP-led NDA government meant it needed a new task.

Missionaries had been a traditional Hindu nationalist target, particularly for the VHP, which was created on the occasion of a visit from the Pope to India to oppose his proselytizing activities. The Bajrang Dal attacked not only missionaries but also the faithful with unprecedented violence. Its hate campaign against Christians climaxed when some of its members led by Dara Singh burnt to death Australian missionary Graham Staines—who had been working among leprosy patients since 1965—and his sons, Philip, 9, and Timothy, 6 while they slept overnight in a jeep in Orissa's Keonjhar district on 22-23 January 1999.

As condemnation poured in from all over India and abroad, the BJP leadership and the RSS sought to distance themselves from the crime. The usual ambivalence was employed. The then Prime Minister A.B. Vajpayee, while saying the guilty would be punished, declared it was time to debate the issue of religious conversions. Taking the cue from him, Katiyar accused Orissa's Congress government of 'framing' the organization to camouflage its 'failings on the law and order front', while VHP working president, Ashok Singhal, claimed Dara Singh was not connected with the Bajrang Dal. The killing of Catholic priest Arul Das and the destruction of churches in Phulbani district followed the murder of Staines and his sons.

Simultaneously in 1998, Gujarat saw a series of attacks on Christian institutions and missionaries in remote areas as well as in cities such as Rajkot and Ahmedabad. In 1998, for instance, a gang led by VHP functionary Niraj Jain and others belonging to both the VHP and Bajrang Dal attacked a five-day national convention of Christians in Vadodara. Around Christmas that year, VHP leaders Janubhai Pawar and Swami Aseemanand led a group that destroyed seventeen churches in south Gujarat's Dangs district.[30]

In December 2003, a new BJP government led by Vasundhara Raje took charge in Rajasthan and provided the impetus for the rapid growth of Hindutva organizations such as the Bajrang Dal, while absorbing into the state machinery persons ideologically sworn to the RSS worldview. On 8 January 2004, tribal development minister Kanak Mal Katara threatened to issue a government order to exclude tribal people converted to Christianity from constitutionally provided reservation benefits. No state government is empowered to formally change the criteria for the scheduled tribe category, but reports from the state indicate that government departments at the district level have been instructed to exclude Christian tribals from reservation benefits.

A visit to Banswara in December 2003 by VHP chief Ashok Singhal—who blessed the birth of the Bajrang Dal—followed by a VHP-Vanvasi Kalyan Ashram camp from 25 December 2003 to 1 January, 2004 focused RSS attention on Banswara and Udaipur. In the months since, nuns were intimidated, tribal children forced to stop attending missionary schools, and locals compelled to stay away from church-sponsored maternal and child health care camps. On 25 December 2003 the Vanvasi Kalyan Parishad launched its campaign to reach more than 100,000 tribal persons and Dalits by distributing lockets of Hanuman or Shiva to compete with the crosses local nuns and Christians wear, as well as to make it easy to target those not wearing the Hindu lockets. This is a pattern followed in the Madhya Pradesh tribal districts as well.

Violence against Muslims

The favourite target of the Bajrang Dal and other Hindutva organizations has been Muslims, partly because of Partition, the myth of the fifth column, and the Kashmir issue. In recent years, the VHP-Bajrang Dal has combined *trishul* distribution and other so-called religious programmes in Rajasthan, Madhya Pradesh, Gujarat, and Maharashtra with a violent anti-minority rhetoric which has led to an increase in physical assaults on Muslims. The terrorist attack at the World Trade Center in New York on 11 September 2001 and the subsequent bombing of Afghanistan coincided with the banning of the Students' Islamic Movement of India by the Indian government. The Bajrang Dal now had international examples to bolster its stereotyping of Muslims as terrorists. Indeed, a Congress government in Rajasthan at the time was forced to ban a pamphlet entitled, 'The Bajrang Dal's volunteers are defending the nation with swords in their hands and a storm brewing in their hearts'.

The brazen attempts by the VHP and the Bajrang Dal—as well as some others such as the Shiv Sena—to form private Hindu armies violates the Indian Constitution, but the BJP-led government at the Centre (1998-2004) prevented action being taken against them. Only the CPI (M) and the Congress demanded a curb on these activities: on 21 January 2000, the Left Front government in Kerala issued an ordinance imposing strict restrictions on the martial training imparted at RSS camps. The following year, Madhya Pradesh and Rajasthan asked the union government to ban the Bajrang Dal, but to no avail.[31] Both states had been targeted by the Hindu right wing; both had Congress leaders defeated in December 2003 by the BJP in state elections.

In July 2001 Digvijay Singh of Madhya Pradesh wrote to the then union Home Minister, L.K. Advani, giving a chronological account of the Bajrang Dal's activities in his state, stressing that 'they were aimed at inciting members of other communities, specially the Muslims and Christians'. In August 2001, Ashok Gehlot the Chief Minister of Rajasthan wrote to the then Prime Minister Atal Behari Vajpayee: 'The language and tone of the proclamations made by Bajrang Dal in its public meetings sharply reflect the non-secular and fundamentalist nature of its ideology which will undoubtedly lead to disruption of peace and tranquillity of our country . . . [This] distribution [of *trishuls*] has all the potential of creating a dangerous situation in the country.' Offering to send a sample of the trishuls to Vajpayee, Gehlot said they were crafted to escape the provisions of the law but could be used as weapons against innocent people. He warned Vajpayee, 'We have examples elsewhere in the world where the forces which encouraged terrorist groups have themselves had to face attacks from the same groups. If the government is lax in dealing with organizations such as the Bajrang Dal, there may come a time when these very organizations will prove to be a threat and danger to your party, the BJP itself, and the whole country.'

What happened in Gujarat was the result of concerted work over the years by the RSS family, including the Bajrang Dal, VHP and Vanvasi Kalyan Ashram. In August 2000, terrorists—believed to be trained by Pakistan's ISI—shot down 33 Hindu pilgrims in Kashmir and, in the ensuing cross-fire with security forces, another 100 died. On 1 August VHP leader Pravin Togadia announced at a press conference in Ahmedabad, 'We will give a fitting reply to these killings here in Gujarat.' For the next ten days, VHP and Bajrang Dal activists, led by elected BJP representatives, destroyed Rs. 150 million worth of Muslim property across several cities in Gujarat.

This was not all: Muslims were forced into ghettos. For instance, on 8 February 2000, VHP and elected BJP municipal officials led a gang of young men and ransacked the homes of Muslims who had moved into Paldi, a posh and predominantly Hindu-inhabited locality in Ahmedabad. Similarly, in late 2001, 550 Muslims from Chanasma in Patan district were forced to migrate to Patan city after many of their fellow villagers were killed, traditional Waqf Board-owned *dargah* land called Navgajapir was forcibly taken over by the Bajrang Dal, and the Navgajapir *dargah* replaced by a Hindu temple. The Ahmedabad-based Council for Social Justice, which submitted its report on the incident in September 2001, added that Bajrang Dal volunteers had also surrounded Indiranagar's Muslim homes sword in hand, hurling violent threats at the Muslim women.

Not content with forcing Muslims out of Hindu-dominated localities, the Hindutva organizations started printing hate pamphlets to urge social and economic boycott of Muslims. One such pamphlet circulated in Gujarat in 2002, signed by a 'true Hindu patriot', exhorted readers:

The only solution is financial boycott. Anti-national elements are using the money they earn with our co-operation to weaken us. They buy arms and molest our sisters and daughters. Come, let us resolve:/I will not buy anything from any Muslim shopkeeper./I will not sell my goods to these elements./Neither use these traitors' hotels or garages/I will give my car to Hindus' garages only./From a needle to gold, do not buy anything made by a Muslim nor sell anything made by us to them./Boycott movies casting Muslim heroes/heroines. Banish films of traitor producers./ Never work in Muslims' offices and do not employ Muslims.

The Gujarat government's plans for an ethnic cleansing drive included a selective census of Christians and Muslims; a selective census of the scheduled castes and tribes to ascertain 'when they converted to Islam or Christianity'; and a directive to the state police to 'investigate' every case of inter-religious marriage. This last followed spurious propaganda by the RSS-VHP-Bajrang Dal combine that Muslims were abducting and marrying Hindu girls in order to convert them to Islam, while Christians were guilty of forced conversion.

All this had an impact on civil society: during the genocide in February/March 2002, ordinary men and women participated in the violence, along with the Bajrang Dal and other Rightwing Hindu organizations. During the provincial elections, most Hindu voters across the state justified the genocide directly and indirectly.

What happened in Gujarat in 2002 was unprecedented. On 27 February 2002, the setting on fire of coach S-6 of the Sabarmati Express carrying a trainload of supporters and sympathizers of the Ram Temple movement at Godhra, resulting in 58 deaths sparked off a violent anti-Muslim backlash. This despite the fact that police investigations revealed it was not 'pre-planned' by Muslims as alleged by Hindutva forces from the chief minister to the lowliest Bajrang Dal worker.

The Godhra carnage triggered off anti-Muslim violence in 16 of Gujarat's 24 districts with the (not so) passive support of the BJP state government led by Narendra Modi. The attacks were meticulously planned as Muslim homes, shops and factories—listed in advance—were systematically targeted. Indeed, the inhumanity and barbarism, which included gang-rapes of women, the killing of children and the burning alive of whole families, has few parallels in Indian history. The official death toll was less than 800, the unofficial estimates 2,000, with the unofficial list of missing persons touching another 2,500. Close to 100,000 Muslims sought refuge in 101 relief camps around the state, with 10,204 homes and 10,429 shops burnt, 1,278 shops ransacked and 2,623 vendors losing the carts on which they sold their wares.

In addition to violence against Muslims and Christians, in the 1990s, the Bajrang Dal found a new target. Now, Hindus too began to be at the receiving end of their violent methods, with the Bajrang Dal donning the garb of a cultural police.

A CULTURAL POLICE PROMOTING HINDU ORTHODOXY AND ORTHOPRAXY

In India, the notion of a cultural police is usually associated with Muslim or Sikh fundamentalists who have been known to impose restrictions on free speech and certain items of food and alcohol, and to enforce a code of good conduct through vice squads.[32] On the contrary, Hinduism's boast has been that as a religion of tolerance which believes that all spiritual paths lead to God. But the last few years have seen the Bajrang Dal emerge as Hindutva's cultural police. With thousands of activists trained in hand-to-hand combat and the use of firearms, the Bajrang Dal devotes its efforts to repressing all those it considers deviant. Several categories can be identified here and, by implication, the Bajrang Dal implements a whole array of methods of social control.

'*Erring Artists*'

Historically, the Bajrang Dal's primary target among Hindus has been artists who, it feels, do not show Hindu culture enough respect. The Bajrang Dal's first instance of cultural policing was aimed at a celebrated Muslim artist Maqbool Fida Hussain in 1996, when militants attacked Ahmedabad's Herwitz gallery where his works were on display. They destroyed paintings and wall hangings worth Rs. 15 million representing the Buddha, Hanuman, and Ganesh. But the official cause of their fury was a canvas dating from 1976 that depicted the goddess Saraswati too scantily clad for their taste.[33] Three days earlier, the Maharashtra authorities had recorded a complaint against Hussain which accused him of encouraging, through his work, inter-community hatred and insulting Hinduism.

Hussain was again a victim of the Bajrang Dal on 2 May 1998 when militants ransacked the painter's apartment in Bombay in protest against his canvas, 'Sita Rescued', which depicted the famous scene in the *Ramayana* where Sita is freed from Ravana. Officially, the vandals said they were attacking the liberties the artist had taken in representing Sita scantily dressed; in private, they did not conceal their indignation that a Muslim artist had dared to reproduce a moment in Hindu mythology.[34]

Hussain was not the only artist targeted by the Bajrang Dal for his 'immoral' treatment of Hindu divinities. In February 2004, militants from the movement filed a complaint against canvases a Hindu artist, Shail Choyal, had painted for an information campaign of the NGO CARE about nursing newborn children. They criticized the painter's depiction of Hindu divinities such as Ganesh and Krishna. On 10 February their complaint was registered by the police who, in the company of some 50 Bajrang Dal militants, searched the offices of the director of the Udaipur Lok Kala Mandal, the art centre where the canvases were stored, seized the paintings and put the director and the artist behind bars. They were later released on bail, but the Bajrang Dal organized a protest march during which their effigies were burned.[35]

The wrath of this cultural police is not reserved for famous painters: it even hunts down amateur artists at the local level. For instance, in Gwalior (Madhya Pradesh), an Indian Institute of Tourism and Travel Management employee was accused by the Bajrang Dal and the Durga Vahini of having staged a play, 'Kal, Aaj, aur Kal', that showed disrespect for Sita, Ram, and Laxman. On 14 March 2004, members of these two organizations burst into her home to blacken her face in public as punishment. Her father and brothers and sisters stepped in. They were beaten and thrown out of their house, while their home was ransacked, all under the passive gaze of police officers.[36]

To provide a comprehensive inventory of all such acts is well high impossible, but a final incident should be related. On 29 January 2004, a gang of Bajrang Dal militants stormed the Garden Art Gallery in Surat and destroyed eight canvases by M.F. Hussain, K.H. Ara, N.S. Bendre, and Chittrovanu Mazumdar. Significantly, the instigators of this act of destruction put forward no justification: this violence thus targeted artistic creation as essentially deviant.[37] What's more, while the first to react against this was a group of artists, SAHMAT, who protested against such acts in the name of creative freedom, no political party took up the issue.[38]

'*Iconoclastic*' *Creators*

It is not 'anti-Hindu' art alone that provokes the Bajrang Dal. The attacks they make on Hindu social traditions are another. Faithful to the Brahmin-inspired conservatism of the Sangh Parivar, the Bajrang Dalis are easily angered by challenges to the caste system. 'Ponga Pandit', a play criticizing the social system, particularly the status of the untouchables, was their target in 2004. On 18 August Bajrang Dal militants prevented the director, Habib Tanvir, from staging it in Gwalior even as the local Superintendent of Police and District Magistrate watched as part of the audience. The trouble makers objected to the apparent transgression of sacred taboos, such as the depiction of a man entering a temple with his shoes on.[39] For the Bajrang Dal, it was bad enough that the play's author was a Muslim; worse, a conversation between a Pandit (Brahmin) and his Jamadarin (an untouchable assigned the most thankless cleaning tasks) hinted that it was not birth but merit that should determine a person's place in society.

The role of women in society, too, has resulted in strong-arm tactics by the Bajrang Dal. In 2000, Indian-Canadian director Deepa Mehta chose to make a film on the life of Hindu widows in Varanasi in the 1930s. At that time—and even now, to a lesser extent—these women were condemned to celibacy and begging. Usually they gathered together in 'homes' where they lived on public charity and eked out a living by making fuel out of cow dung. The screenplay showed the 'illicit' relationship between a Brahmin widow and an untouchable and the rape of another. The VHP president immediately declared that the film insulted 'ancient Indian culture and traditions'[40] and threatened 'more violent protest' if Deepa Mehta tried to shoot in India. She did so nevertheless, after having secured all the necessary authorizations from the central government and the authorities of Uttar Pradesh. The set that was built on the banks of the Ganges was totally ransacked by Bajrang Dal militants. Deepa Mehta then decided to continue shooting in Madhya Pradesh where she couldn't have been more warmly welcomed by the head of government at that time, Digvijay Singh. But here again, the Bajrang Dal resorted to force to prevent the shooting from taking place.

Deepa Mehta's previous film, *Fire*, had already ignited the anger of Hindu nationalists, as it depicted the life of two lesbians. The same theme was taken up in *Girlfriend*, a Bollywood film, which sparked an even more violent Bajrang Dal campaign in 2004: posters were torn down and screenings were prevented in most of Mumbai's theatres, a sign that this organization saw itself as a vice squad allegedly protecting Hindu values.[41]

Westernization of Customs

In his indictment against the film *Water*, Singhal had said it was a 'conspiracy by the votaries of western culture to tarnish the image of widowhood in India'—probably because Deepa Mehta was based in Canada. Opposition to the Westernization of culture is in any case part of the Hindu nationalists' cultural police repertoire.

This translates into violent protests during celebrations or holidays associated with the West, either because they are Christian in origin (such as Christmas) or do not correspond to the 'national' calendar (such as New Year's Eve).[42] The event that receives most attention, however, is Valentine's Day. Every year, this celebration of romance is criticized by the Bajrang Dal as a symbol of Western depravity: young people who celebrate the day together are beaten up, shops selling Valentine's Day iconography or decorated with it are ransacked by the organization.

The other embodiment of Western decadence that Hindu nationalists routinely target is the popular pageant held to elect Miss India—not to mention male variants of this big media circus.

The Bajrang Dal's attempt to police reflects an intolerance uncharacteristic of Hinduism. True, this religion cannot be dissociated from the most rigid form of orthopraxy, embodied by the caste system, but dogmatism and prudishness have never been among its salient features. Sculptures of goddesses that adorn Hindu temples are not just scantily clad, but their eroticism is legendary. If Hussain's Saraswati is naked, it is because she has often been depicted this way, as many sculptures, some of which date as far back as the twelfth century, attest.[43] Far from being attuned to the tradition they claim to defend, the Hindu nationalists are annotating a purely ideological score.

CONCLUSION

Today, the Bajrang Dal may not be the only rightwing Hindu organization contributing to the systematic militarization of Indian civil society, but it is certainly the most powerful of its kind. In the six years between 1998 and 2004 in which the BJP headed the NDA coalition in India, Bajrang Dal stormtroopers were the foot soldiers of the divisive ideology that they both subscribe to, an ideology that exploits religion and religious symbols for political ends. The fact that the party was also in power in major states across the Ganges belt, north of the Vindhya mountains, helped the BJP successfully create the space and the environment for the rise of a militant organization like the Bajrang Dal. This, in turn, took the first steps towards militarizing civil society in some parts of the country. For the Bajrang Dal does not content itself with attacking traditional targets such as Muslims and Christians, but harasses so-called deviant Hindus too. And the violent methods of this cultural police contrast stands in stark contrast to the quietist ethos of the RSS. Yet such aggression is perfectly in tune with another Hindu nationalist tradition that has been running through India for several decades, the tradition embodied by Shiv Sena. The rise of the Bajrang Dal thus reflects the growing influence of methods initiated by the Shiv Sena on the Sangh Parivar.

More generally speaking, it is in tune with the modus operandi of an ever increasing number of Hindu chauvinist groups which act as vehement censors of the best way to write the history of India. This issue is not new. Already in the 1970s, Hindu nationalists in the Morarji

Desai government had protested against the use of history textbooks written, according to them, by biased Marxists.[44] The same accusation was made against the same authors in the 1990s when one of the most reactionary Hindu nationalists of the Vajpayee government, Murli Manohar Joshi, was made education minister. But none of these controversies gave rise to violence, in contrast to what we saw recently. On 5 January 2004, it was an entirely different story indeed when a group of individuals claiming to belong to a till then unheard-of organization—the Sambhaji Brigade—attacked the Bhandarkar Oriental Research Institute (BORI) in Pune which conserved ancient manuscripts of inestimable value, most of which were simply destroyed. The assailants wanted to protest against BORI granting aid to a British author, James Laine, for a book on Shivaji[45] in which he addressed rumours circulating about the true identity of the father of this historic hero.[46] Rewriting history in this way was pure blasphemy for the Hindu nationalists, who ransacked BORI and forced the publisher to withdraw the book. As a result, social scientists are directly —and not only indirectly—concerned by the new kind of threat the Hindu brigades are posing to democracy in India.

While 'deviant' Hindus have become one of the targets of the Sangh Parivar, Muslims do not appear to be such a systematic enemy for some of the components of this network. The strategy of some of the BJP leaders is interesting in this respect. Not only did L.K. Advani visit Pakistan in June 2005, giving additional legitimacy to this country the proponents of Akhand Bharat would like to abolish, he also gave credit to Jinnah by describing him as a secular leader. Such diplomatic words were uttered in view of the Indo-Pakistani rapprochement that A.B. Vajpayee had initiated as prime minister and with an eye on the Muslim voters the BJP had alienated. But the other Hindutva leaders have retained their traditional anti-Muslim bias, as evident from the reaction of the RSS chief, K.S. Sudarshan, to Advani's statement. Predictably, these views will prevail and the BJP will fall in line, especially if its allies within the NDA, sever their link with this party lest it reasserts a pro-active Hindutva-oriented strategy. Muslims, therefore, might well be the primary target of all the Sangh Parivar once again.

NOTES

1. On the many Hindu militias which were active at that time, see C. Jaffrelot, 'Opposing Gandhi: Hindu Nationalism and Political Violence', in Eric Meyer, Gilles Tarabout and Denis Vidal (eds.), *Violence/Non-Violence: Some Hindu Perspectives*, Delhi: Manohar, 2003, pp. 299-324.
2. See W. Andersen and S. Damle, *The Brotherhood in Saffron*, Delhi: Vistaar, 1987, p. 105.
3. For details, see C. Jaffrelot, *The Hindu Nationalist Movement and Indian Politics*, Delhi: Penguin India, 1999, Chapter 7.
4. Jaffrelot, 'The Visva Hindu Parishad: A Nationalist but Mimetic Attempt at Federating the Hindu Sects', in Vasudha Dalmia, Angelika Malinar and Martin Christtof, eds, *Charisma and Canon, Essays on the Religious History of the Indian Subcontinent*, Delhi: Oxford University Press, 2001, pp. 338-411.
5. This leads Manjari Katju to consider erroneously that Bajrang Dal means 'the army of monkeys' (M. Katju, *Vishwa Hindu Parishad and Indian Politics*, Hyderabad: Orient Longman, 2003, p. 51).
6. http://vhp.org/
7. Interview with Rukun Singh Payal in Bulandshahr, April 2004.
8. V. Katiyar, 'It is a War-like Situation', interview published in *Frontline*, 24 April 1992, pp. 9-12.
9. Interview with Acharya Giriraj Kishore (senior General Secretary of the VHP) in New Delhi.
10. Interview with Surendra Jain in New Delhi, May 2004.
11. Interview with V. Katiyar in New Delhi, May 2004.
12. Interview with Payal.
13. Interview with Prakash Sharma, May 2004.
14. http://vhp.org/
15. Interview with Sharma, May 2004.
16. Interview with Payal, April 2004.
17. Interview with Jain, May 2004.
18. Interview with Sharma, May 2004.
19. Interview with Jain.
20. Interview with Sharma.
21. Interview with Jain.
22. The Valmikis are Dalits named after Valmiki, the bandit-turned-Ram devotee, a connection the RSS family has exploited to mobilize support for its members from the community. Valmikis are often used to tackle Muslims during communal riots by telling them that as Hindus they should protect their religion.
23. Interview with Sharma.
24. Interview with Jain.

25. Quoted by D. Bunsha, 'At a Hindutva Factory,' *Frontline*, 7-20 June 2003.
26. For more details, see 'Militant Hindus and the Conversion Issue (1885-1990): From Shuddhi to Dharm Parivartan. The Politicisation and the Diffusion of an "Invention of Tradition"', in J. Assayag (ed.), *The Resources of History, Tradition and Narration in South Asia*, Paris: EFEO, 1999, pp. 127-52.
27. Quoted in S. Gupta, 'Desi Mossad is Getting Ready at Bajrang Dal's Ayodhya Camp', *Indian Express*, 30 June 2000.
28. H. Vaz 'Empowering Women the VHP Way', *Indian Express*, 21 May 2003 and P. Bhattacharya, 'Hindu Nationalists Give Martial Training Arts to Girls to Protect their Faith', *Neapolitan* (Naples), 7 June 2003.
29. For more details T. Sarkar and U. Butalia (eds.), *Women and the Hindu Right, A Collection of Essays*, Delhi: Kali for Women, 1995.
30. For more details, see C. Jaffrelot, 'The BJP at the Centre: A Central and Centrist Party?', in T.B. Hansen and C. Jaffrelot (eds.), *The BJP and the Compulsions of Politics in India*, Delhi: Oxford University Press, 2002, especially the section 'Gujarat, a Laboratory for Hindu Nationalism', pp. 356-63.
31. *The Organiser*, Diwali Special, 1964, p. 15.
32. India became one of the major countries of Muslim mobilization against freedoms that Salman Rushdie had taken in his description of the Prophet in *The Satanic Verses* and the Khalistani militants went on a campaign against places where alcohol was sold in the 1980s in Punjab.
33. P. Swami, 'Predatory Pursuit of Power', *Frontline*, 23 May 1998.
34. See 'BJP–The Saffron Years', Sabrang Alternate News Network (*http://www.countercurrents.org/commsann290603:htm*) and K.S. Narayan, 'When Might is Right', *Deccan Herald*, 1 July 2001.
35. PUCL, Cultural policing by Bajrang Dal and the Rajasthan police (*http://www.pucl.org/Topics/Religion-communalism*).
36. P.S. Tripathi, 'A Law Unto Itself', *Frontline*, 23 April 2004, p. 41.
37. R. Hoskote, 'The Mob as Censor', *The Hindu*, 11 February 2004.
38. People's Democracy, 8 February 2004. SAHMAT stands for for Safdar Hashmi Memorial Trust. It is an organization founded in memory of a theatre personality, Safdar Hashmi, murdered because of his radical political stand.
39. A. Herdenia, 'Sentimental intolerance', *Deccan Herald*, 31 August 2003.
40. Quoted in *The Hindu*, 5 February 2000.
41. The Bajrang Dal has not spared the media either. Soon after the BJP returned to power in Rajasthan, Bajrang Dal members attacked journalists of the Jhalawar bureau of India's largest selling Hindi daily, saying that now that they were in power the newspaper would have to report according to their dictates. Jhalawar, incidentally, used to be Chief Minister Vasundhara Raje's constituency as long as she was an MP—her son, Dushyant Singh, now represents Jhalawar. Perhaps they were taking their cue from the chief minister herself who had the cameras of Jain TV smashed when its reporters asked her uncomfortable questions.

42. The intimidatory tactics of the Bajrang Dal and another RSS-affiliate, the Hindu Jagran Manch, to discourage Hindus from participating in New Year festivities were first recorded in Lucknow in 2000 (A.Tripathi, 'Saffron Threat Fails to dampen Spirits', *The Times of India* [Lucknow], 31 December 2000).
43. P. Swami, 'Predatory Pursuit of Power', op. cit.
44. See Lloyd and Suzanne Rudolph, 'Cultural Policy, the Textbook Controversy and Indian Identity', in A.J. Wilson and D. Dalton (eds.), *The States of South Asia*, London: Hurst, 1982.
45. James W. Laine, *Shivaji: Hindu King in Islamic India*, Delhi: Oxford University Press, 2003.
46. Laine for instance wrote: 'Maharashtrians tell jokes naughtily that Shivaji's biological father was Dadaji Kondeo Kulkarni'. For a thorough account of the controversy, see: *The Complete Review*, 5(1), February 2004.

10

The RSS and Citizenship: The Construction of the Muslim Minority Identity in India

VASUNDHARA SIRNATE

This paper seeks to explain the extent to which the Rashtriya Swayamsevak Sangh (RSS) in India redefines notions of citizenship, deviating from the liberal normative position and uses cultural markers like language and history to define who cannot be a citizen of India. The paper specifically addresses the issue of the demonization of Muslims and conceives of this as a larger disenfranchisement of the Muslim community. The evidence for this process of demonization is found in the written record of the Hindu right and includes the *Organiser*, some pamphlets and textbooks of the Gujarat State Board of Education. The first section of the paper addresses theoretical questions about the RSS notion of citizenship and contrasts it with the liberal view, while stating the influence of German cultural nationalist thought on Hindutva ideologues. The second section of the paper presents the evidence of demonization which supports the particular, organic view of citizenship advocated by the RSS.

An important political development in India in the 1990s was the ascendance of the Hindu nationalist movement led by the Bharatiya Janata Party (BJP) and the RSS which grew into an influential bloc of political and cultural organizations in the country. Hindu nationalist agendas, discourse, and institutions gradually penetrated everyday life and acquired a growing, if contested, social respectability in contemporary Indian society.[1] Post Pokhran[2] and the Kargil proxy war, the BJP emerged on the domestic scene as the resolute champion and defender of the country's pride and national interests.

Since the 1999 electoral triumph of the BJP, political scientists have been hard-pressed to explain the rise of the Hindu nationalist movement and the reasons behind its success in both electoral and social spheres. Recent literature suggests two strands of academic theorizing about the ascendance of this movement. One set of theories explains this phenomenon as the result of decades of systematic, painstaking, organizational work and imaginative political strategy[3] while the second strand interprets Hindu nationalism in cultural and historical terms, arguing that the Hindu nationalists drew on older reserves of 'religious nationalism' that were always central to most forms of Indian nationalism.[4]

The broader idea behind Hindu nationalism is to deconstruct the existing socio-political order and rebuild a new one that derives its discipline and ethos from a superior ancient past. Its understanding of that past is, not surprisingly, a narrow one.[5] The Hindu nationalists want what Hansen calls a 'conservative revolution' based on a broad democratic transformation of politics and public culture.[6] With its emphasis on grassroots mobilization the RSS has managed to effectively penetrate the public realm and popular culture, which is the space where communities vie for recognition through expressions of culture and political representation. Hindu nationalists think in terms of reinvigorating the Indian nation by resurrecting a strong majoritarian call for Hindutva, which combines well-established paternalist and xenophobic discourses with democratic and universalistic discourses on rights and entitlements, and has thus successfully 'articulated desires, anxieties and fractured subjectivities in both urban and rural India'.[7]

The purpose of my paper is to (a) explore the manner in which the RSS and the BJP 'other' and essentialize Muslims and (b) ask what the repercussions of this process are for the conceptualization of citizenship. The implications of this process tend to be deeply political and violent for the demonized communities concerned. 'Othering' has political and social consequences and this paper highlights the political renegotiations involved in this process. These include the rewriting of a new communal history, the elaborate production of myths and legends about Muslims that are translated into narrow political ideologies, and the final debate about the status of Muslim citizenship.

In this paper[8] othering/demonization/essentialization is understood as a political act that aims specifically at the social and political exclusion of Muslims from mainstream politics and national life. The hypothesis developed here is that by exploiting the fractures between Hindu and Muslim groups and othering Muslims, the Hindu Right not only pushes ahead its agenda of political exclusion, but also redefines the idea of citizenship. This paper, it is hoped, spells out how the political disenfranchisement of Muslims is taking place.

OTHERING AND THE IDEA OF CITIZENSHIP

We can look at citizenship in a legal framework where it is defined through legislative measures like the Constitution of a country. Or else we can think of it as a broader theoretical notion is linked to the achievement of freedom for individuals—and in the case of civic republicanism, the good of the community.[9] Citizenship, as understood in the modern sense, is essentially a form of membership of an individual in relation to a larger collective, the nation-state. However, most individuals have other group affiliations as well, which can contradict one's supposedly overarching identity as a citizen.

Modern citizenship theory is primarily derived from liberal thought. One of its earliest meanings can be traced back to Athens, where citizenship implied the act of belonging to a community of equals. If we think of citizenship as a concept that has been historically embedded, we find that the site of embedding of citizenship has been changing. While it was in the Greek *polis* and the Roman Empire in olden times, it became the Roman town in the Middle Ages and finally the modern state.[10] What scholars now consider deeply problematic about citizenship is the idea of exclusion, inherent from the very inception. In the Greek city-state women and slaves were not considered citizens as it was believed that they did not possess the necessary mental or physical faculties. With the Renaissance came the interrogation of feudal notions[11] of exclusionary citizenship and the French revolution in particular struggled to define citizenship in terms of belonging to an all-powerful collective called the nation, where the individual's identity as a citizen was to be privileged over other competing identities.[12] Citizenship therefore had evolved with an inherited notion of exclusion, justified on the basis of a property quotient.

In the US citizenship was enshrined in a Constitution that drew from social contract theorists and considered natural rights as inalienable and self-evident. In the social contract framework various forms of deficiency (like lack of property) were identified to make citizenship exclusive. This exclusion was enforced by denying certain groups the right to vote. For instance, in the US women and black people were two groups denied franchise for being 'weak and of less intrinsic worth'. More recently, John Rawls revisited the liberal position with the equation of justice as fairness practised in the public sphere. In Rawls' framework the archetypal 'moral person' is the democratic citizen, who is free, self-originating, and responsible in exercising his rights and duties.[13] The citizen operates in the political arena to uphold it through the practice of cooperative virtues.

The communitarian or republican view of citizenship, meanwhile, seeks to conceive of it as an activity and not as a status of membership. Not individual rights but the pursuit of the 'common good' is to be privileged and hence this view incorporates the ideas of duty and obligations to political life and the development of civic virtues. Rawls (liberal) and Oldfield (communitarian) attempt to find a middle ground between these two, suggesting that there are alternative versions of the good life, given the diversity of individuals and that rights complement the common good.[14]

T.H. Marshall conceived of citizenship as an expansionary concept and as a process which allowed for the inclusion of new groups (like the working classes in England) into the body politic. He distinguished between civil, political, and social rights of citizenship. Civil rights were important for individual freedom in the eighteenth century, while political rights became important in the nineteenth century as they guaranteed the role of the individual in the exercise of political power. Marshall's addition of social rights of citizenship make possible the establishment of economic welfare and security as a part and parcel of normative citizenship. Critics of Marshall held that social citizenship has often been used as a substitute for civil citizenship and they cite fascism as a classic case where civil rights were suspended while social citizenship was pursued.[15]

Modern citizenship, with its emphasis on civil rights, emerged simultaneously with the growth of nationalist consciousness in Europe. With the French revolution the democratic nation and the civil rights of its citizens were rendered inseparable. Yet with the growth of cultural nationalism in Germany, nations came to be identified as collections of people sharing a language, religion, and history. Individuals were then required to prove an eternal loyalty to the nation-state at the price of the denial of civil rights.[16] Brubaker has shown that in France and Germany, territoriality and blood ties came to be the determinants of citizenship. The idea behind this was to create a homogeneous nation state.

Let us stay with Brubaker. Brubaker studied the effect of the increased post-war immigration of people into Europe and the manners in which the French and German states responded to this. He observed that while the French were more ready to confer citizenship rights on the immigrants, Germany was more exclusionary and restrictive. For Brubaker, citizenship was, normatively speaking, supposed to be egalitarian, sacred, democratic, unique, and consequential—while also being tied to a cultural community. Reality, however, presented a different set of facts. European countries had different mechanisms of defining citizenship. For instance in Sweden and Belgium all that was required for citizenship was a simple declaration, while in Germany there were no special provisions for second generation immigrants. The act of acquiring citizenship in France and Germany became a political act mediated by country-specific institutions.

For Brubaker the overarching notion of the nation state did not exist. What existed were approximations of the ideal which were also rooted in specific historical trajectories and definitions of cultural community. The French state then bore the marks of its revolutionary rebirth and this political unity was bolstered by the striving for a cultural community. French citizenship then was based on assimilation through institutional mechanisms like the educational system. The German idea of nationhood was, contrary to the French, 'particularist, organic, differentialist and Volk-centred'. German nationhood was defined by ethno-cultural unity and citizenship exclusively by descent, which Brubaker asserts is manifest in the political structure even today. This emphasis on *jus sanguinis* as contrasted with *jus soli* has since been challenged on the grounds that many immigrant peoples can under the former system spend their entire lives in a territory without being citizens of it.[17]

This specific notion of citizenship is to some extent echoed by the RSS and especially in the writings of V.D. Savarkar and M.S. Golwalkar who were heavily influenced by German cultural nationalists Fichte and Herder. Golwalkar's *We, Our Nationhood Defined* and Savarkar's *Hindutva—Who is a Hindu?* the primary texts of the RSS, open up a plethora of analytical questions. To what extent can we can draw parallels between the RSS notion of exclusionary citizenship and larger ideas of cultural nationalism where the ultimate test of citizenship was the demonstration of loyalty to the nation? It is argued here that while RSS ideologues were in fact deeply influenced by the German and Italian traditions, the reason why they were able to adopt, so successfully, ideas about the purity of race, is because the existing caste system offered a readymade structure which could be used to engineer exclusion. The myth of the divine birth of the upper castes as opposed to the commonplace birth of lower castes and 'strangers' in the country could be adequately mobilized to create the idea of a superior race to which the nation belonged.

Many of the key political ideas being propagated today by the RSS originated in the 1930s in the thought of Savarkar. Briefly, these ideas include the belief that Hindus constitute 'one nation', about Hinduism under threat of 'extermination' from a 'fifth column' of Muslims, about the threat of forced conversions of Hindus to Islam or Christianity, and also critiques of pseudo-nationalism (which is now a critique of pseudo-secularism), and the politics of vote banks. Also included are ideas about the imperative to militarize Hindudom, reduction of all Muslim culture to Koranic injunctions that would in the long run be treacherous to the nation, and a rejection of the view that communalism was a product of British colonialism.[18] Savarkar was acutely aware of the Orientalist project which sought to construct Hindus as a monolithic entity, directly reducible to Hinduism on the basis of religious belief and practice. His notion of Hindutva then came to embody other elements but also drew heavily from Orientalist discourse on Hinduism; he constructed a primordial view of Hinduness, the essence of which was elusive.[19] Savarkar borrowed the idea of the Aryan invasion from

Aryanist thinking in Germany (and Britain) where the active masculine principle was the defining feature of the Aryan presence.[20] The mingling of Aryans with an inferior people, it was argued, tended to raise the physical and other qualities of the indigenous populace.[21] Another key idea that accompanied this thought was that if the blood of Aryans were to be 'polluted' Indian civilization would weaken and begin to disintegrate.

Savarkar asserted that Aryan mingling with the indigenous population begat the Vedic–Hindu civilization. This Hindu nation, for Savarkar, degenerated during the reign of Ashoka due to the expansion of Buddhism and its doctrines of non-violence. Buddhism had sapped the nation of its virility which had to be regained. This critique of Buddhist non-violence was also a critique of the Indian national movement principles of civil disobedience and *ahimsa* (non-violence). According to Savarkar, Hindutva was the only ideology which could combat 'invaders', Hun, Muslim, or British.[22] He combined this with an explicit account of the geographic boundaries of India that extend from 'Kashmir to Ceylon' and from 'Attock to Cuttack'.[23] Savarkar then telescoped a thousand years of Indian history (1000-1900) into an account of repeated invasions by Muslims and then the British.

The first mark of Hindu identity for Savarkar was citizenship by paternal descent within the geographical space called India. The second criterion was the 'bond of common blood', being born to Hindu parents.[24] This second criterion can be directly linked to the *jus sanguinis* of the German model as discussed by Brubaker. Hindus were not only a 'nation' (*rashtra*), but a 'race' (*jati*), argued Savarkar, and the blood of their illustrious Aryan ancestors flowed through their veins.[25] In a unique turn, Savarkar tried to link the four varna layers by describing how the same blood flowed from one caste to another (from a Brahmin to a Chandal). In this manner he tried to interrogate the British idea of racial difference between castes, even though at one level his version of caste was not very different. He still defended the purity of the upper caste.[26] He wrote:

> We are not only a Nation, but a Jati, a born brotherhood. Nothing else counts. . . . We *feel* we are that same ancient blood that coursed through Rama and Krishna, Buddha and Mahavir, Nanak and Chaitanya . . . that courses from vein to vein, pulsates from heart to heart. . . . (we are) a race bound by the dearest ties of blood. . . .[27]

This dimension of Savarkar's thought is found in the RSS ideology even today: consider the emphasis on the 'essence' of the Hindu community and the projection of a 'complete' Hindu people.

The third criterion of citizenship was participation in a uniquely bounded culture. For him, Muslims in the country were actually Hindus who had lost themselves in their conversion to Islam and needed to be brought back into the Hindu fold. This too is a recurring facet of RSS ideology if we take into account the debate on the rituals of re-conversion or *shuddhikaran* (purification) that it urges Muslims and Christians to undergo. In sum, then, Savarkar held that Hindus were not a religious community but a civilization, an idea most famously propagated by Friedrich Max Müller. Muslims and Christians were, for him, religious communities, not civilizations. So even if they were a part of the territory and race of Hindus, they were still not part of the Hindu 'nation'. For him

> their (Muslims and Christians) Holyland is far off in Arabia and Palestine. Their mythology and Godmen, ideas and heroes are not the children of this soil. . . . Their love is divided. They to a man, set their Holyland above Fatherland in their love and allegiance. . . . Mohammadan or Christian communities possess all the essential qualifications of Hindutva but one and that is they do not look upon India as their Holyland.[28]

In 1938 Savarkar drew parallels between Indian Muslims and German Jews. He valorized Nazism and this was followed by most of his successors, including Golwalkar, with open praise for Hitler's 'final solution' to the Jewish 'problem' in Germany. They also openly praised the Nazi revival of the Indo-Vedic tradition and symbols (the *swastika*) in 1939. That the Muslim League at this time was ascendant in India is also an important aspect which governed the direction of Savarkar's thought, in that the League became an organizational parallel to German Jewry. In 1939, M.S. Golwalkar (the sarsanghchalak of the RSS in 1940) published *We, Our Nationhood Defined* in which he openly praised Germany its othering of the Jews and their subsequent persecution, even while asserting that India had to learn from this example. He wrote,

> To keep up the purity of the Race and its culture, Germany shocked the world by her purging the country of the Semitic races—the Jews. Race pride at its highest has been manifested here. Germany has also shown how well-nigh impossible it

is for Races and cultures, having differences going to the root, to be assimilated into one united whole, a good lesson for us in Hindusthan to learn and profit by.[29]

Today, Golwalkar's text is considered the founding statement of the RSS. Savarkar and Golwalkar between them laid down the exclusivist and organic notions of the Indian–Hindu nation, and this is echoed with little change today. Let us now see how the RSS spreads the idea of Muslims being inherently treacherous to the Indian nation.

THE CITIZENSHIP OF 1947

The post-Independence debate on citizenship centred around a major question: in a newly independent and industrially backward country, what would citizenship mean to anyone? Independence was supposed to bring an end to socio-economic coercion. The ideas of citizenship as understood in Western scholarship were only upheld by a handful of the Indian intellectual elite, who hoped to telescope the various stages in the development of citizenship in the West, and ensure political freedoms for everyone.[30] The paradox India entered into in 1947 was that of universal suffrage and political liberty combined with a crippling absence of those socio-economic changes that had begotten these in the West. In the West citizenship expanded in theory and practice as countries progressed industrially and there was need to include the hitherto excluded ranks of people into the political mainstream. In India, in the absence of strong institutions, slow industrial growth and market change, the chasm between Bharat and India grew as citizens were enfranchised only to have this franchise rendered a shibboleth by the lack of economic and social progress that was a prerequisite of its strength. This was coupled by the incapacity of the state to provide social welfare to a majority of its citizens and the emergence of state capture by powerful local elites who crippled the state machinery at local levels. In such a scenario, the only survivors were the pre-existing social relationships and the inequalities and domination they described. Viewed from the lens of later liberal theory, citizenship in India was therefore only half-hearted, partial and fragmented, which meant that very often the public domain was subjected to revivals of ascriptive identities.[31] One may argue that citizenship in some senses is always embedded in a set of socio-political and economic realities. Citizenship becomes a function of power relations in society and often mimics social hierarchies, losing its effectiveness both as a tool for political articulation and as an organizer of society. In doing so, citizenship instead becomes vulnerable to the process by which inequalities are perpetuated.

In India there were Hindu nationalists and secular nationalists. In the years immediately after Partition, Muslims remained Muslim, with the exception of a few secular nationalists. Linked with this issue was the definition of what constituted a minority. In India, numbers were not crucial to the determination of a minority, but the sense of marginalization in political life was. The minority Muslims, who had chosen not to migrate to newly created Pakistan, had to support their choice by constant and perpetual affirmations of loyalty to the nation. Even in the *Constituent Assembly Debates*, Pakistan was referred to as the homeland for Muslims and the question then arose of thinking of India as a homeland for Hindus. The idea, as Gyanendra Pandey understands it, was to find and define a 'genuine, unambiguously loyal citizen'.[32] This loyalty to the nation was tested only for those who are not deemed 'natural' citizens.

In the Constituent Assembly debates there was a dilemma between the recent history of the creation of Pakistan on the basis of religious identity and the concomitant citizenship it granted, on the one hand, and the intellectual idea of universal citizenship in the Western tradition (in the new Indian state) on the other. S.P. Deshmukh and Shibban Lal Saksena were among those who spoke about the need to conceptualize India as a homeland for Hindus and Sikhs as opposed to Pakistan.[33] J.R. Kapoor held that those who had migrated to Pakistan and 'kicked this country', if they returned to India, should be treated as foreigners and should claim no rights of citizenship.[34] Citizenship was therefore a privilege to be conferred, and later to become an inheritance.[35] Thakur Das Bhargava, for his part, felt that for aliens to become citizens they should demonstrate their discharge of obligations to the nation. There was also a general assertion that those who had demonstrated their loyalty to Pakistan by migrating there had forfeited the privilege of Indian citizenship.

There is evidence that suggests that even the Constituent Assembly looked at Muslim refugees with a sense of paranoia. Thakur Das

Bhargava made the assertion that certain Muslims had entered India with the purpose of bolstering the numbers of the Muslim population.[36] It is interesting to note that even the *Constituent Assembly Debates* on citizenship reveal an urge similar to that of the Hindu right today. For instance, the fear of increased Muslim numbers is found in the contemporary articulation of the RSS which sees any increase in absolute numbers of Muslims as a sign of future Muslim domination. Mahboob Ali Baig and Brajeshwar Prasad challenged the assumption of Pakistan returnees as traitors and chastised the Assembly for thinking in terms of exclusionary citizenship, and conceiving of India as a homeland for Hindus and Sikhs.[37] Nehru, for his part, argued against the line taken by Deshmukh and Roy, and attacked those who considered that the Congress government was following a policy of Muslim appeasement.[38]

A key factor that can be isolated in the *Constituent Assembly Debates* is the linking of Indian citizenship to those who could prove they had no loyalty towards Pakistan. Strangely this test of loyalty was only for individuals of the Muslim community. In fact in every speech Pakistan figured prominently. There was a constant refrain of Pakistani refugees and returnees and the citizenship rights to be given to them. Refugees, returnees, and Muslims who had stayed behind were accused of supporting the demand for Pakistan and by extension were classified as anti-Indian. Implicit in the Constituent Assembly was the unsaid—can we really think of Muslims as Indian citizens? The fact that a similar debate did not rage about the granting of citizenship to Christians and Parsis, only served the purpose of isolating Muslims as constituting a somewhat special community, perhaps with the implication that they should be treated differently. In Gyanendra Pandey's own rendition of the same question, he asserts that the division between the Hindu/Indian and the Muslim/Other was created in the elaboration of Indian nationalism after Independence.[39]

In this analysis, it would appear that the Hindu Right's own understanding of citizenship is predicated on two rudiments. First, citizenship is identified in the tradition of cultural and ethno-nationalism and the idea of identity forming the basis of one's inclusion in the state. Second, citizenship is defined through an exclusion of communities (like Muslims) on the assumption that the Muslim community can never be loyal or patriotic to Hindu India. In this sense, this version of citizenship is closer to the practice of citizenship in Germany where romantic/ cultural nationalists used distinctive cultural characteristics such as language, religion, and history to identify who could and could not be a citizen. Nations in this view are seen as embedded into the identity of its members, who are called upon to demonstrate an ever-growing loyalty to the nation state at the price of an ever-growing denial of their individual rights.[40] The idea of India as the land of Hindus and Sikhs had many adherents in the Assembly. Ambedkar remained silent as the debate raged and it was perhaps the strong influence of Nehru (who turned down such interrogations into citizenship) that seemed to be the deciding influence on the debate.

The citizenship issue includes the denial of state protection, and turns entire sections of Muslims from citizens to non-citizens. In this view the Indian state (*rashtra*) is a passive entity unable to protect itself against home-grown Muslim subversion, supported by Pakistan. This portrayal of the state as helpless in one sense but ruthless and strong when dealing with Muslim Pakistan is an unresolved paradox. The Muslims in India have been placed on trial by the Hindu Right, who have amassed overwhelming evidence against this community as is evinced in a reading of the *Organiser*. That this evidence is fabricated and constructed will be illustrated in the second section of this paper.

EXPLAINING THE EVIDENCE

Organiser

The RSS publication, *Organiser*, was chosen for in depth study. As of 2004, *Organiser* claims its circulation has reached the 500,000 mark and boasts of a network of 2,000 vendors across twenty states.

The idea behind this study was to establish that the RSS had been continuously demonizing Muslims. Existing scholarship tells us that the Hindu right demonizes religious minorities, yet evidence is presented in the form of pamphlets and other isolated writings. This study begins with their official propaganda paper and works, and moves to other forms of evidence such as pamphlets and rewritten textbooks. Taking all of these together it is possible to arrive at a nascent theory about (a) how effective this process really is and (b) whether is in fact a concerted effort as is usually implied by most scholars.

Over a period of nine years (between 1989 and 2001; with 1991-3 records only partially available) the *Organiser* seemed to be in a constant state of refining its agenda.[41] I made a list of 32 topics and noted their frequency (in terms of articles pertaining to them) from 1989 onwards. It was decided to focus on the *Organiser* from 1994 onwards and the frequency of articles and their persistence since then was used to judge what issues were addressed more consistently than others and therefore, what issues were more important.[42] The criteria for categorizing an article as pejorative or not were:

(i) the absence or presence of factual evidence in the article and scholarly references.
(ii) the style of writing, i.e. use of the words 'right', 'wrong', 'threatening', 'anti-Indian', 'un-Indian', 'anti-national', 'involved in conspiracy', 'evil', 'villainous', etc.

This was done to record the frequency with which certain varieties of articles appeared and to isolate key factors in them that suggest a bias against Muslims, Christians, and Dalits. The results were rather surprising. While newer topics were added as the years went by, there were some issues that died out while some others persisted. A distinction was then made between persistent and non-persistent issues. The former were those issues that were mentioned in the *Organiser* on an average of four times a month or once every week, translating into approximately 20-5 mentions over a half-year period. The non-persistent issues were identified as those that were mentioned sporadically with weeks passing without their making the pages of the *Organiser.* The persistent issues are the ones that shape this study, since they suggest various academic possibilities about the content and focus of the *Organiser* and by extension the RSS and BJP. The extension is made to the BJP since a lot of the articles build up on the BJP and its electoral and political agenda. Between 1994 and 1999 there were approximately 145 articles that were clearly identified as focused on the BJP's political agenda. The following is a detailed description of the findings:

(i) The *Organiser* has consistently positioned itself against central governments, with the ferocity of this positioning depending on what government was in power at the centre. For instance, in 1989 the *Organiser* positioned itself against the Rajiv-led Congress government. In the last half of 1989, there were 40 articles against the government criticizing various issues of policy and foreign relations. Many of the articles were, however, in the nature of personal attacks on Rajiv, a development which ceased with his assassination in 1991. The attacks on the Congress government continued till 1995, albeit in a more restrained manner. Between the last half of 1994 and the first half of 1995 there were only 20 articles attacking the government. With the Congress out of power the attacks continued in the nature of anti-Congress vendetta. I had stated earlier that Savarkar had positioned himself against the Congress and Gandhi at key moments. That the RSS chooses to do the same is significant.

(ii) Another 'persistent' issue in the *Organiser* is that of Islam–Pakistan–Indian Muslims. In the last six months of 1989 there were 13 articles against Pakistan and 22 against Muslims in general. In the first half of 1990 there were 45 articles that mentioned Pakistan pejoratively and 28 articles mentioning Muslims as being oppressive to women, anti-national, intolerant, threatening India or being loyal to Pakistan. In the last half of 1994, there were 12 anti-Pakistan articles and 28 anti-Muslims articles, in the first half of 1995 there were 20 anti-Pakistan articles and 23 anti-Muslim articles. In 1997 there were 33 anti-Muslim articles and the number fell to 15 in the first half on 1999 due to the increase in the number of articles about Christianity. In 1999 a record number of 61 articles were published against Christianity, the Pope, missionaries, and Christian educational institutions. The average in the previous years for such articles had been 5 in a six month period. Simultaneously, in 1999 the anti-Pakistan agenda seems diffused, primarily as a consequence of Vajpayee's 'bus diplomacy'. This however, ceases around June (due to Kargil) when a record 19 articles are published in one month against Pakistan, followed by 22 in July. What this demonstrates is that in many ways the *Organiser* devotes a significant portion of its space on Pakistan–Islam and Muslims. In fact, one of the problems the study faced was deciding which articles could be classified as anti-Pakistan, anti-Islam, or anti-Muslim as all three aspects are interwoven into most. It was found that with the exception of 1999 (when most articles were about Christians), the maximum number of articles were against Muslims. In later pages references are made to some articles of the *Organiser* which give an instance of the content of these articles. The idea behind the articles is to incorporate as many issues as possible within the space devoted to one article, thereby making it extremely difficult to gauge who or what ideology the article is directed against. That an article is directed towards a Muslim-related issue, is however, amply clear. To cite an example, an article about the dismal state of women in Pakistan will suggest itself as being pro-women, but anti-Pakistan, anti-Islam on a larger basis and also anti-Muslim as a whole across the world. The article will then nosedive back into India and make cursory references to the manner in which Indian Muslims may act the same way towards women and how if there were to be a Hindu state, women would be in a better position to interrogate such oppressive tendencies. A reader then is goaded into thinking along several parallel axes, each of which reinforces the idea of a Hindu nation and a 'bad Muslim'.

(iii) It is interesting to note that when the Congress was in power, the *Organiser* also sporadically tried to position itself as the champion of minorities, seemingly to protect them from Congress exploitation. This did not seem to resonate well with the rest of the articles and was given up in time.

(iv) While the *Organiser* remains the RSS mouthpiece, little space is devoted to events taking place within the RSS. Most of the articles are about specific issues related to communities and the only political party that gets a positive platform in its pages is the BJP. Surprisingly, the Ayodhya temple issue does not find a persistent mention in the *Organiser*. It is the focus of 52 articles between 1994 and 1996 and finds no mention at all in the first half of 1999. Perhaps this can be explained if we consider the temple issue as being the brain-child of the VHP. Significantly that organization as a whole finds negligible mention in the *Organiser*. This also alerts us to the fact that the Hindu Right is not homogeneous.

(v) The frequency of certain types of articles depends on the current political context of India. For instance, the sudden increase in articles against Christians can be explained as a response to the impending Papal visit and the killing of Graham Staines, which, incidentally, is neither mentioned, deplored, nor supported in the *Organiser.*

(vi) The articles written in criticism of Muslims and Christians focus on the possibility of hidden conspiracy against India in these communities. Therefore, by isolating nationalism as an important factor in their ideology, the Hindu Right is able to paint Muslims and Christians as anti-national and thereby throws up issues of their loyalty to the country.

Here are a few examples. In an editorial Muslims are referred to as those who 'rule the terrorist roost all over the world'.[43] Shri Kant Joshi a regular columnist of the Organiser states, 'Hindu victory is not recorded in our history books . . . and events in which the Muslim invaders are victorious are very gloatingly recorded. . . .'[44]

He believes that Muslims aim at establishing Islam and the Shariat law all over the world. 'Muslims have to follow individually and collectively the three stages of Jihad—persuasion and quiet pressurization, terrorism and military war. . . .'[45]

Muslim proselytization is also viewed in the global context with V.P. Bhatia (another regular columnist) pointing to the fact that in the USA ethnic minorities are converting in some numbers to Islam: 'a couple of papers have revealed some interesting facts and figures about the work of Islamic conversions going on "quietly"'.[46]

In another article Bhatia argues that 'madrassas are modern militant Islam's most deadly weapons to subvert the Kafir countries. . . .'[47] The same article attacks the 'pseudosecularists' for their Nehruvian generosity that is not helping Muslims but breeding resentment among Hindus. This dovetails with the point made earlier in relation to Savarkar's critique of pseudo-nationalism (represented by Gandhi and the Congress). In contemporary discourse not only the Congress but also the Left parties in India are termed pseudosecularists. This enables the RSS to position itself, and for electoral purposes the BJP, as the alternative for those who are disgruntled with the Congress and the Left. In yet another article it is stated that Hinduness is the 'spinal force' of India which has kept it together in the face of the 'destructive onslaughts' of Islam and Christianity.[48]

The Pamphlets

Religious nationalisms at one level tend to recreate and reinterpret history as it exists and deliberately reinsert into that history revisions that help construct a new idea of the past. This is often politically expedient and caters to immediate political realities and problems. What results are misinterpretations and falsifications that are not just bound to ignorance but are also a product of ideological preference.[49] The RSS has used this tool to further its xenophobic agenda by valorizing the Hindu in the course of a chequered history. It sees India's political history as a chronological record of Hindu resistance to invaders from different parts of the world. Specifically, the last one thousand years are seen as a period of constant struggle between Hindus and Muslims. These myths find their way to the common people in the form of pamphlets and journals circulated by Hindu right wing organizations and as a result have gained a certain social acceptability.[50]

Romila Thapar and K.N. Panikkar point out that the history of Ayodhya that was put forward at the time of the Ramjanmabhoomi campaign testifies to the creation of an alternative religious history. For instance some pamphlets were entitled *Shri Ram Janmabhoomi ka Rakt Ranjit Itihaas*,[51] and the argument made in such pamphlets was usually the same—the matter of the birthplace of Ram is a matter of faith for every true Hindu, and that there was a temple at the disputed spot is an 'indisputable' fact. Panikkar argues that this religious interpretation of the past can be seen to have a contemporary political content as it tries to stereotype non-Hindus as hostile foreigners. Therefore, all minorities in India are aggressive, alien 'others' at whose hands the Hindus have suffered in the past.

The RSS has used the traditional networks of civil society to spread its communal message. The most recent example that can be cited is that of Gujarat where independent fact-finding commissions discovered

Gujarati pamphlets inciting people to hatred. The *Communalism Combat* report of the pogrom in Gujarat cites many such pamphlets that contain instructions for Hindus to attack Muslims, and kill their women, children, and infants. Every recipient of the pamphlet was also asked to make copies and circulate them.

Appeals to the Hindu masses are made directly through public speeches, door to door canvassing, pamphlet distribution, and acts of social service. Excerpts from various pamphlets show the existence of one of the most systematically planned and executed ideological strategies ever seen. For instance,

> This was the nation of heroes, now it is filled with frightened people
> They escape from our control and the poor innocent is sacrificed
> If the Hindu Youth is angered there will be a rain of shoes on their heads
> Hindu wake up now and chase away the Muslim[52]

The same pamphlet goes on to give local members of the RSS instructions that include

> When fighting the Muslim change your appearance so you are not recognized
>
> Guard your temple
>
> Have irregular relations with Muslim women so that you have the opportunity to increase the Hindu population
>
> Deform new born babies of Muslims[53]

Other pamphlets inciting Hindus to violence also ask the Hindus to boycott the Muslims economically and calls them terrorists. Another pamphlet asks Hindus not to watch films starring Muslim actors. Yet another pamphlet categorically states,

> We do not want to see a single Muslim alive in Gujarat. . . .[54]

The RSS spreads half-truths.

> The terrorist activities all over India are conducted form a madrasa in Akwada.
> Muslims do not pay any taxes and live at our expense in our country . . .
> The Muslim population has increased form 7 per cent to 32 per cent since 1947
> In all madrasas Muslim children are taught to be fanatics . . .[55]

Possible solutions to the above 'problems' [*sic*] include

> Attack the Akwada Madrasa and destroy it
> Report all tax-evading Muslims

Teach the children about the great people of our culture and create in them a sense of courage . . . teach them to be fanatical Hindus . . .
Oppose the Haj subsidy[56]

This final statement that testifies to the dissemination of the communal message,

Make at least ten copies and distribute them[57]

The Text Books

Perhaps the most potent form of propaganda comes in history text books rewritten from a new and factually incorrect perspective, a fact established by an investigation into these text books by leading historians.[58] A new development in this regard is that of the saffronization of education and the re-writing of history textbooks which can contribute to the growth of a communal consciousness.[59] The RSS is one organization that has established *shakhas* and schools that are called Saraswati Shishu Mandirs and Gyan Bharatis.[60] Today there are over 6,000 such schools imparting education to around 50 lakh students. These schools have the freedom to follow their own curriculums and investigations into their curricula have found the textbooks contain explicit communal propaganda.[61]

All Right-wing movements regard education as a tool to selectively erase a historical memory and substitute it with a constructed one. Be it the Muslim Right in Iran or Pakistan, or the Taliban in Afghanistan that believes in reconstructing a historical past, education for all such movements seems to be the post powerful apparatus for social conditioning. The Sangh had thought this through as early as 1952, when they set up the first Sangh School at Gorakhpur in Uttar Pradesh. A Shishu Shiksha Prabandh Samiti was set up to coordinate the primary schools, while Bal Mandirs began to develop at high school levels.[62] By the 1990s, Vidya Bharti, a nodal coordinating organization, was running the second largest chain of schools in the country, controlling about 4,000 schools, 40 colleges, a total of about 36,000 teachers, and 10 lakh students. The regular schools are located in areas that have an RSS centre and a VHP-controlled temple usually attached to the school premises. The school is thus embedded within what Tanika Sarkar calls a 'tight and comprehensive range of institutions' that would coordinate the child's leisure, education, ideological growth, and religious understanding.[63]

The textbooks used by these schools are true to Savarkar's definition: Hindutva, as a continuous historically stable cultural essence unifies India. All those who live outside its orbits are non-Indian or enemies.[64] History is randomized and leads to events being placed anachronistically. For instance Ram's enemy is not only the mythical Ravana (a demon) but also Babur. Therefore, demons and Muslims flow into each other and are 'free-floating signifiers'.[65] The school hymns and mantras invoking militant and militarized nation worship are modern ones though composed in Sanskrit.[66]

Gujarat was one of the states where the BJP initiated a change in curricula with an agenda that seemed to suggest the imposition of unhistorical claims and cultural values militating against Muslims. The Gujarat Board tried to give a distinct sectarian slant to education by sending out various instructions involving subscriptions to the RSS magazine *Sadhana* and by asking schools to send their teachers to Sanskrit training camps.[67]

Meanwhile, the syllabi followed by the various Vidya Bharatis and Shishu Mandirs in other parts of the country continue to disseminate knowledge through a revision of historical facts. The following examples would further illustrate the argument:

- Our land has always been seen with greedy eyes. This story of invasion and resistance is our 3000-year long Gaurav Gatha. When this proud tradition began is difficult to say as no books were written in this period but we believe that the first man was born on this land.[68]
- To our ancestors those marauders were like mosquitoes and flies that were crushed.[69]
- Lakhs of foreigners came during these thousands of years but they all suffered humiliating defeats. The Mughals, Pathans and Christians are some of these people.[70]

The *Sanskar Saurabh* textbook for Class V presents Sati as a Rajput tradition that Hindus should be proud of since the valour attached to it demonstrates the highest sacrifice.[71] Another edition of the same series for Class IV reveals that it is because we are the children of Manu that we are called *manushya*.[72] A chapter of the same book calls Muslims 'butchers' and 'killers of cows'.[73] Afghanistan, Tibet, Nepal, Bhutan,

Myanmar, Sri Lanka, Pakistan, and Bangladesh are shown as parts of India and the student is urged to pray to a picture of this Akhand Bharat and pledge that he will achieve this shape for our country.[74]

We could probably mention these historically inaccurate instances as well:

- Bharat is the most ancient nation in the world. Our original ancestors Manu and Shatrughan gave life to the earth. The Indian ocean in referred to as the Hindu Mahasagar.[75]
- The Hindu belief is characterized as Dharma while Sikhism, Christianity and Islam are described as sects.[76]
- Urdu is not an independent language. It is Hindi written in a different script.[77]

Today almost all of the RSS and the affiliate Sangh's politics use images of the past as both 'referent and justification'.[78] The debate about the textbooks takes on two mantles. One can think of it as a debate about documented and evidence-supported history or factually incorrect history. A second order of debate would be to think of it as the construction of a prejudiced history. This paper supports the view that by distorting key facts and making value judgements on the history of Muslim rule in medieval India, the idea of Muslim invasion becomes a locus around which current and future political debate can be structured.

CONCLUSION: CONSTRUCTING THE MUSLIM 'OTHER'

The above discussion highlights the creation of the abstract demonic Muslim first in the cultural sphere and its subsequent transposition to the political as a larger disenfranchisement of the Muslim community. The process begins with the creation of an order of myths that become the defining features of the Muslims in India. Literary support enables the Right to influence the public sphere and is provided by written material in the form of periodicals, pamphlets, and school books.

Every social and political struggle has its heroes and enemies. Where no enemies exist it must create them or the struggle will lose its meaning. The 'socially assembled' enemy becomes the focus of a struggle.[79] Stanley Tambiah notes in his analysis of ethnic conflict, the 'rites of violence' in religious riots in South Asia have led inevitably to the 'demonizing of victims and their expulsion or annihilation in the idiom of exorcism'.[80] Juergensmeyer focuses on the issue of identifying enemies in an ethnic war, but can be perhaps be extended to explain the project of the Hindu Right in India. The contention is that in the absence of concrete reasons needed to identify an enemy 'the attempts to make satanic beings out of relatively innocent foes become more creative'.[81] Overarching characterizations of an identified enemy make the process of dehumanizing them easier and hating them as a collective enemy is easier than targeting individuals against whom one has no personal antipathy. What emerges, argues Juergensmeyer, is a 'faceless collective enemy' that could be representative of a 'system' or they could be a 'stand-in for a more diffuse notion of evil, a sort of enemy-in-general'.[82]

For the RSS the Muslim may be a citizen in the letter of the Constitution but is not a part of the nation which is defined through an exclusion of anyone who is not Hindu. To recapitulate the argument made in the first section, the RSS (echoing Savarkar) holds that invasions by Muslim kings and proselytizing Christians have alienated the people from their culture. Once this religious wall of identification is demolished there will be no separation between Hindus, Indian Muslims, and Indian Christians. Therefore, the target of hostility of Hindus is not the Christian or the Muslim but their religions. The Christians and Muslims have been deceived and alienated and in their minds there exists a deep hatred of their own ancestral culture. The objective then is to bring back to the Hindu fold the sheep that have strayed.[83]

> We have to finish Islam from this country, not Muslims. . . . A Muslim who actually believes in the theology of Islam can never be a member of the Hindu Nation. . . .[84]

This emphasis on 'bringing the stray sheep back in' translates into a radical understanding of secularism. Essentially it refers to the recognition of one dominant religion (Hinduism) by minorities in India. This religion permeates the state and its apparatus and while ideally Muslims and Christians should be Hindus once again through a process of cleansing (*shuddhikaran)*, if they don't, they will always have a less than equal status in the state.

The 1990s saw the revival of the 'birthplace of Ram' issue. The contestation between the Hindu Right and Muslims assumed a spatial dimension with Ayodhya representing a 'humiliation' which could be healed only by the removal of the Babri Masjid and the construction of a Ram Mandir on the spot. The politics of the Ramjanmabhoomi agitation was to identify an enemy that acted against the religious interests of Hindus. The Babri Masjid was seen as a violation of the rights of the Hindu majority, which gave rise to the anti-Congress and anti-establishment idiom of 'pseudo secularism' and 'minorityism'. Hindutva was seen as the balm that would organise the enjoyment of the Hindu community. In the process Ram became the crusader of all Hindus and became an agitational device. Ram also became the metaphor of Indian culture and its essence of Hinduness. In this view, the Ramjanmabhoomi agitation was seen as the latest battle of an ancient war. The Masjid was seen as

> an eternal blot on the secular face of India . . . Hindus over the centuries have been subjected to aggression, tyranny and indignities. Thousands of temples have been destroyed. . . . Muslims beat Hindus time and again, not because Hindus lacked bravery or sacrifice, but just for one reason, disunity. . . . Hindus now want to possess what is theirs. . . .[85]

The RSS and the rest of the Sangh Parivar, through the collective worship of Ram, have tried to identify the positive 'core' of Hindus and not see the community as a series of absences as is usually seen in the Orientalist discourse. The final layer in the Ramjanmabhoomi agitation was the discourse on the 'Muslim'. As Hansen argues, this was done by not identifying one but two 'others'—Pakistan and the Muslim world which was the external 'other'; and, Indian Muslims posited as the internal one. The idea was that the *otherness* of the Muslims and its threat had made the Hindus self-conscious about their culture. The identification of the 'Hindu self' was at the same time furthered and inhibited by having a militant Muslim neighbour, a permanent insult in the form of the Babri Masjid, a history of Muslim invasions and Muslim resistance to uniform civil legislation.[86]

In this scenario, Muslims were depicted as being antithetical to the Indian nation; they were seen as intolerant and unfit to live under conditions of democracy,

> Democratic and secular India has gone soft in the face of Islamic subversion. They (Muslims) use the secular pretext to strike at India's very cultural roots. . . . Muslim society here has failed to imbibe the Indian spirit . . . they can destroy the very system ultimately. . . .[87]

In this discourse, Islam is seen as intolerant and a threat to Hindu culture, expansionist, and aggressive. Faith for a Muslim means identifying with the doctrines of Islam, which by implication means that any Muslim has the capacity and the tendency to be violent, secretive, and dominant. This secretive, mystical, well-knit Muslim community is an immediate threat. The Muslims are also seen as being primitive, and this view is supported by the RSS by pointing out to the Muslim resistance to birth control and the Uniform Civil Code.

The negotiation of normative and actual citizenship is an important tool for the RSS. Even though constitutionally Muslims are citizens, the RSS has managed to deprive them of the effective expression of citizenship, making the case that the possession of full political rights depreciates in value without socio-economic empowerment and impartial legislative mechanisms. The ideology of the RSS responds to a created anxiety about strangers and enemies who are internal to the country, not external. Of course, related to this main theme is the question of the BJP's success in the Hindu heartland states and its relative weakness in the southern states. This brings issues of linguistic boundaries of states, influence of socialist movements and lower caste movements which may have effectively challenged Hindutva agendas. Also, one can see the Hindu nationalist movement as an exercise in the capture of state power which will enable it to mobilize resources for certain states in the Hindu heartland. Perhaps the success of the BJP in five key states in 2004 then has something to do with the Centre's financial patronage under the previous BJP-led government. This however can be the subject of another paper.

The written record of the Hindu Right shows that the process of othering Muslims is as yet unceasing and has only suffered a temporary setback in the recent electoral defeat of the BJP. The idea that certain people who have lived all their lives in India can suddenly not be regarded as Indians is a troubling one since it raises a number of questions about the nature and functions of a democratic state, the viability of poly-ethnic societies and the applicability of citizenship as a mediating force between state and individual. This interrogation has undoubtedly impacted on India's much-examined secular credentials and far more acutely on the Muslim community.

NOTES

1. See T.B. Hansen, *The Saffron Wave: Democracy and Hindu Nationalism in Modern India*, Princeton: Princeton University Press, 1999, p. 3.
2. In May 1998 nuclear tests were conducted at Pokhran in Rajasthan.
3. See Christophe Jaffrelot, *The Hindu Nationalist Movement and Indian Politics: 1925 to the 1990s*, Delhi: Penguin, 1996.
4. See Peter van der Veer, *Religious Nationalism*, Berkeley: University of California Press, 1994.
5. See T.B. Hansen, *The Saffron Wave: Democracy and Hindu Nationalism in Modern India*, Princeton: Princeton University Press, 1999, p. 4.
6. Ibid.
7. Ibid.
8. The *Organiser's* English edition has been studied for this paper. The pamphlets and some textbooks have been translated from the Gujarati language.
9. See David Held, *Models of Democracy*, 2nd edn., Stanford: Stanford University Press, 1996, and Carter and Stokes, *Democratic Theory Today: Challenges for the 21st Century*, Cambridge: Polity, 2002.
10. See Gershon Shafir, *The Citizenship Debates: A Reader*, Minneapolis: University of Minnesota Press, 1998, p. 13.
11. Feudal notions of citizenship refer to the property quotient that was a criterion for deciding who had the most stake in managing the affairs of the state. Since most land was concentrated in the hands of men, the landless and women were often excluded from the ambit of politics as they did not fulfil this criterion.
12. See Michael Walzer, 'The Civil Society Argument', in Shafir (ed.),*The Citizenship Debates: A Reader*, Minneapolis: University of Minnesota Press.
13. See Shafir (ed.), *The Citizenship Debates*, op. cit., p. 8.
14. See John Rawls, 'Justice as Fairness in the Liberal Polity', in Shafir (ed.), *The Citizenship Debates*, op. cit.
15. See Shafir, 1998, *The Citizenship Debates*, op. cit., p. 15.
16. Ibid., p. 16.
17. Roger Brubaker, *Citizenship and Nationhood in France and Germany*, Cambridge: Harvard University Press, 1992.
18. See Chetan Bhatt, *Hindu Nationalism: Origins, Ideologies and Modern Myths*, Oxford: Berg, 2001, p. 78.
19. Ibid., p. 86.
20. Ibid., p. 87.
21. This thesis is originally found in Friedrich Schelegel's *On the Language and Wisdom of The Indians* (1808) and also in Joseph Arthur de Gobineau's *Essay on the Inequality of Human Races*.
22. Ibid., p. 90.
23. V.D. Savarkar, *Hindutva: Who is a Hindu*?, Bombay: Veer Savarkar Prakashan, 1923, 1989, p. 34.

24. Ibid., p. 110.
25. Ibid., p. 85.
26. See Chetan Bhatt, *Hindu Nationalism: Origins, Ideologies and Modern Myths*, Oxford: Berg, 2001.
27. See V.D. Savarkar, *Hindutva: Who is a Hindu*?, op. cit., p. 90.
28. Ibid., p. 113.
29. M.S. Golwalker, *We, Our Nationhood Defined*, Nagpur: Bharat Publications, 1939, rpt. 1942, p. 43.
30. Sunil Khilnani, *The Idea of India*, Harmondsworth: Penguin, 1998, p. 65.
31. N. Kabeer, 'Citizenship, Affiliation and Exclusion: Perspectives from the South,' *IDS Bulletin*, vol. 33(2), 2002.
32. Gyanendra Pandey, 'Can a Muslim be an Indian?', *Comparative Studies in Society and History* 41.4, 1999, pp. 608-29.
33. *Constitution Assembly Debates*, Book 4, vol. IX, 30 July-18 September 1949, Lok Sabha Secretariat, pp. 355-6 and 376-8.
34. Ibid., pp. 366-7.
35. Ibid., p. 369.
36. Ibid., p. 382.
37. Ibid., pp. 396-7.
38. Ibid., pp. 398-401.
39. Pandey, 'Can a Muslim be an Indian?', op. cit.
40. Roger Brubaker, *Citizenship and Nationhood in France and Germany*, Cambridge: Harvard University Press, 1992; Shafir, *The Citizenship Debates*, op. cit., pp. 16-17.
41. Because of the missing records it was decided to eliminate these issues from the study and start from 1994, since partial information would at best only approximate the real evidence.
42. The study started out with a value neutral take on all issues like 'Muslims', 'Pakistan', 'Christians', etc. However, it was found that most of the articles about such issues were pejorative and negative in nature, which helped shape the larger idea that there was in fact some demonizing or othering going on in these articles.
43. Sheshadri Chari, *Organiser*, Independence Day Special, 20 August 2002.
44. S. Joshi, *Organiser*, Independence Day Special, 20 August 2002.
45. *Organiser*, 31 December 2000.
46. V.P. Bhatia, 'Global Drive of Islamic Conversions', *Organiser*, 9 February 2003.
47. Ibid., 'Are the Indian Muslims Really Backward', *Organiser*, 17 September 2000.
48. Ibid., 'Hinduise all Politics, Militarize Hindudom', *Organiser*, 2 February 2003.
49. K.N. Panikkar, *The Concerned Indian's Guide to Communalism*, Delhi: Viking, 1999.

50. Ibid., p. xi.
51. Translated, it means 'The Bloody and Glorious History of the Birthplace of Ram'.
52. RSS Pamphlet Sample 5 cited in the Gujarat Carnage Special Issue of *Communalism Combat*, April-May 2002.
53. Ibid.
54. Pamphlet Sample 2.
55. Pamphlet Sample 5.
56. Ibid.
57. Ibid.
58. Tanika Sarkar, 2003, 'The Historical Pedagogy of the Sangh Parivar', *Seminar* No. 522, February; and also Kumkum Roy, 2003, 'What Happened to Confucianism?' *Seminar* No. 522.
59. Saffronization refers to the rewriting of history textbooks according to a glorified Hindu perspective which is at odds with documented history and seeks to portray Hindu civilization as the most advanced of all ancient worlds. It also includes the process where textbooks are made to include anti-minority and more specifically anti-Muslim 'facts'.
60. Saraswati is the Hindu goddess of learning and wisdom. The term literally translated means 'Goddess Saraswati's Temples for Infants'.
61. Panikkar, op. cit., p. xi.
62. Council for the Administration of Children's Education.
63. Tanika Sarkar, op. cit.
64. Roshni Sengupta, 'Saffronising the Mind of India' accessible at http://www.countercurrents.org/comm-sengupta110304.htm. In this article the author does a nuanced job of documenting most of the anachronistic portrayals of history and pontificates on the process of re-writing a new communal historiography.
65. See Tanika Sarkar, op. cit.
66. Ibid.
67. After minority educational institutions protested this circular was withdrawn.
68. Page 8, *Gaurav Gatha*, for Class IV, Shishu Mandirs.
69. *Gaurav Gatha*, p. 9.
70. *Itihaas Gaa Raha Hai*, Class V, Shishu Mandirs.
71. Chapter 28, *Sanskar Saurabh*, Book 3 for Class V.
72. 'Manu aur Manav', Chapter 3, *Sanskar Saurabh*, Class IV.
73. Page 57, *Sanskar Saurabh*, Class IV.
74. Pages 31-2, *Sanskar Saurabh*, Class IV.
75. Page 1, *Akhil Bharatiya Sanskriti—Gyan Pariksha Pradhnotri*, ed. Vidya Bharati, Class 8.
76. Page 16, ABSGPP.
77. Page 65, *Sadachar ki Batein*, Class IX.
78. Tanika Sarkar, op. cit.

79. Mark Juergensmeyer, *Terror in the Mind of God: The Global Rise of Religious Violence*, Berkeley and LA: University of California Press, 2000.
80. Stanley Tambiah, *Leveling Crowds: Ethnonationalist Conflicts and Collective Violence in South Asia*, Berkeley: University of California Press, 1996, pp. 310-11.
81. Mark Juergensmeyer, op. cit., p. 172.
82. Ibid., p. 175.
83. Abhas Chatterjee, *The Concept of Hindu Nation*, Delhi: Voice of India, 1995, p. 28.
84. Ibid.
85. Daljit Singh, *Organiser*, Deepavali Special, October 1990.
86. Hansen, op. cit., p. 178.
87. V.P. Bhatia, *Organiser*, Republic Day Special, 1993.

DOCUMENTS AND REPORTS

Gujarat Carnage Special Issue of *Communalism Combat*, April-May 2002.

Human Rights Watch Report on the Gujarat Riots entitled *We Have No Orders to Save You*, vol. 14, no. 3 (c), http://www.hrw.org/reports/2002/india.

The Report of the National Human Rights Commission on the Gujarat Riots, *Final Order on Gujarat dated 31 May 2002.*

Gujarat Carnage, A Report to the Nation by An Independent Fact Finding Mission: Dr. Kamal Mitra Chenoy, S.P. Shukla, K.S. Subramanian and Achin Vanaik, 11 April 2002.

Organiser

Constituent Assembly Debates, Book 4, vol. IX, 30 July-18 September 1949, Lok Sabha Secretariat.

11

A Malevolent Embrace?

The BJP and Muslims in the Parliamentary Election of 2004

NIRAJA GOPAL JAYAL

The Indian parliamentary election of 2004 was an election of many firsts: it was the first Lok Sabha election of the twenty-first century; it was the first election in which political communication came to be conducted in the corporate vocabulary of image-making, branding and marketing; it was the first election after the first ever non-Congress government completed a full term in office; and it was the first election after which the elected leader of the single largest party declined the prime ministership and nominated another. It was also arguably the first general election in which the minority vote was assiduously courted by a party whose very identity was, since the early 1990s, defined by its hostility to minorities.

It is no secret that the Bharatiya Janata Party (BJP), with its genetic ties to the Rashtriya Swayamsevak Sangh (RSS), has practised a particularly exclusionary brand of politics: conceiving and launching the Ramjanmabhoomi agitation; violently tearing down the Babri Masjid in December 1992; and, above all, perpetrating the most horrific violence upon innocent Muslims in Gujarat a decade later. It has consistently held that, if elected to power on its own, it would enact a Uniform Civil Code (i.e. do away with the special provisions of Muslim, and other, personal law), build a temple in Ayodhya on the site of the destroyed Babri Masjid, and remove Article 370 (providing

* First published in *India Review*, vol. 3, no. 3, July 2004, pp. 183-209.

the state of Jammu & Kashmir with a special status) from the Constitution. This paper will analyse the failed attempt of the BJP to reinvent itself as a moderate and inclusive party in the election campaign of 2004, and the response of the Muslim community to this initiative. It will also examine the results of the election in constituencies where the Muslim population exceeds 10 per cent, including the nomination of candidates, party strategies, and the final outcomes.

While many explanations of the electoral verdict have been offered (and each strongly contested), these could be classified into three broad strands. The first is a political economy strand, encompasses two conflicting explanations: the first views it as a verdict on an urban-centered economic reforms programme, best exemplified in the 'India Shining' advertising campaign which alienated more voters than it attracted. This claim has been rebutted by a second argument: that the verdict actually expressed popular dissatisfaction with the reforms not having gone far enough, and with 'the extent of achievement compared with the magnitude of expectations'.[1] Likewise, a micro-level study of women voters—belonging to a self-help group engaged in a micro-credit programme funded by the World Bank—in Andhra Pradesh showed how the vote against former Chief Minister Chandrababu Naidu was 'not a mandate against the World Bank programmes espoused by the incumbent *but for it, and more of it*'.[2]

The findings of the National Election Study, a post-poll survey conducted by the Centre for the Study of Developing Societies (CSDS), confirm the ambiguity noted above. Since the economic reforms were not placed before the electorate as the primary issue, and only 19 per cent of the more than 25,000 respondents had even heard of a change in economic policy, the verdict could not strictly be interpreted as a mandate against the reforms. However, unemployment was identified as the most important problem, and the BJP-led National Democratic Alliance (NDA) coalition government was seen to have a pro-rich image. The condition of the poor may have worsened in the last five years, but there was no evidence of the resentment about this being directly related to the economic reforms. The fact that the poor are not part of the elite consensus on economic reforms was made apparent by the survey, but that they voted on the basis of this is much less clear.[3]

The second explanation sees the verdict as a decisive rejection of the BJP's Hindutva agenda and the communal violence against the Muslims in Gujarat in February 2002. This explanation must of course contend with the fact that, in the assembly elections held in Gujarat in December the same year, the Modi government was swept back into power, defying the almost invincible law of anti-incumbency that plays such an important role in Indian politics. More importantly, the way the state of Gujarat voted in 2004 had much to do with conflicts internal to the Sangh Parivar, especially the dissatisfaction of the Bharat Kisan Sangh (the farmers' unit of the RSS). Some allies of the BJP—including the Trinamool Congress, the Telugu Desam Party, the Janata Dal (U) and even the Shiv Sena—have, in their post-election analyses, attributed the defeat of the NDA to the Gujarat riots. The most recent voice to join this chorus is none other than that of just ousted former Prime Minister Atal Behari Vajpayee himself who, in an interview, said that the BJP was contemplating the removal of Narendra Modi for the chief minister of Gujarat, because the electoral defeat was largely on account of the 2000 Gujarat riots. This sparked off a controversy with the party apparatchiks as also with the RSS and Vishwa Hindu Parishad (VHP), reacting sharply and negatively to Vajpayee's statement, perhaps signaling the long-term marginalization of the Vajpayee line of relative moderation within the BJP. Nevertheless, a distinction must be made between the rejection of Hindutva and the condemnation of the riots, as the one does not necessarily entail the other. There is a difference between communal ideology and the willingness to engage in communal violence: it is arguable that a large number of citizens who would subscribe to the first would recoil with horror at the second. In other words, there is no necessary compatibility between entertaining communal beliefs, on the one hand, and the willingness to practice or justify violence against minorities, on the other.

To cite the findings of the CSDS National Election Study once more, the survey showed a substantial agreement—of 83 per cent—among people of all communities with the statement that—'Government should protect the interests of the minorities'. Predictably, of course, 89 per cent of Muslim respondents and 85 per cent of Christian respondents agreed, while the extent of agreement among Hindu respondents was 83 per cent.[4]

The third explanation for the election result views it as an aggregation of state-level verdicts. As such, the cumulative result is an outcome of some strategic, and other not-so-clever, alliances entered into by the Congress and the BJP respectively. On the whole, the Congress party made effective alliances, which enabled it to increase the total number of seats won despite a drop of 2 per cent in vote share from 1999. Congress contested 417 seats out of 543, leaving 36 more seats for its allies than it did last time. This was how its allies could contribute as many as 74 seats, apart from adding 9 per cent to the vote share. The BJP's alliance with the All-India Anna Dravida Munnetra Kazhagam in Tamil Nadu, by contrast, showed very poor judgement on its part, while its ally in Andhra Pradesh was completely decimated in the Assembly election held almost simultaneously, an anti-incumbency vote also reflected in its Lok Sabha tally.

The way in which religious minorities in general, and the Muslims in particular, voted is of course not central to any of these explanations. Even the second explanation refers to the more widespread abhorrence of communal violence in the electorate rather than the insecurity of the Muslim voters as such. As an attempt to understand the place of the minorities in the election, therefore, this paper seeks neither to establish nor to commend the second explanation. Its purpose is limited to a marshalling of the evidence on how the Muslim minority was courted, and what the concrete electoral outcomes demonstrate about the place of Muslims in the polity as well as in Indian political discourse.

The next section of this paper seeks to provide a background understanding of the extent of Muslim under-representation in parliament from independence to the present, and the way in which the majoritarian first-past-the-post electoral system tends to entrench this under-representation. It also provides a brief background to relevant political events, chiefly the violence against the Muslims in Gujarat in 2002 and its aftermath. Section III provides an account of the BJP's attempt at recasting itself as an inclusive party, and seeks an explanation for this. It also deals with the response of the Muslim community as expressed in the statements of clerics, as well as in sections of the Muslim press. The election manifestos of the BJP and the Congress party are compared for their discourse on minorities. Section IV of the paper examines and analyses the election results in over one hundred constituencies where the percentage of Muslims in the population is above 15 per cent, and specifically the performance of the BJP in these. As may be expected, the result varies depending upon a variety of factors, including the proportion of Muslims in the electorate; the strategies of the leading political parties; the particular regional configuration of the electoral battle; the practice of strategic voting by the Muslim electorate, and so on. The result also takes into account the preliminary findings reported by the CSDS post-poll survey, suggesting how Muslims *actually* voted in this election. The concluding section V examines the extent to which the Muslim voter remains central to the polity and political discourse in a post-BJP India.

II

As the second largest religious community in the country, the Muslims—at 12.12 per cent of the Indian population—account for two-thirds of all the religious minorities taken together. This is despite the fact that, at the time of partition in 1947, Muslims accounted for 24 per cent of the country's population, exactly double of what it is today. While the 1991 Census was not conducted in the state of Jammu & Kashmir, in the 1981 Census, Muslims accounted for 64 per cent of the population of the state. They also comprise 95 per cent of the Union Territory of Lakshadweep. Muslims are the main minority in the states of Assam, West Bengal, Bihar, Uttar Pradesh, and Kerala, in all of which their proportion of the population ranges between 15 and 28 per cent. They are also the largest minority group—though with smaller proportions—in the states of Rajasthan, Maharashtra, Andhra Pradesh, Madhya Pradesh, Gujarat, Karnataka, Haryana and Delhi, in each of which their number exceeds one million. Altogether, the number of Muslims in India makes this the second largest Muslim community in the world after Indonesia, and larger than the Muslim population of Pakistan. Though just three states (Bihar, Uttar Pradesh and West Bengal) account for more than half the population of Muslims in India, there are Muslim communities in many regions and, more importantly there is considerable variation between them of region, culture and language, making it difficult to speak of Muslims in India in terms of a monolithic or homogeneous category.

If their proportion in the population is taken as the decisive criterion, then Muslims have been consistently under-represented in parliament. In the first Lok Sabha, elected in 1952, they constituted 4.4 per cent of the house, and in the just-constituted Fourteenth Lok Sabha—with 35 Muslims returned to the house—they stand at 6.45 per cent. The highest representation achieved by Muslims was in 1980, when they accounted for 9.2 per cent of Lok Sabha members. The table below details Muslim representation in the Lok Sabha for the period preceding that for which data has been generated in this paper.

TABLE 1: MUSLIMS IN THE LOK SABHA (1952-99)

Year	Total no. of seats	No. of Muslims in Lok Sabha	Muslims expected on the basis of population	Deprivation (%)
1952	489	21	49	57.14
1957	494	24	49	51.02
1962	494	23	53	56.60
1967	520	29	56	48.21
1971	518	30	58	48.28
1977	542	34	61	44.26
1980	542	49	59	16.95
1984	543	46	62	25.81
1989	543	33	60	45.00
1991	543	28	65	56.92
1996	543	28	66	57.56
1998	543	28	66	57.56
1999	543	32	66	51.52
Total		405	770	47.45

Source: Iqbal A. Ansari, 'Muslim Representation in Legislatures: 1952-2002', Mimeo, Delhi: Jamia Hamdard University, 2003, p. 24.

In the election to the Fourteenth Lok Sabha, the focus of this paper, the total number of Muslim candidates elected was 35, slightly higher than that in 1999. Notably, of these, 25 members were elected from constituencies with a Muslim population of over 15 per cent, while the remaining 10 were elected from constituencies with Muslim populations of less than 15 per cent.

On the whole, the representation of minorities in the Lok Sabha has remained more or less constant, registering no sharp increase or decline. The Sikhs, Christians and Jains are represented roughly in proportion to their percentage in the population. An examination of the results of the last decade shows that, at 1.94 per cent of the population, Sikhs had representation ranging between 1.84 per cent (in the tenth Lok Sabha, elected in 1991) and 2.20 per cent in the Thirteenth. Similarly, at 2.34 per cent of the total population, Christians too were represented to the extent of 2.94 per cent (in the Tenth Lok Sabha) and 2.02 per cent (in the Thirteenth). Only Muslim representation that continues to be abysmally low, almost stationary in the region of 5 to 6 per cent, though their percentage in the population is considerably higher at 12.12 per cent.

This pattern is explained partly by the demographic distribution of Muslims as compared to other religious minorities, and partly by the sharply polarized intercommunal situation prevailing in the country. The only state in which Muslims constitute a majority is Jammu & Kashmir, which has six Lok Sabha constituencies, inevitably shared between Muslims, Hindus and Buddhists in the ratio of 3:2:1, based upon the religious demography of the state's territory. The island of Lakshadweep has a Muslim majority population of 95 per cent and the single parliamentary seat here is reserved for a Scheduled Tribe (ST) candidate. In addition, three constituencies in West Bengal, two in Kerala, and one each in Bihar and Assam have a Muslim population of over 50 per cent. As states, Assam and West Bengal have a high concentration of Muslims, but even Assam—with a 28.43 per cent Muslim population—returned Muslims in only two seats (in percentage terms, 14 per cent of its 14 seats in the Lok Sabha) in the thirteenth as well as the fourteenth Lok Sabhas.

This under-representation can only partially be explained by the majoritarian first-past-the-post electoral system, which helps minorities that are geographically concentrated, and conversely disfavours minorities that are *not* geographically concentrated. Thus, for instance, members of the Scheduled Tribes do manage to win seats in excess of the quotas reserved for them largely due to the concentrated character of the ST population in those states of central India and the north-east where they are present in larger numbers. This however is not true of Scheduled Castes, who are more evenly distributed across the country, or of Muslims, who are geographically more dispersed.

Historically, the Congress party has projected itself, and been viewed, as the protector of minorities, and as the guarantor of a secular state that recognizes minority rights as of foundational importance. Unsurprisingly, the Congress has historically been the party most favoured by Muslim voters. Lloyd and Susanne Rudolph have, however, argued that since the shifts in Muslim voting patterns from 1977 to 1984 parallel the regional and national outcomes in these elections, this raises 'the question of whether the minorities purported support for Congress results more from a special relationship based on Congress's commitment to equal citizenship and secular values or from a perception of Congress as the dominant party and as such the likely winner and prospective governing party.'[5] They express doubts about the validity of the thesis that there is 'a special relationship' between the Congress and the Muslim voter. While this may have been true of Nehru's time, it appears to be less and less the case from the early 1960s onwards, based on evidence from the parliamentary constituencies that have Muslim populations of 10 per cent or more. Here, Rudolph and Rudolph found that in three consecutive elections—1977, 1980 and 1984—Congress received a lower percentage of votes in these constituencies than in others. Further, in 1977 and 1980, it won a lower proportion of seats in Muslim constituencies than it did overall.[6]

Indeed, a recent study has argued that the Congress must shoulder the blame for the under-representation of Muslims, because the percentage of Muslim nominations by the party has been consistently low. In the first five Lok Sabha elections (1952-71), the Congress nominations for Muslims remained between 4.29 and 5.74 per cent. In these elections, Muslim candidates belonging to the Congress managed to win even in constituencies where the Muslim population was between 3 and 18 per cent only.[7] It was in the 1977 (post-Emergency) election that the Congress, for the first time, nominated 7.52 per cent Muslim candidates. Interestingly, in this particular election, the Muslim vote conformed to the general pattern and went against even Muslim candidates if they were Congress nominees.[8] The popular explanation for this has been the excesses of the programmes of forced sterilization, and the bulldozing of homes of poor Muslims in the Turkman Gate area of Delhi.

In the next two general election (1980 and 1984), however, the number of Muslims elected reached their highest number. Both these elections saw a massive pro-Congress wave in the country as a whole that was also echoed in the Muslim vote. Beginning with the 1989 election again, there has been a downward curve of Muslim representation, repeated in 1991, 1996 and 1998. These elections have seen a spread of the Muslim vote across many parties, including most notably the Smajwadi Party and the Bahujan Samaj Party in Uttar Pradesh, and the Rashtriya Janata Dal in Bihar. Thus, the 28 Muslim MPs elected in 1998 represented 12 different parties. The corresponding figure for 1991 was six parties and seven for 1996. In the 1996 election—which, not unimportantly, was the first parliamentary election after the demolition of the Babri Masjid, in which the Congress Prime Minister Narasimha Rao was perceived to have deliberately chosen a Nero-like strantegy of inaction—the Congress lost Muslim support by four percentage points. The drop in the Muslim vote for the Congress in the 1996 election was, in no small measure, due to a feeling of betrayal in December 1992 when the Babri Masjid was violently torn down, and the Narasimha Rao government was perceived to have watched silently and therefore complicitly. In the next election, and indeed more forcefully in the Assembly elections in Uttar Pradesh in 1993, Muslims decided that their interests were more secure with the Samajwadi Party, which was voted into power in UP that year, albeit in an alliance with the Bahujan Samaj Party that lasted barely two years.

In the parliamentary elections of 1998 and 1999, it appeared that the Muslim anger had somewhat subsided and there was a return to the Congress. In the thirteenth Lok Sabha, elected in 1991, there were 32 Muslim MPs, up from 28 in each of the previous three Lok Sabhas, and representing 11 different parties. The Congress nominated 33 Muslims, of whom 10 were elected.[9] As far as the Muslim vote for the Congress is concerned, the data on seats is corroborated by data on vote share based on the National Election Studies' post-poll survey, conducted by the CSDS.

There are at least two ways of addressing under-representation: the political and the electoral. As we have seen, political parties, including the Congress, were never particularly enthusiastic about putting up more minority candidates. As the current climate of heightened communalism in the country does not hold out immediate hope of the

TABLE 2: MUSLIM VOTES FOR THE CONGRESS
LOK SABHA ELECTIONS 1991-9

Year	1991	1996	1998	1999
Vote Share %	38	34	43	50

Source: Yogendra Yadav, 'The New Congress Voter', *Seminar*, No. 526 (June 2003), p. 65.

former, some have suggested remodeling the electoral system. Suggestions include a range of methods: adopting a form of proportional representation according to the Mauritius model of allocating a number of additional seats that are uncontested but allotted to the best losers from among women, minorities and the most backward castes; encouraging political parties to give fair representation to disadvantaged groups in their party organization as well as in nominations for elections; and redrawing of constituencies such that constituencies presently reserved for the Scheduled Castes and Scheduled Tribes, in which the Muslim population exceeds the percentage in the country or the concerned state, are dereserved.[10]

Several other strategies that have been recommended belong to neither of the two categories identified above. One is a proposal for treating Muslims as a 'Backward Class' and so entitled to the benefits of affirmative action.[11] While this suggestion comes from a veteran Muslim leader, Syed Shahabuddin, it is an argument that has actually been used *against* the elites of the Muslim community—which would arguably include Shahabuddin himself—as it is claimed they have monopolized the benefits of even token representation. The 2001 publication of a book—*Masawat ki Jung* (War of Equality), sparked off an intense debate among Muslims as to the status of internal discrimination against backward castes among the Muslims. This account of Muslims in Bihar society and politics provided detailed data on the composition of various boards and committees of community organizations to show the overwhelming preponderance of the 'forward castes' among the Muslims.[12] In the last Bihar Assembly (Vidhan Sabha) election of 1995, for example, it showed that of the 42 Muslim candidates put up by the Congress party, only 13 belonged to the lower 'castes'. In all Bihar Assembly elections in independent India, between 1952 and 1995, there were a total of 245 Muslim candidates who won the election. Of these, 197 belonged to the higher 'castes'—the Shaikh, Sayyad and Pathan *jatis*. The backward Muslims, on the other hand, got barely 19.2 per cent of the seats.[13] The author's claim is that the marginalization of the backward castes among the Muslims is of the same order (80–20) as the marginalization of Muslims as a whole vis-à-vis the Hindus.

An alternative view holds that instead of seeking quotas in the civil service, Muslims should pursue the path of social mobility through private entrepreneurship. In this area, they already have inspiring models of prosperity in the form of the Bohras of western India, the Aga Khani Khojas, the Memons, and various other traditional mercantilist Muslim groups in various parts of the country. Additionally, greater decentralization, along with the creation of districts and constituencies where Muslims are in a majority, would effectively address the distortions of the electoral process, and this could be further supplemented by reserving such seats for Muslims, as is currently done for the scheduled castes and scheduled tribes.[14]

III

Unlike the Congress, which was almost the natural party of Muslim affiliation, the BJP has never been a plausible candidate for the Muslim vote. Its politics of Hindu nationalism has thrived on demonizing of the Muslim (and occasionally Christian) minority, on the view that minorities are not entitled to special rights, and with the allegation that the Congress and other parties that claim to be secular are actually practizing a politics of 'appeasement' and 'pseudo-secularism'. The two most compelling images of the BJP's virulent anti-Muslim sentiment are without doubt the destruction of the Babri Masjid in 1992, and the violence against the Muslims of Gujarat in February 2002. While the former was justified in terms of religious fervour, the latter was justified as a 'natural reaction' to the 'action' in which forty-odd Hindu pilgrims were burned alive in a train coach at Godhra. This became the pretext for systematic violence against Muslims in many cities and towns of Gujarat, with murder, rape, loot, plunder, and many other unimaginably gruesome forms of violence being perpetrated. The riots also made obvious the complicity of the state apparatus—from the lowest functionary in the police station to the highest executive office in the state government—as Muslim citizens could get no protection from the violence. Nor, subsequently, has it been easy for them to obtain justice, let alone compensation for their property. Reassuringly, the Gujarat law courts have recently invited the wrath of the Supreme Court, now holding out some hope that justice will eventually be done. Senior party leaders of the BJP remained unperturbed by these events as strident justification rather than contrition was the preferred public attitude of party functionaries. This is only a capsule account of why the BJP was the most unlikely party to attempt to project itself as inclusivist in the weeks preceding the election of 2004.

It is indeed hard to recall any previous election in which *any* national party has so unabashedly (and so unconvincingly) advertised its courting of the largest religious minority in the country. Even a decade or two ago, it was quite customary for the Congress to ceremonially share the platform with the Shahi Imam of Delhi's Jama Masjid at election time, but these gestures were merely public affirmations of longstanding ties that were presumed to exist anyway, and had not been forged specially for purposes of the election.

Four aspects of the BJP's attempt to woo the Muslim voter bear detailing here: its election manifesto; its seeking out of prominent Muslim politicians to recruit and sponsor as candidates; its election campaign, particularly the campaigns of Prime Minister Vajpayee and Deputy Prime Minister Advani; and its Minority Development Convention in February 2004. The document through which the BJP sought to re-invent itself was not officially a manifesto, but was nevertheless released with all the fanfare that usually attends the launch of one. Indeed, the BJP's 'Vision Document'[15] was released even before the election manifesto of the NDA alliance. Not without abundant symbolism, this was done on the Hindu festival of Ramnavami (March 30), promising 'Ram Rajya', literally meaning the Kingdom of Rama, and metaphorically a 'paradise of good governance'. The first part of the Vision Document tried to convey the impression that the BJP's commitment to three most contentious issues was now characterized by a more consensual and moderate approach. These three issues are the construction of the Ram Temple at Ayodhya, the enactment of a Uniform Civil Code, and the abrogation of Article 370 of the

Constitution, and together they have loge served as a popular shorthand for the BJP's communal and anti-minority agenda. But according to the new vision. Document, the BJP would respect the judicial verdict on the Temple, and would be committed to dialogue in an atmosphere of mutual trust and goodwill as the way forward. Secondly, the earlier belligerence on the enactment of a Uniform Civil Code—doing away with the personal laws governing marriage and inheritance rights that minority communities enjoy—was replaced by arguments couched in terms of gender justice, emphasizing the desirability of social and political consensus on this issue. Third, Article 370 of the Constitution (which accords a special status to the state of Jammu & Kashmir, the abrogation of which has long been one of the most controversial features of the BJP's political programme) found no mention at all. The state of Jammu & Kashmir, however, was mentioned, with the major challenges in that state being identified as those of terrorism, development and the strengthening of governance.

A subsequent chapter, following the 'vision' statement, outlined 'The BJP Agenda for the Next Five Years'. This was marked by a conspicuous silence on all the three issues, suggesting a conscious attempt to differentiate between the BJP's long-term vision and its short-term agenda. Why did the BJP produce a Vision Document when the common manifesto of the NDA alliance was in the offing? The answer may lie in the BJP's compulsions, both electoral and ideological, to reassure the RSS, the VHP and other members of the Sangh Parivar, that its commitment to their common ideals remained firm, and also perhaps to remind its core constituency in the electorate that these were not altogether forsaken or forgotten. While the core commitments stood, the subtle shift in the way in which these issues were articulated, encouraged the view that the BJP was seeking to occupy a centrist space in the polity, and had moved from a hard-line position to a softer approach based on consensus.

Even as the Vision Document hinted at a moderation of the BJP's stance on these controversial issues, the NDA manifesto appeared to lurch in the opposite direction. The Ayodhya Temple issue figured in its manifesto for the first time, though with the expected caveats about abiding by the judicial verdict and preferring a dialogue based on mutual trust and goodwill. Thus, even as the BJP seemed to be trying to reinvent itself as a mainstream party, its alliance partners seemed to be signalling their willingness to partake of some of its controversial core agenda. The family likeness between the two documents was unmistakable and telling.

Nevertheless, the NDA manifesto did make the token promises for minorities: a minorities development agenda within six months to focus on education, economic upliftment and empowerment (the 3 Es); addressing especially the needs of those belonging to poor backgrounds; the reorientation of the Minorities Commission to focus on developmental and welfare issues; continued encouragement to the promotion the Urdu language and the modernization of *madrasa* education; and 'a concerted effort . . . to increase minorities' representation in administration and public bodies'.[16]

If the NDA manifesto envisaged a broadly 'promotional' strategy, the Congress manifesto can be characterized as 'protective' in nature. The section on minorities in the latter was obviously a response to the events in Gujarat, as it emphasized the promotion of peace and communal harmony, the enactment of a comprehensive law on social violence, and prosecution by special courts. It envisaged affirmative action at the national level for religious minorities, stating that it had already made such provision in Kerala and Karnataka. It also committed itself to the establishment of a Commission for Minority Educational Institutions; to the setting up of new technical institutions that can provide direct affiliation for minority professional institutions to central universities; and direct lending by the National Minorities Development Corporation and the parallel state bodies. On Ayodhya, of course, it reiterated the party's stand that the verdict of the courts must be abided, and if the issue is resolved through negotiations, all parties in the dispute must be included.

Shortly before the election, the BJP—perhaps realizing the rather unconvincing, and even callow, image of its token Muslim MPs, party spokesman Mukhtar Abbas Naqvi and central minister Shahnawaz Khan—seemed to be scurrying around for Muslim leaders of stature whom they could co-opt and sponsor for the election. An apparent feather in the party's cap was the induction of one of the best-known Muslim leaders, Arif Mohammed Khan. Khan had shot to fame, and won public accolades in 1986, when he resigned as a minister from the Congress government of Rajiv Gandhi because he disagreed with the government's decision to enact a law overturning a liberal Supreme Court judgement on maintenance for a Muslim woman divorcee. Rejecting the retrograde interpretation of Muslim Personal Law, which the government had sought to entrench through this law, Khan had then taken a principled position on gender justice. He later joined the Bahujan Samaj Party, and contested the 1999 election from Bahraich in eastern Uttar Pradesh on a BSP ticket, but lost narrowly to the BJP candidate. This time, solicited by both the Congress and the BJP, he joined the latter, was given the BJP ticket from Kaiserganj in UP, but once again lost the election. When questioned about his decision to join the BJP, he replied that if the BSP could legitimately capture the Muslim vote, and then enter into a governmental alliance with the BJP in Uttar Pradesh, what was so wrong about Muslims joining the BJP directly?[17] In another interview, he justified his decision thus:

> Suddenly I realised the BJP is telling me 'you come into the party, we want to correct the distortions in our image, we want to take everyone along.' . . . They are extending their hand, they say they want to correct the situation. We have to catch hold of this extended hand.[18]

Another prominent Muslim leader who seemed to be inclined towards the BJP was Najma Heptullah, a Congress MP for four terms and Deputy Chairperson of the Rajya Sabha. Heptullah quit the Congress shortly before the election, and though she did not formally join the BJP, the public perception was clear about her proximity to that party. This has since been confirmed, with the BJP nominating her as one of its candidates for the election to the Upper House of Parliament, the Rajya Sabha. The most prominent Muslim leader to move to the Congress party was Syed Shahabuddin, the former diplomat, former Janata Party parliamentarian, and former editor of the influential monthly *Muslim India*.

As far as the election campaign is concerned, the BJP was for the first time seen to be engaging in an active courting of the Muslim vote, especially in Uttar Pradesh. The Atal Behari Vajpayee Himayat Caravan (Sympathizers' Committee), a committee consisting of Muslim intellectuals and clerics, was formed, which worked to mobilize support for the prime minister through a 17-day election tour on a bus. The prime minister addressed the committee, affirming his belief that the country could not progress unless Hindus and Muslims learnt to live together, and it was in this spirit that he was appealing for votes, rather than from greed for short-term political benefits. He also cited the success of his peace initiative with Pakistan as an example of his good intentions, though this statement was criticized for its implicit equating of the welfare of Muslim citizens with the India–Pakistan relationship.

The election campaign of Deputy Prime Minister L.K. Advani was conducted in a mode reminiscent of his *Rath Yatra*[19] of 1990, the road trip which gave the first impetus to the Ramjanmabhoomi agitation by creating a wave of popular opinion in favour of the construction of the Ram Temple at Ayodhya, and energizing the BJP and its affiliate organizations, the RSS and the VHP, for the demolition of the Babri Masjid. This time, though, his campaign had a very different theme, that of 'India Rising', a phrase metonymically and otherwise recalling the 'India Shining' campaign that was ostensibly a governmental, rather than a party, campaign. Unlike in the 1990 *Rath Yatra,* the image Advani sought to project in 2004 was that of a national statesman and leader of a plural society. On his *Bharat Uday Yatra*,[20] Advani travelled 8,000 kilometres (4,970 miles), visited 121 parliamentary constituencies in 12 states—from Kanyakumari in the south to Pathankot in the north, and from Porbandar in western India to Puri in the east. His *yatra* was launched in the state of Kerala (where the BJP has virtually no political presence) with the BJP's token Muslim leaders, along with some local Muslim clerics and a few Christian priests. As his 'chariot'—a luxurious vehicle equipped with every creature comfort imaginable—travelled north and west, Advani delivered speeches announcing his commitment to the diversity of India. Drawing closer to the areas where BJP enjoys electoral support, and especially in Ayodhya, he reiterated the continued commitment of the BJP to the construction of the Ram Temple in Ayodhya. Thus, Hindutva was deployed where it had a known resonance, and issues of economic growth, development and governance everywhere else.

The BJP also attempted to play the old Congress hand of getting the influential Imam of Delhi's Jama Masjid, Syed Ahmed Bukhari, to encourage Muslim voters to support the BJP. It has long been customary for the Imam to issue a *fatwa* on the eve of elections, advising Muslims on how they should vote. On this occasion, Bukhari gave an interview to a national English daily stating that he had come to terms with the 'bitter truth' that the BJP was the only party capable of ensuring communal harmony in the country. In the past, he said, none of the parties supported by Muslims had done anything for them in return. He pointed to the low presence of Muslims in public employment, as also to their lower levels of educational attainment, to reinforce his argument. The BJP, unlike these other parties, he said, was different insofar as it had never concealed its animosity towards Muslims, was clearly a party that said only what it meant, and that therefore if it was now offering promises of a development package for the Muslim minority within six months of coming to power, these promises should be taken at their face value. The BJP had, he affirmed, clearly softened its stance in the last one month![21]

Fourthly, in February 2004, the BJP organized a 'Convention of Minorities' in Delhi. Significantly, the Convention thanked the prime minister for his successful initiatives on peace with Pakistan, normalcy in Jammu & Kashmir, and cross-border counter-terrorism. The assumption—frequently articulated in BJP pronouncements—that peace with Pakistan, or a friendly cricket match between the two countries, carries an assurance of the welfare of Indian Muslims, is deeply problematic and resented by Muslim opinion. Implicitly, such a claim hints that the Muslim citizens of India are Muslims first and Indians second, that their loyalty lies with the Muslims of Pakistan, and that they can be mollified and enticed to vote for the BJP if they are offered peace with Pakistan and normalcy in Kashmir as a bait and as a proxy for their own security. That this identification of Indian Muslims with their co-religionists in Pakistan may be offensive to Muslim citizens is not generally acknowledged.

• At the Convention, an appeal was also made to Muslims to change the course of Indian history by voting for the BJP. It was claimed that

> there has been a significant reduction in incidents of communal violence during the NDA rule. . . . Minorities are safe and have faced no discrimination under the NDA Government. . . . On the contrary, the BJP-led Government has provided more support and resources for the promotion of Urdu language and modernization of Madarsa [*sic*] education in the past five years than the previous governments did in 50 years.[22]

The Convention also adopted a three-point Action Plan that explains some of the initiatives discussed so far.

1. The BJP calls upon well meaning and prominent public figures belonging to minority communities to come forward to join the BJP *along with their followers.*
2. 'Support Atal Behari Vajpayee Committees', comprising people belonging to minority communities, should be set up in every town and village. This Convention calls upon respected community leaders, *who may or may not join the BJP*, to become the convenors of these committees.
3. This Convention calls upon BJP workers to make intensified efforts to reach out to their *minority brethren* in their neighbourhoods, communicate the achievements and initiatives of the NDA Government as well as the BJP's Vision for the future, and mobilize their support for the BJP and its allies.[23]

It is easier to explain the support for the BJP from Muslim clerics like the Shahi Imam than it is to explain the sudden decision of the BJP to court the Muslim vote. The former is of a piece with the general perception, in the months preceding the election, that the BJP was likely to return to power. However, as far as the latter is concerned, the BJP had probably realized that the Gujarat riots, and the party's refusal to replace the chief minister, may prove to be a liability in the election, and chose to embark upon an adventurous strategy of damage-limitation, howsoever unconvincingly. Indeed, as BJP ideologue and journalist Swapan Dasgupta wrote: 'The BJP has not forsaken Hindutva. It has merely shifted its strategic role, a shift that has been entirely prompted by the context of the polls.'[24]

Dasgupta argued that the RSS and the VHP have no quarrel with economic growth and developing infrastructure, but they do ask this question of the BJP: what distinguishes the party from the Congress, which could as easily pursue the same policies? In other words, the ideological distinctiveness of the BJP comes not from its developmental and governance agenda, but from Hindutva. Otherwise, there is little to suggest why it should be seen as different from, or better than, the Congress.

Arguably, the peculiarity of the political situation in the state of

Uttar Pradesh—a state in which the Congress has had its foothold converted into the merest toehold, and the BJP's vote-catching abilities are even lower—also encouraged the BJP to try and play the spoiler in a series of triangular and quadrangular electoral contests. Till the demolition of the Babri Masjid during the premiership of the Congress P.V. Narasimha Rao, the Muslim vote in UP traditionally went to the Congress party. After this event, the Muslim voter—provoked by a sense of betrayal and fear—shifted his support to the Samajwadi Party and the Bahujan Samaj Party, each of which had come to represent the interests of different, though sometimes overlapping, disadvantaged caste groups. The electoral contest in UP is invariably three- or four-cornered, fought by the BJP, the Congress, the Samajwadi Party, and the Bahujan Samaj Party, and has contributed to the fracturing of the vote, leading to a series of hung assemblies in the last decade. While the BSP has a dependable core constituency of Scheduled Castes, the Samajwadi Party depends largely upon a combination of the Muslim and Yadav vote. In courting the Muslims, the BJP may not have expected to win their support, but was certainly trying to split the Muslim vote so as to prevent it from consolidating in favour of any of the others.

Eventually, as we shall see, the Muslim voters of Uttar Pradesh voted largely for the Samajwadi Party, to which they have been loyal for several years now. It is a measure of the insecurity faced by Muslim citizens that they did so despite two disturbing developments. The first of these pertained to the circumstances under which, in 2003, the Samajwadi Party was, with the covert support of the BJP, installed in government in Uttar Pradesh, and retained suspiciously accommodative attitude toward the BJP. The second related to a campaign poster in which the sacrifices of Mulayam Singh Yadav, the leader of the Samajwadi Party, were compared with those of the grandson of the Prophet during the Karbala tragedy 1,400 years ago. Widely published in Urdu newspapers, this advertisement appalled and angered clerics as well as others by its sheer audacity. If the Samajwadi Party succeeded in obtaining the lion's share of the Muslim vote despite these incidents, it was surely because it was perceived as the most likely guarantor of Muslim security.[25] Another episode involving the Samajwadi Party was the election-eve announcement, by Mulayam Singh Yadav, that all government-run or government-aided schools and colleges would end their classes by noon on Fridays to enable Muslim students and teachers to offer the *namaz-e-Juma* or Friday prayers. Significantly, this government order was opposed by Muslim leaders, theologians, and various Muslim organizations on the grounds that if the state government had serious intentions of improving the Muslim welfare, they should produce concrete plans for their educational and economic development instead of creating disharmony between Muslim students and their Hindu peers.[26] As a result of the controversy, the order was quickly withdrawn.

The response of the opinion of Muslim clerics, intellectuals and journalists has been intermittently recorded in the foregoing pages. One issue thus far unmentioned is the plan to set up a separate Muslim political party to promote Muslim interests. The plan, it was reported in the Urdu press, had been encouraged, if not positively supported, by the BJP. The report was given credence by the fact that the NDA government at the centre had spoken of such a party at the time it created a joint parliamentary committee to look into the 'mismanagement' of the Ajmer *dargah*.[27] The move to launch a Muslim party was naturally fiercely opposed by the Jamiat-ul-Ulama-i-Hind (or the JUH), which has its own fairly large network across the country. The reason for the opposition was partly that the formation of such a party would only sharpen Hindu chauvinism, and also that it would divide Muslim voters further instead of uniting them against the BJP, which was the need of the hour. However, the president of the JUH, Maulana Asad Madani, stated that the creation of a common secular party to represent all religious minorities, dalits, adivasis, and backward castes, would be desirable.[28] Predictably, given the propensity of the political class, this alternative proposal was perceived to have been supported by the Congress! In the event, all these reports proved to be no more than the usual pre-election speculation.

IV

The interpretation of the results of the 2004 parliamentary election, insofar as they pertain to Muslims, can be approached in two ways. The first involves an analysis of the total number of Muslims elected to the Lok Sabha; the percentage of Muslims in the population of the constituencies that elect Muslim candidates; the parties and candidates elected by constituencies which have a sizable Muslim population; the nomination of candidates—Muslim or otherwise—by the various parties; and the trends that emerge regarding the constituencies, states, and political parties from which Muslim candidates win or lose. There is also a second category of evidence which pertains to the way in which Muslim voters actually voted in the election, regardless of whether the candidates contesting in their constituencies were Muslims or not. This is important because it not only illuminates Muslim voting behaviour, but also the practice of tactical or strategic voting. This second type of evidence can, however, be gleaned only from surveys which are suggestive rather than definitive. At the present, the only such credible data are to be found in the post-poll survey findings of the National Election Study 2004—a survey of approximately 25,000 voters—conducted by the CSDS, referred to above.

As has already been noted, 35 Muslim candidates were elected to the Fourteenth Lok Sabha.

Table 3 shows that one-third (11) of these belong to constituencies where the Muslim population is over 40 per cent, and another one-third to constituencies where it is between 20 and 30 per cent. It is also notable that the largest number of Muslim candidates were elected from constituencies where the Muslim population is less than 20 per cent.[29] The 35 Muslim MPs elected belonged to a diverse range of parties, as demonstrated in Table 4. Which shows that the 35 Muslim

TABLE 3: MUSLIM POPULATION IN 35 CONSTITUENCIES THAT ELECTED MUSLIM CANDIDATES TO THE FOURTEENTH LOK SABHA

Number of Muslim candidates elected	Percentage of Muslims in the population of the constituency
9	Over 50
2	40
4	30-9
4	25-9
4	20-4
12	Below 20

Source: Government of India, Election Commission, www.eci.gov.in.

TABLE 4: PARTIES FROM WHICH MUSLIM CANDIDATES WERE ELECTED TO THE FOURTEENTH LOK SABHA

Political Party	Number of Muslim MPs elected from constituencies with a Muslim population of over 15 per cent and above
Indian National Congress	10
Samajwadi Party	7
Communist Party of India (Marxist)	5
Bahujan Samaj Party	4
Rashtriya Janata Dal	2
Janata Dal (U)	1
Dravida Munnetra Kazhagam	1
Majlis-e-Ittehadul Muslimeen (MIM)	1
Muslim League (MUL)	1
Jammu & Kashmir National Conference	2
Jammu & Kashmir People's Democratic Party	1
All parties	35

Source: Government of India, Election Commission, www.eci.gov.in.

MPs elected belong to 11 different parties: 10 belong to the Congress Party, 7 to the Samajwadi Party, 5 to the CPM, 4 to the Bahujan Samaj Party, 2 each to the Rashtriya Janata Dal and the Jammu & Kashmir National Conference, 1 each to the JKPDP, the JD(U) and the DMK, and 1 each to the two main Muslim parties, the AIMIM and the MUL. Unlike those belonging to the Samajwadi Party or the Bahujan Samaj Party, the Congress candidates belong to several states, notably excepting Uttar Pradesh, but including Andhra Pradesh, Assam, Bihar, Maharashtra, Tamil Nadu, and West Bengal. The SP and BSP candidates—11 in all, or close to a third of the total number of Muslims elected all over India—belong exclusively to Uttar Pradesh. The converse also holds true, in that all the Muslims elected from UP belong to either of these two parties. Let us turn to an examination of the way in which constituencies with more than 15 per cent Muslim populations voted in the election of 2004.

Tables 4 and 5 make it abundantly clear that, despite all its last-minute efforts at wooing the Muslim vote, not a single Muslim was elected from the BJP. Table 6 provides data on those seats won by the BJP, though with Hindu candidates, in constituencies that have a sizeable Muslim population. It is worth bearing in mind the findings

TABLE 5: HOW CONSTITUENCIES WITH A MUSLIM POPULATION OF OVER 15 PER CENT VOTED

Muslims in constituency	Total number of constituencies	No. of Muslim elected	No. of non-Muslim elected	Parties from which Muslim candidates were elected	States
Over 50	11	9	2	JKN, JKPDP, INC, CPM, RJD, MUL, JD(U)	J&K, Kerala, West Bengal, Lakshadweep Bihar, Assam,
40-9	6	2	4	INC, SP, CPI	Assam, West Bengal, UP
30-9	13	4	9	INC, SP, BSP, AIMIM	Andhra Pradesh, Assam, UP
25-9	18	4	14	INC, SP, BSP, CPM	UP, Bihar Kerala
20-4	19	4	15	SP, RJD, CPM	UP, Bihar, West Bengal
15-19	33	2	31	INC, SP	Karnataka, UP
All constituencies with over 15% Muslim population	100	25	75		

Source: Government of India, Election Commission, www.eci.gov.in.

of the CSDS National Election Study data, which shows that the BJP's own share of the Muslim vote was 3 per cent in 1996 and 5 per cent in 1998. With its allies, the BJP obtained 14 per cent of the Muslim vote in 1999, which however dropped to 11 per cent in 2004.[30]

Neither of the BJP's star Muslim candidates—Shahnawaz Khan, who had been a minister in the outgoing government, nor Arif Mohammed Khan, who joined the party shortly before the polls—managed to win the election. Quite apart from the fact that not a single Muslim candidate was elected from the BJP, the Table 6 suggests that the chances of any BJP candidate succeeding are higher as the proportion of Muslims in the population declines. Thus, in constituencies with over 30 per cent Muslims in the population, the BJP could not win a single seat, a clear pointer, if any were needed, of minorities' distrust in the BJP. In constituencies where the Muslim population ranges between 24 and 29 per cent, the BJP has slightly

TABLE 6: SEATS WON BY THE BJP IN CONSTITUENCIES WITH OVER 15 PER CENT MUSLIM POPULATION

% of Muslim in the constituency	Number of constituencies	Seats won by the BJP	States
Over 50	11	0	-
40-9	6	0	-
30-9	13	0	-
25-9	18	4	Bihar, UP
20-4	19	3	Bihar, Assam, UP
15-19	33	14	UP, Gujarat, Karnataka, MP, Rajasthan, Maharashtra, Haryana
10-14	9	7	Rajasthan, MP, Maharashtra

Note: All non-Muslim candidates.
Source: Government of India, Election Commission, www.eci.gov.in.

better chances of success. There are 37 such constituencies, of which the BJP won seven. It is when we examine constituencies with Muslim populations in the range of 15 to 19 per cent that we observe the BJP winning close to half the seats, though of course with Hindu candidates. There are 33 such seats, of which the BJP won 14, dispersed across a wide range of states including Rajasthan, Madhya Pradesh, Gujarat, Karnataka, Uttar Pradesh, Maharashtra and Haryana.

Thus, in constituencies that have 30 per cent Muslims, the BJP is completely unsuccessful. In constituencies which have between 20 per cent and 30 per cent Muslim, it is relatively more successful (and that too in Bihar and UP). It is most successful in constituencies which have less than 20 per cent of the population is Muslims. In the latter category, we may also perceive a wider spread in terms of states, including Rajasthan, Madhya Pradesh and Karnataka, where the overall trend was in any case fairly positive for the BJP.

It also appears that the BJP's allies are happy to renounce contesting seats in which the BJP can create a polarization of the vote along community lines. Thus, for instance, of the 16 seats contested by the BJP in Bihar, it won five. Four of these had a Muslim population of over 20 per cent, and in the remaining one the BJP candidate came second. That the avowedly socialist JD(U), the BJP's ally in Bihar, chose not to contest in any constituency with a significant Muslim population could suggest that these seats were left for the BJP to manage through communal polarization, however uncertain a strategy this may be. The success that attends strategies of communal polarization is attested by the fairly respectable winning margins of the BJP. In Uttar Pradesh, for instance, of the 10 seats won by the BJP, its winning margins hovered around 7.5 per cent. Further, the BJP came second in eight constituencies, in all of which it lost by less than 8 per cent of the vote. Indeed, in three constituencies, it lost by less than 2 per cent of the vote.

Overall, the results suggest that constituencies with a higher proportion of Muslims will generally elect candidates from parties with secular credentials like the Congress or the CPM, or else confessional parties like the MUL or the AIMIM. This should imply that Muslim voters would tend to trust either confessional parties (though these are thin on the ground) or else parties that have a secular orientation and therefore offer some hope of security. Even in constituencies with a Muslim population of between 30-50 per cent, it is the avowedly secular parties that dominate. The result as a whole does not privilege any one factor but rather a combination of politics at the level of the state (for instance, in Uttar Pradesh, parties like the SP and BSP invariably tend to do better than the Congress, whereas in other states, Congress tends to do better); candidates (whether or not they are Muslims); and the proportion of Muslims in the population.

In 1987, Susanne and Lloyd Rudolph argued that Muslims tend to vote for 'national centrist parties', at that time Congress and the Janata Party, wherever they are a vulnerable minority (10-20 per cent in the population), but wherever they approximate a plurality (over 20 per cent), they tend to vote for confessional parties. They posited an inverse relationship between the proportion of Muslims in the population and Muslim voter support for national centrist parties: that is, the lower the proportion of Muslims, the more likely it is that Muslim voters will vote for national centrist parties.[31] In the period analysed by the Rudolphs, of course, the BJP (or its predecessor, the Bharatiya Jana Sangh) was not the substantive political player that it has subsequently become. The present study, the focus of which is close to two decades later, in an era defined by the communalization of politics, supplements the Rudolphs' thesis by showing that the BJP's chances of winning improve as the Muslim population declines. The most obvious explanation for this is, of course, that while Muslim voters prefer secular parties, the more substantial numbers of the non-Muslim population lead to the trumping of the Muslim population, and its preferences.

This study also suggests that there is perhaps no such phenomenon as 'the Muslim vote'. As is well known, Indian Muslims are diverse and heterogeneous, with their ways of life differing across region, language group, and even sectarian divisions. Despite this, however, the Muslim vote is, to a larger extent than the non-Muslim vote, not merely an accumulation of many local votes. Thus, and especially in the climate of fear and anxiety produced over the past few years, contributing to the defeat of the BJP and its allies is very likely to be an important concern for the Muslim voter, regardless of region, language, or sect. On the other hand, this is obviously a local vote in the way in which the decision about which candidate or which party to vote for is arrived at, strategically designed to defeat communal parties. In West Bengal, for instance, a sitting BJP candidate was defeated because of the Gujarat violence, on which subject he was heard openly complaining about the insufficient attention given to the Godhra incident. In 1999, the BJP-Trinamool Congress alliance had won nine out of the 42 Lok Sabha seats in West Bengal; in 2004, it won just one, and that was party supremo Mamata Banerjee's own seat. Clearly and predictably, the allies also paid the price for Gujarat, and it is therefore unsurprising to hear leading members of the Shiv Sena, the Trinamool Congress, and the Telugu Desam now attributing the electoral defeat of the NDA to the Gujarat riots.

As far as allies are concerned, those of the Congress—such as the Dravida Munnetra Kazhagam and the Rashtriya Janata Dal—won quite easily. Of the BJP's many allies, none of them could win a constituency with a substantial Muslim population. Indeed, in constituencies with a substantial Muslim population, over 50 per cent for example, *all* parties have an incentive to put up Muslim candidates, and indeed the combination of party and candidate determines the win. In such constituencies, even if the right party puts up a non-Muslim candidate, that candidate can win. This explains the election of the only two non-Muslim leaders, both Congressmen, to have been elected from constituencies with a Muslim population of over 50 per cent, Priya Ranjan Das Munshi and Pranab Mukherjee, both from West Bengal. Even in constituencies where the Muslim population is slightly lower, the party appears to be the determining criterion, and it matters little whether the candidate is a Muslim or a Hindu.

The survey data from the NES 2004[32] suggest that the Congress is the party preferred by Muslim voters, unless they have a strong alternative available. For the entire country, 47 per cent of Muslims preferred the Congress, 11 per cent the BJP, and 42 per cent 'Others'. In Delhi, the Muslim support for Congress was 94 per cent (despite Imam Bukhari's appeal). In Bihar, Maharashtra, and Tamil Nadu Muslim support for Congress was in the region of 75 per cent, and in Gujarat, Andhra Pradesh, and Assam, over 60 per cent. Only in Jammu & Kashmir, unsurprisingly, that the Congress vote was a mere 24 per cent, on account of the presence of regional parties. For the same reason, it was as low as 15 per cent in Uttar Pradesh and 26 per cent in West Bengal.

As always, the Muslim vote exemplifies the typical behaviour of a minority, namely, a search for security from the most credible party likely to deliver it. With the exception of states such as UP and West Bengal, where the Muslim vote continues to go substantially to the Samajwadi Party, the Bahujan Samaj Party and the CPM, the pre-eminence of the Congress is apparent. Even in Bihar, where Muslim candidates supported by the RJD have won seats, the survey data show that 75 per cent of voters prefer the Congress.

V

It is truly ironic that the Muslim vote received such visibility for the first time, and in an election fought by an incumbent government led by the BJP, whose credentials vis-à-vis the Muslim community are weaker than those of almost any other (with the possible exception of the Shiv Sena, which may be considered to be its fraternal partner). Equally ironic is the fact that the post-election process of revamping the BJP has centred crucially on its position on the Gujarat riots of 2002. While the RSS has taken the position that the BJP lost the election because it abandoned its core agenda of Hindutva, former Prime Minister Vajpayee has criticized this argument, saying that 'The impact of the Gujarat riots was felt nationwide. This was unexpected and hurt us badly. Narendra Modi should have been removed after the incident.'[33] The party spokesperson issued a sharp denial, saying that Vajpayee had clearly been misinterpreted, that this issue had already been settled at the Goa party conference in 2002, and that there was no question of reopening it now. Vajpayee backtracked, and the issue of the removal of Modi was deferred.

However, at the meeting of the BJP's National Executive in Mumbai from 21–3 June, the party rededicated itself to Hindutva and strongly reaffirmed its bonds with the RSS. Its leadership decided that the party should abandon the project of being an 'ordinary' political party and reclaim and recover its identity as 'a party with a mission'.[34] Despite a token statement that its efforts to reach out to the minorities would continue, this meeting signaled quite conclusively the end of the brief flirtation between the BJP and the Muslims. The reaffirmation of its commitment to Hindutva may seem to be the best way of holding the cadres—especially of fraternal organizations—together, but it is also likely to be the least effective way of obtaining the popular vote.

NOTES

1. Sanjaya Baru, 'Political Economy of the 2004 Result', *The Financial Express*, 14 May 2004.
2. Srikrishna Ayyangar, 'Andhra Pradesh: Why Women Did Not Vote for TDP', *Economic and Political Weekly*, vol. XXXIX, no. 20, 15-21 May 2004, pp. 1992-3 (emphasis in original).
3. Yogendra Yadav, 'Economic Reforms in the Mirror of Public Opinion', *The Hindu*, 13 June 2004, p. 16.
4. Abhay Datar, 'A Vote for Secular Politics', *The Hindu*, 20 May 2004, p. AE-2.
5. Lloyd I. Rudolph and Susanne H. Rudolph, *In Pursuit of Lakshmi: The Political Economy of the Indian State* (Delhi: Orient Longman), p. 187.
6. Rudolph and Rudolph, *In Pursuit of Lakshmi*, p. 194.
7. Iqbal A. Ansari, 'Muslim Representation in Legislatures: 1952-2002', Mimeo, Delhi: Jamia Hamdard University, 2003, p. 134.
8. Ibid., p. 18.
9. Ibid., p. 23.
10. Ibid., p. 136.
11. Syed Shahabuddin, 'How and Why the BJP is Wooing Muslims?' *The Milli Gazette*, 16-31 March 2004, p. 12.

12. Ali Anwar, *Masawat ki Jang* (Hindi), Delhi: Vani Prakashan, 2001, p. 137.
13. Ibid., pp. 170-1.
14. 'Minority View', Interview with Omar Khalidi, *The Times of India*, 15 June 2004.
15. Bharatiya Janata Party, 'Vision Document', www.bjp.org/Press/mar_3104a.htm.
16. National Democratic Alliance, *Agenda for Development, Good Governance, Peace and Harmony*, 2004, www.bjp.org/Press/NDA%20Agenda.htm.
17. *India Today*, 8 March 2004, p. 28.
18. Interview with Arif Mohammed Khan, *The Indian Express*, 10 March 2004.
19. The term *Rath Yatra* is generally used for a procession in which deities are taken out on a chariot, thronged by large numbers of devotees. The most famous such *yatra* is the Jagannath *Yatra*, the origin of the word 'juggernaut' hinting at the scale of the procession.
20. The term 'Bharat Uday' translates as 'India Rising', not dissimilar from the name of the controversial advertisement blitz that the NDA government ran for a few months until the electoral code of conduct came into force. India Shining, which sought to project the economic successes of India, was widely criticized for the fact that, being funded by taxpayers' money, it seemed to be subsidizing what was effectively an advance election campaign for the BJP/NDA. It was also criticized for its class bias, and its insensitivity toward the persisting issues of poverty, hunger and farmers' suicides.
21. 'Lotus Eater', Interview with Syed Ahmed Bukhari, *The Times of India*, 26 April 2004.
22. *BJP Today*, 16-31 March 2004, www.bjp.org.
23. Ibid. (emphasis added)
24. Swapan Dasgupta, 'Whatever Happened to Hindutva?' *Seminar*, No. 533 (January 2004), p. 43.
25. This is confirmed by the initial findings reported by the National Election Survey 2004 (CSDS), which suggest that while Muslims in many states voted overwhelmingly for the Congress party, wherever there was a strong regional alternative, they chose it instead. Thus, while 72 per cent of Muslims in Maharashtra and 85 per cent of those in Rajasthan voted Congress, only 15 per cent of Muslims in UP did the same. See Sanjay Kumar and Alistair McMillan 'Caste Matters, but So Do a Whole Lot of Other Things', *The Hindu*, 20 May 2004, p. AE-7.
26. 'Mulayam's Muslim Appeasement Backfires', *The Milli Gazette*, 15 March 2004, p. 4.
27. 'BJP plans 'secular' Muslim party', *The Milli Gazette*, 1-15 January 2004. p. 4.
28. 'No Separate Muslim Political Party: JUH', *The Milli Gazette*, 1-15 February 2004, p. 6.

29. Tables 3-6 have been generated from the data provided by the Election Commission of India on its website, www.eci.gov.in. Research assistance by Ravindra Karnena in sorting this data is gratefully acknowledged.
30. Yogendra Yadav, 'Vote Banks Didn't Sink BJP: Vote Blanks Did', *The Indian Express*, 30 May 2004.
31. Rudolph and Rudolph, *In Pursuit of Lakshmi*, p. 194.
32. Kumar and McMillan, 'Caste matters'.
33. 'Atal Blows Hot, Modi Catches Cold', *The Times of India*, 14 June 2004.
34. 'Back to Basics: Defeated BJP Turns to Hindutva', *The Hindustan Times*, 23 June 2004.

12

The Future of Muslims in India: Views of an Outsider Political Scientist

THEODORE P. WRIGHT, JR.

An essay in predicting the future of Indian Muslims requires first and foremost a typology of ethnic minorities[1] to determine the politically relevant characteristics of each and to search for analogous groups around the world. In social science there are no unique cases.

There are various criteria for categorizing subordinate groups; among them size in percentage and location are clearly important, if not always decisive. Other things being equal, a tiny minority, like the Parsis of India, are very unlikely to be perceived as a threat by the dominants in society, of which many of them may well be a part. A huge minority, like the Chinese in Malaysia or Black Africans in South Africa before 1994 are sure to arouse apprehensions among the rulers.

Alternatively, there is origin: how a group became subordinate, whether by voluntary or involuntary immigration (slavery), ritual pollution, religious conversion, changing boundaries, differential birth and emigration rates, or group status reversal, usually influences relations with the dominant group whether it constitutes a majority or a numerical minority of the population.[2] Geographical distribution, whether evenly distributed or concentrated in certain areas, particularly if the latter are on the border of a state, and most particularly if that border is with another state in which the group in question constitutes a dominant majority, like the Sudeten Germans in Czechoslovakia in 1938, may thus invite secession and foreign intervention.

As a consequence of all these attributes, what are the changing goals of the community's leadership, from secession, to role reversal, to autonomy, integration, assimilation and disappearance, as well as the intent of the state's dominant elites toward this particular ethnic minority, ranging from coercive assimilation, to pluralism, autonomy, subjugation, expulsion and genocide?[3]

With respect to size, Muslims were a quarter of the population of British India[4] but this was reduced to 10 per cent of the population of the Republic of India after 1947. The largest princely states, Hyderabad and Jammu and Kashmir, the former with a Muslim ruler over a majority Hindu population, the latter, conversely, with a Hindu maharaja ruling a two-thirds Muslim population, both fell to India, Hyderabad by conquest and Kashmir by ruler's accession in 1947-8. The remaining Muslims are widely scattered throughout India, with only a few pockets of concentration in Kerala, West Bengal, and Hyderabad city. Of these, only Kashmir and parts of West Bengal are adjacent to Muslim-dominated states that could be tempted to make irredentist claims, as Germany did on Czechoslovakia and Poland in 1938-9, or Turkey on Cyprus in 1972.

Despite or perhaps because of its post-partition poverty, the Muslim population of India has had a slightly higher growth rate than the Hindus, rising from 9 to 12 per cent in a half century. This trend has excited unreasonable fears on the part of Hindu nationalists of an ethnic ratio reversal such as happened in the Lebanon as between Christians and Muslims after 1943, and caused a civil war in 1975-88.[5] Demographers point out the fallacy of projecting trends in group population ratios, given the number of rapidly changing causative factors.[6] Who could have predicted the decline in birth rates in many Catholic countries in the past generation?

Other ways in which the Muslim minority could be transformed into a dominant majority appear to be unlikely in the foreseeable future. 1. Mass conversion of Hindus to Islam as happened with Christians to Islam over a much longer period in Asia Minor, now Turkey, after 1072.[7] A Minuscule conversion of Dalits to Islam in some villages of Tamil Nadu in 1981 occasioned a tremendous furore in north India and the resuscitation of the Vishwa Hindu Parishad;[8] 2. Differential susceptibility to epidemic diseases such as decimated the Native American peoples after contact with Europeans. Could AIDS be such an epidemic in our century?[9] 3. Military conquest by a currently weaker Pakistan, especially if India were to fall apart as predicted by Selig

Harrison in 1960[10] or, conversely, if Pakistan disintegrated further than it did in 1971 and were reannexed by India. 4. Massive differences in emigration/immigration rates such as reversed the French/British ration in Canada between 1760 and 1820[11] or the Hindu/Native Fijian ratio in Fiji.

Not all reversals of minority and majority necessarily cause fear and violence. The United States, for instance, is currently experiencing a rapid decline in the percentage of 'Euro-Americans' with predictions rife of their becoming a minority by the mid twenty-first century.[12] But the sting of loss is reduced by equally rapid increases in ethnic and religious exogamy which portend assimilation into a new nationality rather than a 'zero-sum-game'.[13] This easy way out of the 'ethnic numbers game' seems improbable as between Hindus and Muslims in India who, except for a tiny number in the intelligentsia and entertainment world, practice almost no intermarriage at all because of parental arrangement of marriages and very little even between castes and quasi-castes within each of the two communities.[14]

As to location of Indian Muslims, it has already been noted that the presence of Muslim majorities (Kashmir) or large minorities (West Bengal and Assam) on the borders of Muslim majority countries, arouses fears among nationalist Hindus. The unorganized mass migration from either side of the frontier in the divided Punjab in 1947 eliminated that cause of anxiety, as did the exchange of Greeks and Turks in 1924 and the expulsion of the Ostdeutsch from Czechoslovakia and Poland in 1945.[15] Are either of these drastic 'solution' apt to happen again in the future in South Asia? On the Pakistani side, there are few Sikhs and Hindus to exchange, and in any case the huge numbers of Indian Muslims could never be absorbed by Pakistan. On the eastern wing, there is still a considerable Hindu minority in Bangladesh which has been gradually declining by individual emigration. The agitation of the Shiv Sena and BJP is rather against the uncontrolled immigration of Muslim Bangladeshis into India in search of work.[16] That the Hindutvadis demands are insatiable and not really related to border security, is shown by the cries of 'Another Pakistan; another Partition' when a Muslim majority district of Malappuram was carved out in Kerala, far from either Muslim majority country.[17]

This brings us to the question what difference origin makes in creating or worsening antipathies. I have argued elsewhere[18] that north Indian Muslims are particularly prone to arouse resentment among upper caste Hindus because invading Muslim warriors conquered and ruled the Gangetic plain for some six centuries (AD 1191-1857). They built forts, mosques, palaces, *madrasas* and tombs that are still among the most visible historic monuments. Some of these structures may have been constructed on the sites of destroyed Hindu temples.[19] This was the source of the lethal agitation, demolition and riots over the Babri Masjid in 1992.[20] The campaign to destroy the mosque and rebuild the temple was used by the BJP to propel itself into power and even played a role in the Gujarat pogrom of 2002. Elements of the Sangh Parivar press for similar action in Mathura and Varanasi, claiming to have lists of thousands of other Muslim displacements of Hindu temples. Already, after losing power in the 2004 elections, they are pressing a similar claim in Maharashtra.[21] The similarities to the Zionist claims for the 'temple mount' in Jerusalem to replace the third most holy Muslim mosque are patent.[22]

Southern and coastal India, having on the contrary been settled by peaceable Arab merchants since the eighth century, have not until recently exhibited the syndrome of communal hatred, so one can venture to predict that if the north is ever ethnically 'cleansed' of Muslims like Germany was of Jews after 1932 or Czechoslovakia of Germans in 1945, Islam will survive in coastal pockets, provided the Sangh Parivar does not succeed in communalizing the south.[23]

Coastal Muslims have thus developed into a different type of minority with consequences for their objectives and political behaviour. Communities like the Memons, Khojas, Bohras, Navayats, Marakayyars, Lebais, Rawthers, and Mappillas fall into the category of 'middleman minorities',[24] comparable to Jews, overseas Chinese, Indians, Greeks, Armenians, Parsis, and Jains who find their niche in mercantile enterprise. If successful, they may excite envy, but do not pose a threat to majority dominance. It is no coincidence that the richest Indian Muslim is no longer the feudal Nizam of Hyderabad as before the fall of his state, but Azeem Premji, a computer entrepreneur of Bangalore.[25] Can and will north Indian Muslim youth shift their role models from the quasi-feudal world of music, sports and acting to these technological skills?[26]

Who loom so large in America, are represented only by the coastal 'middlemen' groups, not by industrial labourers except by internal migration as from UP to Bombay. Minorities created by annexation might encompass some Muslims in annexed Muslim princely states like Hyderabad, Bhopal and Junagadh but they are incorporated here in the 'former ruling elite' even if never members of that elite, because of their identification with it. The bulk of Indian Muslims are in Schermerhorn's terms 'mass subjects': poverty-stricken, disproportionately illiterate, and more urban than Hindus are.[27] They are mostly the descendants of lower caste Hindus converted to Islam by Sufis[28] as Hindu nationalists delight to point out. Unless and until they can acquire modern education they are likely to remain marginalized and vulnerable to politically motivated pogroms, like other former elite populations such as the Russian Muslims, WaTutsis, Zanzibar Arabs, and prospectively the Afrikaners of South Africa. Some minorities were subject to enforced assimilation at a low level of society and hence suffered loss of ethnic identity, such as Manchus, Uighurs and the Tibetans of China, non-reservation Amerinds, Fijians, and Maoris. Climbing aboard the 'affirmative action quotas' bandwagon in the path of Scheduled Castes, Tribes and OBCs of India seems to me to be a counterproductive tactic, as it increases the animosity of the upper castes and splits the politically useful alliance with the OBCs.[29] Alternatively, if the Muslim elite is made ineligible, it would divide the Muslim community by social class, as argued by Syed Shahabuddin.[30]

Louis Wirth adumbrated four possible minority goals: assimilation, pluralism, secession, and dominance.[31] Later Richard Schermerhorn by adding dominants' goals for the minority implied some more painful outcomes: subordination, expulsion and genocide.[32] In part, prediction of outcomes depends on external factors such as the state of Indo-Pakistan relations, over which a minority has no control,[33] but it also is contingent upon interaction of changing goals of both minority and majority leadership. This has been painfully apparent in Palestinian-Israeli relations during the second Intifada to the point where a significant proportion of Jewish opinion in Israel has come to favour the expulsion of the Arabs from the West Bank to Jordan.[34] Schermerhorn maps out these relationships in a matrix of four combinations of minority and majority goals for each other: assimilation and pluralism by the former and forced segregation and forced assimiliation by the latter. He calls it 'congruent and incongruent orientations toward centrifugal trends of subordinates as viewed by themselves and superordinates'. Concretely, this means that conflict may result from either dominants trying to force assimilation on unwilling subordinates (Germanization under the Hapsburgs or Ottomanization in Turkey, Russifications under the Czars); or from the opposite: dominants trying to enforce segregation on a minority that wants assimilation, as in the American South before the Civil Rights movement or South Africa under apartheid. What he calls 'integration' may result from either both sides agreeing on segregation as under the *millet* system of the Ottomans or from both agreeing on assimilation as among Euro Americans before the neo-ethnicity and diversity movements of the 1970s.

For most Indian Muslims, except for the Left and the more ardent secularists, I would guess that the main goal has been autonomy/pluralism since 1947, a preference with which the Nehruvian consensus agreed. Those in the Muslim League who had championed Pakistan in the 1940s either emigrated there as Muhajirs to become part of a new dominant group, or accommodated to the ruling Congress party in India.[35] Hence some degree of communal harmony prevailed to the end of Nehru's life in 1964. Symptomatic of this pluralism was the tactic refusal of Congress governments to provide a Common Civil Code as directed in the Constitution. The gradual escallation of communal riots in 1964-92 seems to have had more to do with political party manipulations in an increasingly competitive democracy and with the decay of Gandhian ideals and institutions[36] than with any major change in objectives.

Hindu nationalists, on the other hand, have ostensibly favoured enforced assimilation (Indianization) into a single Hindu-defined Indian nation, somewhat like American policy (Americanization) for European immigrants (the 'tacit compact') from the mid-nineteenth century until about 1970. But then when in power at the centre in

1998-2004, the BJP and its allies revealed a real preference for violent repression, leading in the Gujarat pogrom of 2002 toward mass killing[37] like Ottoman policy towards the Armenians in 1896-1916 in the face of Russian intervention.

The surprising outcome of the 2004 elections has given Indian Muslims a reprieve, but as long as the BJP remains the principal opposition and alternative government, they live under the continued threat of a return to the stark choice presented to them by Golwalker in 1947:

> The non-Hindu peoples in Hindustan must either hold in reverence Hindu religion, must entertain no idea but that of glorification of the Hindu race and culture, i.e. they must not only give up their attitudes of intolerance and ungratefulness towards this land and its age-long traditions, but must also cultivate the positive attitude of love and devotion instead-in a word they must cease to be foreigners OR may stay in the country wholly subordinated to the Hindus nation, claiming nothing, deserving no privileges, far less any preferential treatment-not even citizens' rights.[38]

N.C. Chatterjee added in his address to the Hindu Mahasabha in 1949:

> They (Muslisms) must 1. accept the Ramayana and Mahabharata in place of Arabic and Persian classics. 2. Regard Rama, Krishna, Shivaji, etc., as their heroes and condemn Muslim invaders. 3. Discard Arabic names for Sanskrit origin ones (as in Indonesia). 4. Accept Hindu dress, personal laws. Then they could retain their own religion. We would not much mind their following any path for their personal salvation.[39]

These demands sound arrogant and outrageous in 2004, but to an American of my generation, it gives pause to realize that we 'old immigration' WASPS have required equivalent types of conformity from our religious, ethnic, and racial minorities as conditions for accepting them, if at all, as fully American. The so-called Melting Pot amounted not to a halfway meeting of equals, but to 'Anglo-Conformity'.

This new situation, a minority always being dependent on one major party lest a much worse fate befall them when the other party comes to power in the normal rotation of parties in a democracy, is comparable to that of Tamils in Sri Lanka, or Chinese in Malaysia, Catholics in Northern Ireland, and Jews in Germany in the early 1930s with the rise of the Nazis. At least in a democracy, elections, by making minority votes a subject for party competition and coalition government the norm, may have a mellowing or centripetal effect on the party most antagonistic to minorities, but one cannot ignore the opposite possibility of a centrifugal tendency, polarizing voters and presaging the collapse or paralysis of government as happened to so many European countries in the 1930s during the Great Depression.

After all this gloom, can one envisage a more benign future for Indian Muslims? As I pointed out in 1997,[40] a lot of the historically worse developments for other minorities have not as yet happened to Indian Muslims: literal genocide like the holocaust, mass expulsion (as like from Spain in 1492), deprivation of citizenship (despite proposals by the Shiv Sena), formal residential or occupational segregation (as in Nazi Germany under the Nurnburg laws), forcible religious conversion (as in Spain 1492-1607), loss of mother tongue or script (if one can consider Urdu and Hindi as both variants of Hindustani),[41] educational discrimination by law (instead only by choice and by poverty), expropriation of property (other than emigrants and intending evacuees in 1947), or clothing proscription (as now in France with the veil) or pressure to change names (as in America at immigration).

If India has a 'modern', i.e. rationalistic and developed future, as is already happening in its major metropolises, one can foresee the possibility of a world in which minorities are invisible in their physical appearance, clothing, language, occupation and residence so as to make it difficult for the majority dominants to discriminate openly or commit violence on minority individuals unpunished.

For Muslims, the most conspicuous indicator, making them subject to job and residential discrimination is their Arabic personal and surnames. However, some Muslims on the West coast, especially Ismailis, have adopted ambiguous or even non-Muslim surnames denoting places of origin or occupations. When Arabic first names are then reduced to initials it may render the individual less susceptible if not immune to discrimination. Who would have known that A. Premji, referred to above, is a Muslim? This tactic has been widely and successfully practised by American Jews.[42] How many, for instance, know that among the largely Jewish 'neo-cons' who provoked the US attack on Iraq for the sake of Israel, Lewis Libby, John Bolton and

Bernard Lewis are Jews?[43] Or on the Democratic side, that Richard Holbrook, former US Ambassador to the UN and architect of the Dayton accords with Bosnia, is likewise Jewish?

Another trend among minorities in modern societies, but especially noteable with American Jews, is exogamy or outmarriage. About half of Jewish marriages in the past generation have been with non-Jews,[44] usually with Christians. Very few Indian Muslim marry Hindus.[45] As I pointed out in my 1995 paper, 'How Long Can Ethnicity Survive Exogamy?'[46] and as inveighed against by most Orthodox Jewish rabbis, mass exogamy may be the slippery road to group extinction by assimilation. But in the meantime, intermarriage promotes access to the elite (witness Senator John Kerry), and creates cross-pressures which mitigate prejudicial stereotypes.

Other avenues by which minorities may be able to integrate into majority society without losing their identify are by sports, entertainment, secular schools, residence, profession and military service, if this is open to them.[47] These have been used by Muslims with some success in Bombay.[48]

Aside from these integrative developments, there is another scenario in which the whole paradigm of politics and group relations is shifted to some basis other than religious affiliation. This was archetypically the approach of Marxists and secular liberals like Nehru to the communal conflict. Nehru worked heroically, but with only partial success, to persuade Indians to devote their energies to the material problems of economic and social development. The Marxist parties and intellectuals tried to redirect enmities from religious to class struggle, cross cutting religion. That these policies can work is illustrated by the relative absence of communal riots in West Bengal and Kerala, the two states with powerful Marxist parties.[49] Both Marxists and secular liberals have been on the defensive since the triumph of neo-classical liberal capitalism over the Soviet Union in 1991, but one can foresee a possible recrudescence of class-based politics if laissez-faire policies continue to promote ever widening gaps in income. Muslims as a sizeable component of the poor and landless would benefit disproportionately from a renewal of re-distributive policies.

A less drastic reorientation and one already tried with mixed results is the strategy of Muslim alliance with the Dalit and OBC political parties. Together these groups constitute a large majority of the population, mobilized in recent years against the twice-born upper castes who have dominated Indian politics, business, and land ownership. Unfortunately for Muslims, where this has been tried in Uttar Pradesh, rivalries develop over the spoils of victory and the most 'forward backward' naturally take the lion's share or defect to align with the BJP. Similarly, for Muslims to demand a share of reservations in civil service, university admissions, and legislatures, pits the have-nots against each other and benefits the those fortunate among them who least need help.

The single most important cause clouding the future of Indian Muslims since Partition is the deadly enmity between India and Pakistan. It breeds largely false suspicious of their loyalty in border provinces which politicians are quick to exploit. At the heart of this international feud is the Kashmir controversy. If this could be resolved to the minimal satisfaction of both countries and the Kashmiris, for instance by a kind of confederation, the chance would arise to refocus south Asian enmity on a third nation such as China or the USA and take the heat off of the Muslim minority. If, to the Contrary, an unrestrained nuclear war should break out between the two as almost happened in 1999, the consequences for both parties, and not the least for Indian Muslims, would be catastrophic as they might become the scapegoats.

NOTES

1. R.A. Schermerhorn in *Comparative Ethnic Relations: A Framework for Theory and Research*, New York: Random House, 1970, p. 13, properly makes the point that not all subordinate groups are statistical minorities, so he suggests a fourfold paradigm of size and power: Majority groups (size and power), elites (power but not size), mass subjects (size but not power) and minority groups as such (neither size nor power).
2. Ibid., Chs. 3 and 4.
3. Louis Wirth, 'Problems of Minority Groups', in Ralph Linton, ed., *The Science of Man in the World Crisis*, New York: Columbia University Press, 1945; Theodore P. Wright, Jr., 'The Question of Minority Identity in a Pluralistic Society', in *The Muslim Minority in India*, ed. Syed Z. Abedin, Kalamazoo, Michigan: Muslim Students Association, 1972.

4. Syed Shahabuddin and Theodore P. Wright, Jr., 'India: Muslim Minority Politics and Society', in *Islam in Asia*, ed. John L. Esposito, New York: Oxford University Press, 1987, pp. 152-3.
5. Abdo Baaklini, 'Ethnicity and Politics in Contemporary Lebanon', in *Culture Ethnicity and Identity; Current Issues in Research*, ed. William C. McCready, New York: Academic Press, 1983, pp. 22-3.
6. Theodore P. Wright, Jr., 'The Ethnic Numbers Game in India: Hindu-Muslim Conflict over Conversion, Family Planning, Migration and the Census', in McCready, op. cit., pp. 420-1.
7. S. Vryonis, *The Decline of Medieval Hellenism in Asia Minor and the Process of Islamization from the 11th through 15th Centuries*, Berkeley: University of California Press, 1971, cited in *Conversion to Islam*, ed. Nehemia Levtzion, New York: Holmes & Meier, 1979.
8. Abdul Malik Mujahid, *Conversion to Islam: Untouchables Strategy for Protest in India*, Chambersburg: Anima Publications, 1989.
9. Crawford Young, *The Politics of Cultural Pluralism* Madison: University of Wisconsin Press, 'Latin American Indians: Demographic Change', pp. 436-7; there is some evidence from Africa that circumcized males are less vulnerable to AIDS than uncircumcized males.
10. Selig Harrison, *India: the Most Dangerous Decades*, Princeton: Princeton University Press, 1960.
11. Kenneth McRoberts, 'The Rise of Quebecois Identity', in *The Mobilization of Collective Identity: Comparative Prspectives*, ed. Jeffrey A. Ross and Ann Baker Cottrell, Lanham MD: The University Press of America, 1980, pp. 225-6.
12. Samuel Huntington, *Who Are We? Challenges to America's National Identity*, 2004.
13. Theodore P. Wright, Jr., 'Identity and Changing Status of Former Elite Minorities: the Contrasting Cases of North Indian Muslims and American "Wasps", in *Rethinking Ethnicity: Majority Groups & Dominant Minorities*, ed. Eric P. Kaufmann, London: Routledge, 2004, pp. 31-9.
14. Ibid., 'How Long Can Ethnic Identity Survive Exogamy?', delivered at the 75th anniversary seminar of the sociology department of Bombay University, A.R. Momin, convenor, 28 December 1995.
15. Hellenic Resources Network, 'Convention Concerning the Exchange of Greek and Turkish Populations', Lausanne, 1923.
16. Partha S. Ghosh, *BJP and the Evolution of Hindu Nationalism*, Delhi: Manohar, 1999, pp. 270-1.
17. James Chiriyankandath, 'Kerala and the Limits of Hindu Nationalism', in *The BJP and the Compulsions of Politics in India*, ed. Thomas Blom Hansen and Christophe Jaffrelot, Delhi: Oxford University Press, 1998, pp. 209-10.
18. Theodore P. Wright, Jr., 'Identity Problems of Former Ellite Minorities', *Secular Democracy*, August 1972, pp. 43-51.

19. Richard Eaton has contested the amount and motivation of Muslim temple destruction. *The Rise of Islam and the Behgal Frontier, 1204-1760*, Delhi: Oxford University Press, 1994, pp. 72, 140.
20. Asghar Ali Engineer, ed., *Babri Masjid Ramjanambhoomi Controversy*, Delhi: Ajanta, 1990; for the Hindu Nationalist point of view, Sita Ram Goel, *Hindu Temples: What Happened to Them*, Delhi: Voice of India, 1991.
21. 'Police fear and Ayodhya re-run', *Times of India*, 1 September 2004.
22. Bernard Wasserstein, 'Three Faces of Jerusalem', *Prospect*, 20 December 2001.
23. Theodore P. Wright, Jr., 'The Spread of Communal Violence to the South', *Eastern Anthropologist*, Raghuraj Gupta and Nadeem Hasnain, guest eds., LIII, nos 3-4 (July-December 2000), pp. 367-73.
24. Walter Zenner, *Minorities in the Middle*, Albany: State University of New York Press, 1991.
25. 'Billion Dollar Team: How India's Most Valuable Company WIPRO made Azim Premji the Richest Indian Ever', *India Today*, 16 March 2000.
26. Theodore P. Wright, Jr., 'Muslims Self-Reliance in India: the Model of the Business Communities', *Indian Journal of Politics*, XXI, nos 3-4 (July-December 1997), pp. 49-55.
27. Rajiv Shah, 'Urban Muslims the worst off: Survey', *Times of India*, 9 March 1999.; Omar Khalidi, Indian Muslim Society and Economy', *Oriente Moderno*, Nova Serie, XXIII, 1 (2004), 177-202.
28. M. Mujeeb, *The Indian Muslims*, London: George Allen & Unwin, 1967, p. 21.
29. Theodore P. Wright, Jr., 'A New Demand for Muslim Reservations in India', *Asian Survey*, XXXVII, 9 (September 1997), pp. 852-8.
30. Laura Dudley Jenkins, *Indentity and Identification in India: Defining the Disadvantaged*, London: Routledge Curzon, 2003, p. 118.
31. Theodore P. Wright, Jr., 'Indian Muslims, the Bangladesh Secession and the Indo-Pakistan War of 1971', *Main Currents in Indian Sociology*, III, ed. Giri Raj Gupta, Delhi: Vikas Publishing House, 1978, pp. 128-48.
32. Wikipedia (online) says that the 7 member National Union bloc of three parties in the Israeli Knesset (out of 120) favours exchange of the remaining Arab population of Israel and the West bank with Arab countries.
33. Theodore P. Wright, Jr., 'The Muslim League in South India since Independence: A Study in Minority Group Political Strategies', *American Political Science Review*, LX, 3 (Septmeber 1966), pp. 579-99.
34. Ashutosh Varshney, *Ethnic Conflict & Civic Life*, New Haven: Yale University Press, 2002, Chapter 9.
35. M.L. Sondhi and Apratim Mukarji, *The Black Book of Gujarat*, Delhi: Manak, 2002.
36. Donald E. Smith, *India as a Secular State*, Princeton: Princeton University Press, 1963, p. 466.

37. Ibid., p. 375.
38. Milton Gordon, *Assimilation in American Life*, New York: Oxford University Press, 1964, Chapter 4.
39. Theodore P. Wright, Jr., 'The Indian State and its Muslim Minority: From Dependency to Self-reliance?', in *India: Fifty Years of Democracy and Development*, ed. Yogendra Malik and Ashok Kapur, New Delhi: APH Publishing Co., 1998, Chapter 8.
40. Ibid., 'Strategies for the Survival of Formerly Dominant Languages', *Economic and Political Weekly*, 12 January 2002, pp. 107-14.
41. Robert C. Christopher, *Crashing the Gates; the De-WASPing of America's Power Elite*, New York: Simon and Schuster, 1989, Chapters 2, 9.
42. Elizabeth Drew, 'The Neoconservatives in Power', *New York Review of Book*, vol. 10 June 2002.
43. J.J. Golderg, *Jewish Power*, Reading: Addison-Wesley, 1996, p. 66 reports one survey claiming 52 per cent outmarriage rate.
44. Theodore P. Wright, Jr., 'How Long Can Ethnic Identity Survive Exogamy?', op. cit.
45. Ibid., 'The Tyabji Clan of Bombay: The Impact of Modernization on Muslim Kinship', in *Family, Kinship and Marriage among the Muslims*, ed. Imtiaz Ahmad, Delhi: Manohar, 1976, pp. 217-38.
46. Omar Khalidi, *Khaki and the Ethnic Violence in India*, Delhi: Three Essays Collective, 2003.
47. Theodore P. Wright, Jr., 'Muslim Mobility in India through Peripheral Occupations: Sports, Music, Cinema and Smuggling', in *Asie du Sub: Traditions et Changements*, ed. Marc Gaborieau and Alice Thorner, Paris: Editions du Centre National de la Recherche Scientifique, Collection des Colleques Internationaux, 1979, pp. 271-8.
48. Varshney, op. cit., chart p. 97, shows Kerala and West Bengal with the 4th and 8th least deaths per million of urban population among sixteen states, 1950-95, but this includes West Bengal for the tumultuous period before the Communists came to power in 1977.
49. Imtiaz Ahmad, 'Pakistan and the Indian Muslim', *Quest*, XCIII (January-February 1975), pp. 39-47.

Contributors

AMIR ALI is with the Department of Political Science, Jamia Millia Islamia, New Delhi.

NAWAR ALAM is with the Centre for West Asian and African Studies, Jawaharlal Nehru University, New Delhi.

ARSHAD ALAM is with the Centre for Jawaharlal Nehru Studies, Jamia Millia Islamia, New Delhi.

CHRISTOPHE JAFFRELOT is the Director of Centre d'Etudes et Recherches Internationales (CERI), Paris.

CRAIG JEFFREY is with the School of Earth, Environment and Geographical Sciences at the University of Edinburgh.

MUSHIRUL HASAN is a historian of Modern India. He is currently the Vice-Chancellor, Jamia Millia Islamia, New Delhi.

NIRAJA GOPAL JAYAL is with the Centre for Law and Governance, Jawaharlal Nehru University, New Delhi.

PATRICIA JEFFERY is with the School of Social and Political Studies, University of Edinburgh.

ROGER JEFFERY is with the School of Social and Political Studies, University of Edinbrugh.

S.M.A.K. FAKHRI is with the Department of Political Science, Jamia Millia Islamia, New Delhi.

SMITA GUPTA is currently Political Editor with *Outlook* magazine, New Delhi.

SYLVIA VATUK is with the Department of Anthropology at the University of Illinois, Chicago.

THEODORE P. WRIGHT, Jr., is Professor Emeritus at the Graduate School of Public Affairs, State University of New York, Albany.

VSUNDHARA SIRNATE is a Graduate Student at the Department of Political Science, University of California, Berkeley.

YOGINDER SIKAND is currently with the Centre for Jawaharlal Nehru Studies, Jamia Millia Islamia, New Delhi.

ZOYA HASAN is with the Centre for Political Studies, Jawaharlal Nehru University, New Delhi.

Index